PSYCHOSYNTHESIS

Roberto Assagioli was one of the masters of modern psychology in the line that runs from Sigmund Freud through C. G. Jung and Abraham Maslow. Himself a colleague of all these men, Assagioli was among the pioneers of psychoanalysis in Italy, though he pointed out that Freud had largely neglected the higher reaches of human nature. Over many years until his death in 1974, Dr. Assagioli developed a comprehensive psychology known as psychosynthesis. Psychosynthesis sees man as tending naturally toward harmony within himself and with the world. Dr. Assagioli's concept of the will is a key part of that vision. Penguin Books also publishes Roberto Assagioli's *The Act of Will.*

AN ESALEN BOOK

The Esalen Publishing Program is edited by Stuart Miller

•Available in paperback.

Psychosynthesis

A Manual
of Principles
and Techniques

Roberto Assagioli, M.D.

PENGUIN

ARKANA

ARKANA
Published by the Penguin Group
Penguin Books USA Inc., 375 Hudson Street, New York,
New York 10014, U.S.A.
Penguin Books Ltd, 27 Wrights Lane,
London W8 5TZ, England
Penguin Books Australia Ltd, Ringwood,
Victoria, Australia
Penguin Books Canada Ltd, 10 Alcorn Avenue,
Toronto, Ontario, Canada M4V 3B2
Penguin Books (N.Z.) Ltd, 182–190 Wairau Road,
Auckland 10, New Zealand

Penguin Books Ltd, Registered Offices:
Harmondsworth, Middlesex, England

First published in the United States of America by
Hobbs, Dorman & Co., Inc., 1965
This edition is published by arrangement with the
Berkshire Center for Psychosynthesis, Inc.
Viking Compass Edition published 1971
Published in Penguin Books 1976
Published in Arkana 1993

1 3 5 7 9 10 8 6 4 2

An Esalen Book

LIBRARY OF CONGRESS CATALOG CARD NUMBER: 74–4852

ISBN 0 14 019.460 6

Printed in the United States of America
Set in Linotype Baskerville

PREFACE TO THE PAPERBACK EDITION

Since the publication of this book in 1965, many developments have taken place in the fields of psychology and psychotherapy. In the words of A. H. Maslow in the Preface to the second edition of *Motivation and Personality* (New York: Harper & Row, 1970):

> The humanistic psychologies, the new transcendent psychologies, the existential, the Rogerian, the experiential, the holistic, the value-seeking psychologies, are all thriving and available at least in the United States, though unfortunately not yet in most departments of psychology. . . .

These developments have been too numerous and diverse to be described here, however briefly, or to be given a bibliography. Maslow, a pioneer in this field and its outstanding figure, whose premature death is deeply regretted, contributed much on this subject in his later writings. Interested readers are referred to them, to the *Journal of Humanistic Psychology*, and particularly to the *Journal of Transpersonal Psychology*.

Parallel with this movement, or rather within its main stream, psychosynthesis has been accorded increasing recognition and appreciation. Its techniques are being extensively applied in many countries. The fact that the book has been recommended for use in classrooms has led to requests from various quarters that it be made available at a lower price and in a handier form. This paperback edition is offered in response to these requests.

Typographical reasons and the pressure not to delay publication have prompted me to forgo an ample revision of the text, which, in its present form, has been found to serve its purpose. Nevertheless I have considered it advisable to make a few changes, the chief of which concerns the will. A distinction has been drawn between the stage of *deliberation* and that of *motivation*. The last stage is called the "direction of the execution," to emphasize the fact that the will does not produce results by means of sheer force (as the "Victorian" conception of the will maintained), but through the regulation and harmonizing of the other psychological functions, which it "steers" toward the chosen goal. This process is dealt with in detail in the author's forthcoming book on the will.

The subjects dealt with in Chapter II seem particularly timely in view of the present widespread urge and eager attempts to attain an expansion of consciousness and higher ranges of perception. These aspirations and endeavors can be interpreted and justified by what has been said concerning the *awakening* (pp. 40 – 43). The methods of dealing with the vicissitudes, problems and dangers of that quest are discussed on pp. 43 – 53. Sane and effective ways toward the attainment of the sought-for states of expanded consciousness are indicated in the exposition of various psychosynthetic techniques.

Comments and reports on the results of the application of the various techniques described in this book will be greatly appreciated.

Roberto Assagioli

Via San Domenico 16
50133 Florence, Italy
December 29, 1970

PREFACE

This exposition of the principles and techniques of psychosynthesis has been made, on behalf of the Psychosynthesis Research Foundation, by its Chairman, Roberto Assagioli, M.D. (Florence, Italy), with the valuable assistance of Robert Gerard, Ph.D. (Los Angeles), member of the International Advisory Board of the Foundation.

The Foundation wishes to express its appreciation to Jack Cooper, M.D. (New York City) for his helpful suggestions in the preparation of the manuscript.

Part Two of the book, dealing specifically with various techniques, was made available, in draft form, in 1963, as a "Manual of Techniques" for private use by a selected number of psychiatrists, therapists, and educators, in order that they could make a beginning with the application of the techniques. In response to many requests to make it more widely available the present volume has been prepared.

The Foundation would greatly appreciate any comments and suggestions, as well as reports on the application of psychosynthesis techniques in various settings, and the results obtained. These will be taken into due consideration when future editions are prepared.

The best training for practicing psychosynthesis (as in the case of psychoanalysis) is a "didactic psychosynthesis." When this is not possible, it is most advisable that the therapist undertakes an auto-psychosynthesis (self-synthesis) by applying the techniques to himself before, or at least while, applying them to others.

Roberto Assagioli, M.D.
Florence, Italy

NOTE TO THE SECOND PRINTING

This edition is substantially the same as the first. The inclusion of further material in the text, a careful revision of the index and the enriching of the bibliographies would have entailed a considerable delay in the reprinting which was urgently needed owing to the rapid—and gratifying—sale of the first edition. The many appreciative reviews and private comments indicate that the book, as it is, serves a useful purpose as a general introduction to the principles and the therapeutic application of psychosynthesis.

Some of the subjects mentioned in the book have been dealt with at greater length in several booklets published by the Psychosynthesis Research Foundation, such as *The Training of the Will* (Assagioli), *Approaches to the Self* (Crampton & Taylor), *The Psychology of Woman* (Assagioli).

It seems opportune—in answer to some questions and requests which have been addressed to me—to give more information about the origin and elaboration of the various sections of this book, and at the same time to make more definite acknowledgments and express my grateful appreciation to all those who in various ways cooperated with me in the preparation of this book for publication.

Chapter I, I wrote originally in Italian and it was published as a pamphlet with the title *Psicoanalisi e Psicosintesi*. It was then translated into English and published with the same title in *The Hibbert Journal* in 1934. It was later thoroughly revised and published as a booklet by the Psychosynthesis Research Foundation in 1959 under the title *Dynamic Psychology and Psychosynthesis*.

Chapter II was also originally written and published in Italian, and its English translation was published in *The Hibbert Journal* in 1937, with the title *Spiritual Development and its Attendant Maladies*. It was later modified and carefully revised, with the helpful cooperation of Robert Gerard, Ph.D., to whom due acknowledgment was given in the pamphlet published by the Psychosynthesis Research Foundation in 1961 with the present title *Self-Realization and Psychological Disturbances*.

The basic material constituting Part Two of the book (comprising Chapters III to VI) was gathered by me during many years of therapeutic practice and experimentation and described in my lectures and courses of lessons at the *Istituto di Psicosintesi* and in various unpublished papers. With the establishment of the Psychosynthesis Research Foundation in 1957 the need was felt to organize the material with a view to its publication as a manual of psychosynthetic techniques. For this purpose Dr. Robert Gerard in 1959, by means of a grant by the Foundation, came to Italy and collaborated with me. We discussed together many of the techniques, recording the sessions on tape, and gradually there emerged the general pattern for the description of the techniques: Purpose—Rationale—Procedure—Indications and Applications—Limitations and Contra-indications—Combination with Other Techniques; and this was finally adopted. In this work Dr. Gerard's cooperation proved very valuable and I give him full recognition for it.

The Exercises for Spiritual Psychosynthesis (on the *Legend of the Grail;* on Dante's *Divine Comedy;* on the *Blossoming of a Rose;* and the *Exercise for Evoking Serenity*) were originally written by me.

Part Three (Chapters VII and VIII) were also originally written in Italian by me and then translated into English with the help of various friends, particularly of Mr. Kenneth Leslie-Smith.

Later, the material, including tape transcriptions, thus gathered and still not organized was thoroughly elaborated and coordinated by

Bruno and Louise Huber, who were then doing secretarial work for me. A further careful revision, particularly of the wording and style, was made by Frank and Hilda Hilton; and a final revision, with hekpful suggestions, was made by Jack Cooper, M.D.

As regards the Appendix, the articles *Initiated Symbol Projection** and *Meditative Techniques in Psychotherapy* were translated and adapted by William Swartley, Ph.D., from papers in German by Hanscarl Leuner, M.D., H. J. Kornadt, Ph.D. and Wolfgang Kretschmer, Jr., M.D., as stated on pp. 287 and 304 of the book. I acknowledge with gratitude this valuable contribution by Dr. Swartley.

Roberto Assagioli, M.D.
Florence, Italy
July 1969

---

*Dr. Leuner now prefers to call his method "Guided Affective Imagery", and uses "Initiated Symbol Projection" to refer to the diagnostic aspects of his work.

TABLE OF CONTENTS

Part One

PRINCIPLES

INTRODUCTION | DYNAMIC PSYCHOLOGY AND
PSYCHOSYNTHESIS | SELF-REALIZATION AND
PSYCHOLOGICAL DISTURBANCES

Introduction*

To place psychosynthesis in the context of current thinking—particularly as regards new trends—in psychiatry and psychology, it may be well to offer a confrontation or comparison between psychosynthesis and existential psychotherapy.

I am well aware of the difficulties and limitations of such a comparison. As van Kaam (16) has stated, "Existentialism is a collective name for widely divergent existentialist currents of thought which have only a few characteristics in common." But the difficulty is obviated to a great extent by the fact that I shall not take into consideration the philosophical and theoretical aspects of existentialism—which are those in which their representatives differ most—but only those related to psychotherapy.

However, this exposition does not attempt to be in any way exhaustive, but is meant to be only indicative, and introductive. I shall add that, in a subordinate way, it will implicitly point out also the similarities and differences between psychosynthesis and the other non-existential methods of psychotherapy. Let us first take up the similarities:

A. SIMILARITIES

Most of these are the same as those so lucidly indicated by Maslow (12) in his paper *Remarks on Existentialism and Psychology.*

*This introductory chapter is drawn from two papers given by the author at the Fifth International Congress of Psychotherapy, Vienna, on August the 21st, 1961.

1. The fundamental similarity or, rather, identity is a methodological one, namely the method of starting *from within*, of beginning with the *self* of the individual, with his *presence*. This means to attribute a central importance to the concept and experience of "identity"—an emphasis given also by Maslow and by a group of other American psychologists and psychiatrists, such as Allport (1), Goldstein (9), Fromm (8), Moustakas (13), Erikson (6), etc., representing a trend with which I am mainly in agreement. The same can be said to a great extent concerning the personalistic psychology of Tournier (15), Baudoin (4), Caruso (5), the "personalen" conception of Herzog-Dürk (10), A. Vetter (17) and the "personal-anthropological" one of von Gebsattel (18).

2. The concept, or rather the fact, that each individual is in constant development, is *growing*, actualizing successively many latent potentialities.

3. The central importance of *meaning;* particularly of the meaning which each individual *gives* to life, or is *looking for* in life.

4. The recognition of the importance of *values*, particularly of the ethical, aesthetic, noetic, religious values, so well emphasized by Frankl (7).

5. The fact that each individual is constantly confronted by *choices* and *decisions*, with the consequent *responsibility* which they entail.

6. The need of achieving a clear awareness of the *motivations* which determine the choices and the decisions.

7. The recognition of the depth and seriousness of human life, of the place of anxiety in it and of the suffering which has to be faced.

8. The emphasis on the *future*, and of its dynamic role in the *present*.

9. The recognition of the uniqueness of each individual, Allport's "idiographic psychology" (1), and therefore the need of what I call "differential psychosynthesis," requiring a different combination of the many techniques of therapy in a new *method* for each patient.

B. DIFFERENCES

I should like, first of all, to make clear that these are relative, not fundamental, that there is no real contrast. They consist mostly in different emphasis and in the inclusion of factors, or aspects, or techniques not taken into consideration, or into sufficient consideration, by other therapies.

It is also opportune to point out that certain differences are greater with some representatives of existential therapy than with others. I cannot now indicate these differences, but well-informed readers will be able to easily recognize them.

1. The most distinctive point perhaps is the emphasis put upon, and the central place given in psychosynthesis to the *will* as an essential function of the self and as the necessary source or origin of all choices, decisions, engagements. Therefore, psychosynthesis includes a careful analysis of the various phases of the will, such as *deliberation, motivation, decision, affirmation, persistence, execution,* and makes much use of various techniques for arousing, developing, strengthening and rightly directing the will.

2. A second point of difference from some existentialists concerns the nature of the self and the search for self-identity. In my opinion, the direct experience of the self, of pure *self-awareness* — independent of any "content" of the field of consciousness and of any situation in which the individual may find himself — is a true, "phenomenological" experience, an inner reality which can be empirically verified and deliberately produced through appropriate techniques. An examination of the nature and place of the self in its two aspects is contained in Chapters One and Two: *Dynamic Psychology and Psychosynthesis* and *Self-Realization and Psychological Disturbances.*[a]

3. Another difference from certain existentialist trends is the recognition of the positive, creative, joyous experiences which man may, and often does, have along with the painful and tragic ones. They are those aptly called by Maslow "peak experiences," such as: self-realization, fulfillment, achievement, illumination, peace, and joy. They are phenomenological *lived* experiences, and in psychosynthesis they are actively fostered or induced through the use of appropriate methods.

4. The experience of loneliness is not considered in psychosynthesis either ultimate or essential. It is a stage, a temporary subjective condition. It can and does alternate with, and finally can be substituted by, the genuine living experience of interpersonal and interindividual communications, relationships, interplay; by cooperation between individuals, and among groups — and even by a *blending*, through intuition, empathy, understanding and identification. This is the large field of interindividual psychosynthesis, reaching from the interpersonal relationship of man and woman to the harmonious integration of the individual into even larger groups up to the "one humanity." It can be and has

---

[a]Revisions of published monographs (3).

been expressed in other words as the reality and the function of *love* in its various aspects and particularly in that of "agapé," altruistic love, "charity," brotherhood, communion, sharing: Sorokin (14), Lewis (11) and Fromm (8).

5. The deliberate use of a large number of *active techniques* for:
   a. The transformation, sublimation and direction of psychological energies.
   b. The strengthening and maturing of weak or undeveloped functions.
   c. The activation of superconscious energies and the arousing of latent potentialities.

6. The conscious and *planned* reconstruction or re-creation of the personality, through the cooperation and the interplay of patient and therapist. The amount and the character of such cooperation varies during the development of the therapeutic process and can be described as having three stages, although they are not separated, but often overlap and blend. At first the therapist plays the more active role. Then his influence becomes more and more catalytic: he represents or constitutes a model or a symbol and is introjected in some measure by the patient. In the final stage the therapist gradually withdraws, and is replaced by the Self, with whom the patient establishes a growing relationship, a "dialogue," and an increasing (although never complete) identification.

May I emphasize the fact that the elements and functions, coming from the superconscious, such as aesthetic, ethical, religious experiences, intuition, inspiration, states of mystical consciousness, are *factual*, are real in the pragmatic sense (*wirklich*, to use the significant German word), because they are *effective (wirkend)*, producing changes both in the inner and the outer world. Therefore, they are amenable to observation and experiment, through the use of the scientific method in ways suited to their nature; also they can be influenced and utilized through psycho-spiritual techniques.

At this point the question may arise as to the relationship between this conception of the human being on the one hand and religion and metaphysics on the other. The answer is that psychosynthesis does not attempt in any way to appropriate to itself the fields of religion and of philosophy. It is a scientific conception, and as such it is neutral towards the various religious forms and the various philosophical doctrines, excepting only those which are materialistic and therefore deny the existence of spiritual realities. Psychosynthesis does not aim nor attempt to give a metaphysical nor a theological explanation of the great Mystery—it leads to the door, but stops there.

In the list of the techniques used in psychosynthesis the various phases of psychosynthetic treatment are indicated. The starting point of the treatment is the ascertainment of *the unique existential situation of each patient,* of the *problems* which it presents and of the ways for their solution. This includes naturally a psychoanalytical phase. Then follows the activation of the latent aspects and functions and the development of the weak ones, through the use of the active techniques suitable for each task. After, or rather while this is being done, the harmonization and integration into one functioning whole of all the qualities and functions of the individual must be aimed at and actively fostered—the central purpose of psychosynthesis. Such harmonization and integration both allows and requires the constructive utilization and expression of all the liberated and activated drives and energies of the personality. In its turn this brings up the many problems and psychosynthetic tasks of interpersonal relationships and of social integration (psychosynthesis of man and woman—of the individual with various groups—of groups with groups—of nations—of the whole of humanity).

In actual treatment all these phases are not dealt with separately and in succession, but are carried on in a parallel way. For instance, tackling at the beginning the central existential problem one often finds that it includes ethical or religious conflicts, and their treatment must be taken up at once. In contrast, the analytical investigation can be made at intervals, whenever a block or a resistance has to be eliminated.

A distinctive characteristic of the psychosynthetic treatment is the *systematic* use of all available active psychological techniques. I emphasize the word "systematic," which means a use made according to the specific plan of the treatment and directed towards clearly envisioned aims. Therefore it is not a mere eclecticism as it might appear from a superficial view. I will deal with those techniques in greater detail later (see Part Two) but wish to mention here a few of those which I consider of paramount importance. The basic one, which helps and even makes possible the use of all the others, concerns the arousing and development of the *will.*

The will is, curiously, not recognized as the central and fundamental function of the ego. It has often been depreciated as being ineffective against the various drives and the power of the imagination, or it has been considered with suspicion as leading to self-assertion (will-to-power). But the latter is only a perverted use of the will, while the apparent futility of the will is due only to a faulty and unintelligent use. The will is ineffective only when it attempts to act *in opposition* to the imagination and to the other psychological functions, while its skillful and consequently successful use consists in *regulating* and *directing* all other functions toward a deliberately chosen and affirmed aim.

The will is not only and simply "will power" according to the usual conception. It includes six phases or stages, all necessary for its complete and effective expression.

1. Goal, valuation, motivation; 2. Deliberation; 3. Decision; 4. Affirmation; 5. Planning; 6. Direction of the execution.

Each of these aspects of the will can be developed and used through appropriate techniques.

Another psychological method of the greatest individual and social importance is the transmutation and sublimation of the bio-psychic energies, particularly of the sexual and of the combative or aggressive drives. Modern psychology, and particularly psychoanalysis, has discovered (or more exactly rediscovered) the transformation which those energies can undergo and which they often undergo spontaneously. Thus, a scientific "psychodynamics" is being developed, which aims at discovering the laws under which the transformations take place and the techniques for bringing about those which are desired. It offers the means by which the present enormous waste and deplorable misuse of incalculable amounts of sexual, emotional, and combative energies can be offset and the same forces can be directed and used for creative activities and achievements. It does not seem exaggerated to say that such utilization may gradually parallel that which is being made of the previously neglected or ignored power of electricity.

A different, and in a certain sense opposite, group of procedures are those aiming at the awakening, the releasing and the employment of the potent superconscious spiritual energies, which have a transforming and regenerating influence on the personality. This release may be compared to that of the intra-atomic energy latent in matter.

May I briefly mention that, while psychosynthesis has been developed and is mainly used in therapy, its principles and methods can be and are applied also in other fields. First of all in that of psychological hygiene, or mental health, for the prevention of neurotic and psychological troubles. Then in the field of education where the many techniques which it uses can have wide and fruitful applications Moreover, it can have a special usefulness in the education of gifted and super-gifted children, because in them the superconscious functions are spontaneously awakened or awakening, and their activity needs to be wisely directed and integrated with that of the other functions. Another large field is that of interindividual (interpersonal) and group relationships, which sorely need to be adjusted and harmonized.

Last but not least, psychosynthesis can be applied by the individual himself or herself, fostering and accelerating inner growth and self-actualization, which should be the aim of all and which sometimes is felt as an imperative inner urge, as a vital existential necessity. Such self-psychosynthesis should be practiced, or at least seriously attempted, by every therapist, social worker and educator (including parents). Of course, great help can be given by didactic psychosynthesis; it is therefore advisable, and I strongly recommend such a didactic training—as is done in psychoanalysis.

This introduction, although very cursory, may be sufficient to indicate that psychosynthesis has much to offer; but I should not want by any means to give the impression that it is, or that I consider it as, something already fully developed or satisfactorily completed. On the contrary, I consider it as a child—or at the most as an adolescent—with many aspects still incomplete; yet with a great and promising potential for growth.

I make a cordial appeal to all therapists, psychologists and educators to actively engage in the needed work of research, experimentation and application. Let us feel and obey the urge aroused by the great need of healing the serious ills which at present are affecting humanity; let us realize the contribution we can make to the creation of a new civilization characterized by an harmonious integration and cooperation, pervaded by the spirit of synthesis.

REFERENCES

1. Allport, G.: *Becoming*, New Haven, Yale University Press, 1955.
2. Angyal, A.: *Foundations of a Science of Personality*, Cambridge, Harvard University Press, 1941.
3. Assagioli, R.: *Dynamic Psychology and Psychosynthesis*. Monograph. New York, Psychosynthesis Research Foundation, 1958.

—— *Self-Realization and Psychological Disturbances.* Monograph. New York, Psychosynthesis Research Foundation, 1961.

4. Baudoin, C.: *Découverte de la Personne,* Paris, Presses Universitaires, 1940.

5. Caruso, I. A.: *Psychoanalyse und Synthese der Existenz,* Wien, Seelsorger-Verlag, Herder 1952.
—— *Bios, Psyche, Person,* Freiburg, K. Alber, 1957.

6. Erikson, Erik H.: *Childhood and Society,* New York, Norton, 1950.

7. Frankl, V. E.: *Theorie und Therapie der Neurosen; Einfuehrung in Logotherapie und Existenzanalyse,* Wien, Urban & Schwarzenberg, 1956.
—— *Arztliche Seelsorge,* Wien, Deuticke, 1952.
—— *The Doctor and the Soul: An Introduction to Logotherapy,* New York, Knopf, 1955.

8. Fromm, E.: *The Sane Society,* New York, Rinehart, 1956.

9. Goldstein, K.: *The Organism,* New York, American Book Co., 1939.

10. Herzog-Dürk,: *Mensch sein als Wagnis,* Stuttgart, Klett, 1961.

11. Lewis, C. S.: *The Four Loves,* New York, Harcourt Brace, 1960.

12. Maslow, A.H.: *Cognition of Being in the Peak Experiences.* Monograph. Waltham, Mass., Dept. of Psychology, Brandeis University, 1956.
—— *Remarks on Existentialism and Psychology* (Lecture delivered at the American Psychological Association, Cincinnati, 1959). Mimeographed, from Psychosynthesis Research Foundation, New York.

13. Moustakas, C.: (Editor), *The Self: Explorations in Personal Growth,* New York, Harper, 1956.

14. Sorokin, P.A., et al.: *Forms and Techniques of Altruistic and Spiritual Growth,* Boston, Beacon Press, 1954.
—— *The Ways and Power of Love,* Boston, Beacon Press, 1954.

15. Tournier, P.: *Médecine de la Personne,* Neuchâtel, Delachaux & Niestlé, 1941.

16. van Kaam, A.: *The Third Force in European Psychology: Its Expression in a Theory of Psychotherapy.* Monograph. New York, Psychosynthesis Research Foundation, 1960.

17. Vetter, A.: *Natur und Person,* Stuttgart, Klett, 1950.

18. von Gebsattel, E.V.: *Gedanken zu einer anthropologischen Psychotherapie,* in Frankl-von Gebsattel-Schultz Hb.d. Neurosenlehre in Psychotherapie, Bd. III, S.435-588, Munchen, Urban Schwarzenberg, 1959.

Dynamic Psychology and Psychosynthesis

I begin with a semantic remark and with some historical information. The word psychosynthesis, and expressions such as "mental synthesis" and similar ones, have been used by a number of psychologists and psychiatrists. Considering only the field of psychotherapy, we find first Janet (34), who speaks of "synthèse mentale," then Bezzola (10), Neutra (53), Bjerre (11), de Jonge (16), Trüb (74); and Freud (21) speaks of the synthesizing function of the ego. But they used the word only in the sense of "healing the functional dissociation," that is, re-establishing the condition existing before a split or dissociation due to a traumatic experience or to strong conflicts.

Others, such as Jung (35), who mentions synthesis when dealing with "the transcendental function," Maeder (43), Caruso (15), Stocker (69), and W. Kretschmer, Jr. (38) used the words synthesis, psychosynthesis, synthesis of existence, synthetic psychotherapy in a deeper and wider sense as the development of an integrated and harmonious personality, including both its conscious and unconscious parts. Recently the word psychosynthesis has been adopted by Lepp (40).

The conception and the practice of psychosynthesis which I have gradually developed,[a] while it includes the preceding, is

[a] The history of this development is briefly given in the Appendix, see p. 280.

more comprehensive and at the same time more definite and technical.

When we observe the most obvious characteristics of contemporary civilization, we are struck by its extreme extraversion, its desire to know and master the forces of nature in order to satisfy its ever growing needs and demands. This is indeed the dominating trend of our age, but it is by no means the only one, as a closer study will reveal.

As is well known, in the course of the last seventy years a group of inquirers, which was at first small but which gradually grew more active, turned its attention to the investigation of the phenomena and mysteries of the human psyche. The most important results have not been achieved by academic psychologists, but by independent investigators. Nearly all of them were clinicians, driven by the practical needs of their patients and aided by the greater evidence that certain psychological phenomena acquire when they are accentuated by a morbid condition.

The first scientist to contribute original discoveries in this field was Pierre Janet (34). Starting with the phenomena of "psychological automatism" he found that there are many mental activities taking place independently of the patient's consciousness, and even real "secondary personalities" living behind, or alternating with, the everyday personality.

Soon after Janet a Viennese doctor, Sigmund Freud (21), began his investigations of the unconscious psychological processes. His starting point was Breuer's cathartic method, which consisted in recalling to the consciousness of the patient the forgotten trauma or impressions which had produced the symptoms and releasing the strong emotions associated with them. Breuer used hypnosis for this purpose, but Freud soon found out that the same result could be reached by the use of free association and by the interpretation of dreams, which became the specific techniques of psychoanalysis.

Freud demonstrated that various physical symptoms and psychological disturbances are due to instincts, drives, phantasies, buried in the unconscious and retained there by resistances and defence mechanisms of various kinds. He also found that many manifestations of our normal life, such as dreams, fancies, forgetting, mistakes and lapses of behaviour, and even some kinds of artistic and literary production, are due to the same psychological mechanisms which determine morbid symptoms in the sick. For instance, the curious forgetting of well-known things or words is due, according to Freud, to some connection existing between the forgotten word or fact and some painful or disagreeable event. He gives an amusing illustration of this: one day he could not remember the name of a well-known resort on the Italian Riviera, namely, Nervi. "Indeed," he writes, " 'nerves' (in Italian *nervi*) give me a great deal of trouble."

On this basis Freud developed a wealth of conceptions on the genetic processes and on the structure of the human personality which it is impossible to summarize, the more so because they underwent considerable changes during the many years of Freud's copious production. But his psychoanalytic doctrines are at present well-known and have been expounded or summarized by various writers.[b]

Freud had many pupils and followers, some of whom contributed various developments and modifications, while remaining in the main stream of the psychoanalytic movement; such were Karl Abraham (1), Sandor Ferenczi (19), Wilhelm Stekel (67), Melanie Klein (37), etc. On the other hand, some of Freud's original pupils and co-workers took independent and even antagonistic positions and developed conceptions, methods and even Schools of their own. The more important among them are: Alfred Adler (2) who, in his "Individual Psychology," emphasized the importance of the drive to personal self-assertion, or the will-to-power; C. G. Jung (35), who investigated the deeper layers of the unconscious, where he found images and symbols of a collective character, and also made original contributions to the classification and description of psychological types; Otto Rank (58), who put particular emphasis on the problem of separation and union, and on the function of the will. Later, specific contributions were made by Karen Horney (32), who pointed out the importance of actual conflicts and of the need for security. Erich Fromm (22) put the accent on social pressures on the individual.

---

[b]A comprehensive and objective exposition of Freudian psychoanalysis is that by Ruth L. Munroe in her book *Schools of Psychoanalytic Thought* (50) which also contains a clear exposition and critical comments on the other main exponents of psychoanalytic thought.

Various contributions have been made by French psycho-analysts such as Allendy (3), Hesnard (31), and Baudoin (8). Mention should also be made of "Existential Analysis," put forward and practised by Binswanger (12) and Frankl (20).

If we take into consideration a larger field, which includes both special branches of medicine and of psychology and various independent cultural movements, we find significant and valuable contributions to the knowledge of human nature and to its betterment. Among these are:

1. *Psychosomatic Medicine,* which has increasingly developed in recent years, bringing to light the strong influence of psychological factors in determining troubles of every kind, including many of an organic character.

2. *The Psychology of Religion,* which investigates the various manifestations of religious consciousness and of mystical states. The researchers in this field have been numerous; we can mention, among the first, William James (33), with his classical book — *The Varieties of Religious Experience;* Underhill (75), (*Mysticism*); Heiler (30); Winslow Hall (26); etc. Lately, a number of books have appeared which discuss the relationship between psychology and religion.

3. *The Investigation of the Superconscious* (and its manifestations such as intuition and illumination), of genius and of creative activity; and of highly gifted children. Here we find the study of "cosmic consciousness" by Bucke (13); the contributions of Ouspensky (55), Winslow Hall (26), Urban (76), Maslow (45), Terman (72), etc.; and the group working in the Association for Gifted Children.

4. *"Psychical Research"* or *Parapsychology,* which developed from the classical studies of Myers (52) on the "Subliminal Self" and was developed by earnest scientists such as James (33), Lodge (42), Richet (61), Geley (23), Osty (54), Rhine (60), etc. It has given evidence of the existence of supernormal psychophysical abilities such as extra-sensory perception, mechanical action from a distance (telekinesis), telepathy, and premonition. It has also gathered much material on the problem of survival.

5. *Eastern Psychology* (especially Indian), both ancient and modern. Its valuable contributions are beginning to be integrated with those of Western psychology (62).

6. *"Creative Understanding,"* which emphasizes the creative power of spiritual understanding and of inner significance. Its chief champion was Hermann Keyserling (36) who expounded this approach through many books and through the "School of Wisdom" which was active for many years at Darmstadt, Germany.

7. *The Holistic Approach and the Psychology of the Personality.* This was first promoted by Smuts (65) in his book *Holism and Evolution* and is being adopted by an increasing number of psychologists and psychiatrists such as: Allport (4), Angyal (5), Goldstein (24), Maslow (45), Murphy (51), Perls, Hefferline and Goodman (56), and Progoff (57). The views of the preceding authors were ably summarized by Hall (25). Parallel with this development in America there has been in Switzerland the movement called *Médecine de la Personne,* started by Tournier of Geneva (73), and followed by Maeder (43) and others and, along independent lines, by Baudoin (8). The personalistic standpoint has been also upheld by Stern (68) in Germany.

8. *Inter-individual and Social Psychology and Psychiatry* and the *Anthropological Study of Man.* This is a large movement which includes various independent currents. Here we find Sullivan (70) with his "Inter-personal Theory of Psychiatry," Lewin (41), and then the investigators of group dynamics as at the University of Michigan (14), the researchers into human relations at Harvard (59), the contributions of Sorokin (59) on altruistic love, etc., also at Harvard; while in Europe there is the emphasis on the social and moral aspect in psychiatry by Baruk (7) and Hauser (29). The anthropological approach is ably represented, among others, by Margaret Mead (48).

9. *"Active Techniques" for the Treatment and Development of the Personality.* The comparatively older ones are hypnotism and suggestion and auto-suggestion, described and used

by the two "Schools of Nancy" (Liebault, Bernheim,
Coué) and, with greater scientific accuracy, by Baudoin
(8); then the autogenous training of Schultz (63); Desoille's "Rêve éveillé" (17); the rational approach of Ellis
and Harper (18); Happich's meditation technique (27);
Moreno's (49) psychodrama, and other forms of Group
Psychotherapy of Bach (6) and Berne (9). Moreover
there are the various techniques, too numerous to be
quoted in this rapid survey, for the training of specific
functions such as memory, thinking, imagination and
will.[c]

This vast amount of studies and research offers enough
material for an attempt at co-ordination and synthesis. If we
assemble ascertained facts, positive and well-authenticated contributions and well-founded interpretations, ignoring the exaggerations and theoretical superstructures of the various schools,
we arrive at a pluridimensional[d] conception of the human personality which, though far from perfect or final, is, we think, more
inclusive and nearer to reality than previous formulations.

To illustrate such a conception of the constitution of the human being in his living concrete reality the following diagram
may be helpful. It is, of course, a crude and elementary picture
that can give only a structural, static, almost "anatomical" representation of our inner constitution, while it leaves out its dynamic
aspect, which is the most important and essential one. But here, as
in every science, gradual steps must be taken and progressive approximations be made. When dealing with a reality so plastic and
elusive as our psychological life, it is important not to lose sight of
the main lines and of the fundamental differences; otherwise the
multiplicity of details is liable to obscure the picture as a whole
and to prevent our realizing the respective significance, purpose,
and value of its different parts.

With these reservations and qualifications, the chart is as
follows:

---

[c]This enumeration is merely indicative: the list of the investigators is very incomplete
and apologies are made to those not mentioned. The only purpose of the survey was
to show how manifold and diverse are the approaches to the research into the mystery of man.
[d]This apt term indicating an inclusive outlook has been used by Ruth Munroe (50)
and by Gardner Murphy (51).

Diagram I

1. The Lower Unconscious
2. The Middle Unconscious
3. The Higher Unconscious or Superconscious
4. The Field of Consciousness
5. The Conscious Self or "I"
6. The Higher Self
7. The Collective Unconscious

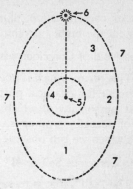

1. The Lower Unconscious

This contains:

  a. The elementary psychological activities which direct the life of the body; the intelligent co-ordination of bodily functions.
  b. The fundamental drives and primitive urges.
  c. Many complexes, charged with intense emotion.
  d. Dreams and imaginations of an inferior kind.
  e. Lower, uncontrolled parapsychological processes.
  f. Various pathological manifestations, such as phobias, obsessions, compulsive urges and paranoid delusions.

2. The Middle Unconscious

This is formed of psychological elements similar to those of our waking consciousness and easily accessible to it. In this inner region our various experiences are assimilated, our ordinary mental and imaginative activities are elaborated and developed in a sort of psychological gestation before their birth into the light of consciousness.

3. The Higher Unconscious or Superconscious

From this region we receive our higher intuitions and inspirations—artistic, philosophical or scientific, ethical "imperatives" and urges to humanitarian and heroic action. It is the source of the higher feelings, such as altruistic love; of genius and of the states of contemplation, illumination, and ecstasy. In this realm are latent the higher psychic functions and spiritual energies.

4. The Field of Consciousness

This term — which is not quite accurate but which is clear and convenient for practical purposes — is used to designate that part of our personality of which we are directly aware: the incessant flow of sensations, images, thoughts, feelings, desires, and impulses which we can observe, analyse, and judge.

5. The Conscious Self or "I"

The "self", that is to say, the point of pure self-awareness, is often confused with the conscious personality just described, but in reality it is quite different from it. This can be ascertained by the use of careful introspection. The changing *contents* of our consciousness (the sensations, thoughts, feelings, etc.) are one thing, while the "I", the self, the *center* of our consciousness is another. From a certain point of view this difference can be compared to that existing between the white lighted area on a screen and the various pictures which are projected upon it.

But the "man in the street" and even many well-educated people do not take the trouble to observe themselves and to discriminate; they drift on the surface of the "mind-stream" and identify themselves with its successive waves, with the changing contents of their consciousness.

6. The Higher Self

The conscious self is generally not only submerged in the ceaseless flow of psychological contents but seems to disappear altogether when we fall asleep, when we faint, when we are under the effect of an anesthetic or narcotic, or in a state of hypnosis. And when we awake the self mysteriously re-appears, we do not know how or whence — a fact which, if closely examined, is truly baffling and disturbing. This leads us to assume that the re-appearance of the conscious self or ego is due to the existence of a permanent center, of a true Self situated beyond or "above" it.[e]

---

[e]The higher Self should not be confused in any way with the super-ego of Freud, which is not a real self but, according to Freud's theory, a construction, an artificial product. It is also different from any "phenomenological" conception of the self or ego.

There are various ways by means of which the reality of the Self can be ascertained. There have been many individuals who have achieved, more or less temporarily, a conscious realization of the Self that for them has the same degree of certainty as is experienced by an explorer who has entered a previously unknown region. Such statements can be found in Bucke's *Cosmic Consciousness* (13), in Ouspensky's *Tertium Organum* (55), in Underhill's *Mysticism* (75), and in other books. The awareness of the Self can also be achieved through the use of certain psychological methods, among which are Jung's "process of individuation" (35), Desoille's "Rêve éveillé" (17), techniques of Raja Yoga (62), etc.

Then we have the corroboration of such philosophers as Kant and Herbart, who make a clear distinction between the empirical ego and the noumenal or real Self. This Self is above, and unaffected by, the flow of the mind-stream or by bodily conditions; and the personal conscious self should be considered merely as its reflection, its "projection" in the field of the personality. At the present stage of psychological investigation little is definitely known concerning the Self, but the importance of this synthesizing center well warrants further research.

7. The Collective Unconscious

Human beings are not isolated, they are not "monads without windows" as Leibnitz thought. They may at times feel subjectively isolated, but the extreme existentialistic conception is not true, either psychologically or spiritually.

The outer line of the oval of the diagram should be regarded as "delimiting" but not as "dividing." It should be regarded as analogous to the membrane delimiting a cell, which permits a constant and active interchange with the whole body to which the cell belongs. Processes of "psychological osmosis" are going on all the time, both with other human beings and with the general psychic environment. The latter corresponds to what Jung has called the "collective unconscious"; but he has not clearly defined this term, in which he includes elements of different, even opposite natures, namely primitive archaic structures and higher, forward-directed activities of a superconscious character. (See C. G. Jung, *Two Essays on Analytical Psychology*, London, 1928, pp. 118-9).

The preceding diagram helps us to reconcile the following facts, which at first appear to contradict and exclude each other:

1. *The seeming duality,* the apparent existence of two selves in us. Indeed, it is *as if* there were two selves, because the personal self is generally unaware of the other, even to the point of denying its existence; whereas the other, the true Self, is latent and does not reveal itself directly to our consciousness.

2. *The real unity and uniqueness of the Self.* There are not really two selves, two independent and separate entities. The Self is one; it manifests in different degrees of awareness and self-realization. The reflection appears to be self-existent but has, in reality, no autonomous substantiality. It is, in other words, not a new and different light but a projection of its luminous source.

This conception of the structure of our being includes, coordinates and arranges in an integral vision the data obtained through various observations and experiences. It offers us a wider and more comprehensive understanding of the human drama, of the conflicts and problems that confront each one of us, and it also indicates the means of solving them and points the way to our liberation.

In our ordinary life we are limited and bound in a thousand ways—the prey of illusions and phantasms, the slaves of unrecognized complexes, tossed hither and thither by external influences, blinded and hypnotized by deceiving appearances. No wonder then that man, in such a state, is often discontented, insecure and changeable in his moods, thoughts and actions. Feeling intuitively that he is "one," and yet finding that he is "divided unto himself," he is bewildered and fails to understand either himself or others. No wonder that he, not knowing or understanding himself, has no self-control and is continually involved in his own mistakes and weaknesses; that so many lives are failures, or are at least limited and saddened by diseases of mind and body, or tormented by doubt, discouragement and despair. No wonder that man, in his blind passionate search for liberty and satisfaction, rebels violently at times, and at times tries to still his inner torment by throwing himself headlong into a life of feverish activity, constant excitement, tempestuous emotion, and reckless adventure.

*   *   *   *   *

Let us examine *whether* and *how* it is possible to solve this central problem of human life, to heal this fundamental infirmity of man. Let us see how he may free himself from this enslavement and achieve an harmonious inner integration, true Self-realization, and right relationships with others.

The task is certainly neither easy nor simple, but that it can be accomplished has been demonstrated by the success of those who have used adequate and appropriate means.

The stages for the attainment of this goal may be tabulated as follows:

1. Thorough knowledge of one's personality.
2. Control of its various elements.
3. Realization of one's true Self—the discovery or creation of a unifying center.
4. Psychosynthesis: the formation or reconstruction of the personality around the new center.

Let us examine each of these stages.

1. Thorough Knowledge of One's Personality.

We have recognized that in order really to know ourselves it is not enough to make an inventory of the elements that form our conscious being. An extensive exploration of the vast regions of our unconscious must also be undertaken. We have first to penetrate courageously into the pit of our lower unconscious in order to discover the dark forces that ensnare and menace us — the "phantasms," the ancestral or childish images that obsess or silently dominate us, the fears that paralyze us, the conflicts that waste our energies. It is possible to do this by the use of the methods of psychoanalysis.

This search can be undertaken by oneself but it is accomplished more easily with the help of another. In any case the methods must be employed in a genuinely scientific manner, with the greatest objectivity and impartiality; without preconceived theories and without allowing ourselves to be deterred or led astray by the covert or violent resistance of our fears, our desires, our emotional attachments.

Psychoanalysis generally stops here; but this limitation is not justified. The regions of the middle and higher unconscious should likewise be explored. In that way we shall discover in ourselves hitherto unknown abilities, our true vocations, our higher potentialities which seek to express themselves, but which we often repel and repress through lack of understanding, through prejudice or fear. We shall also discover the immense reserve of undifferentiated psychic energy latent in every one of us; that is, the plastic part of our unconscious which lies at our disposal, empowering us with an unlimited capacity to learn and to create.

2. Control of the Various Elements of the Personality.

After having discovered all these elements, we have to take possession of them and acquire control over them. The most effective method by which we can achieve this is that of disidentification. This is based on a fundamental psychological principle which may be formulated as follows:

We are dominated by everything with which our self becomes identified. We can dominate and control everything from which we disidentify ourselves.

In this principle lies the secret of our enslavement or of our liberty. Every time we "identify" ourselves with a weakness, a fault, a fear or any personal emotion or drive, we limit and paralyze ourselves. Every time we admit "I am discouraged" or "I am irritated," we become more and more dominated by depression or anger. We have accepted those limitations; we have ourselves put on our chains. If, instead, in the same situation we say, "A wave of discouragement is *trying* to submerge me" or "An impulse of anger is *attempting* to overpower me," the situation is very different. Then there are two forces confronting each other; on one side our vigilant self and on the other the discouragement or the anger. And the vigilant self does not submit to that invasion; it can objectively and critically survey those impulses of discouragement or anger; it can look for their origin, foresee their deleterious effects, and realize their unfoundedness. This is often sufficient to withstand an attack of such forces and win the battle.

But even when these forces within ourselves are temporarily stronger, when the conscious personality is at first overwhelmed by their violence, the vigilant self is never really conquered. It can retire to an inner fortress and there prepare for and await the favourable moment in which to counter-attack. It may lose some of the battles, but if it does not give up its arms and surrender, the ultimate issue is not compromised, and it will achieve victory in the end.

Then, besides repelling one by one the attacks that come from the unconscious, we can apply a more fundamental and decisive method: we can tackle the deep-seated causes of these attacks and cut away the roots of the difficulty. This procedure may be divided into two phases:

a. *The disintegration of the harmful images or complexes.*
b. *The control and utilization of the energies thus set free.*

Psychoanalysis has demonstrated that the power of these images and complexes lies chiefly in the fact that we are unconscious of them, that we do not recognize them as such. When they are unmasked, understood, and resolved into their elements, they often cease to obsess us; in any case we are then much better able to defend ourselves against them. In order to dissolve them we should use the methods of *objectification*, of *critical analysis* and of *discrimination*. That is to say, we must employ cold, impersonal observation as if they were mere natural phenomena, occurring outside ourselves. We should create a "psychological distance" between ourselves and them, keeping these images or complexes at arm's length, so to speak, and then quietly consider their origin, their nature and—their stupidity! This does not mean the suppression or repression of the energies inherent in those manifestations but their control and redirection into constructive channels.

It is well known that too much criticism and analysis are apt to paralyze and even kill our emotions and feelings. This critical faculty, which we often employ indiscriminately and harmfully against our higher feelings and creative potentialities, should instead be used to free ourselves from undesirable impulses and tendencies. But such analysis and criticism are not always sufficient. There are certain strong trends, certain vital elements which, however much we may disparage and condemn them, obstinately persist. This is true especially concerning sexual and aggressive drives. These, when detached from the complexes or diverted from their previous channels, create in us a state of agitation and unrest and may find new but equally undesirable outlets.

These forces, therefore, must not be left to run wild, but should be disposed of in harmless ways or, better still, used for constructive purposes: creative activities of various kinds; the rebuilding of our personality, contributing to our psychosynthesis. But in order to be able to do this we must start from the center; we must have established and made efficient *the unifying and controlling Principle of our life.*

3. Realization of One's True Self—
The Discovery or Creation of a Unifying Center.

On the basis of what we have said about the nature and power of the Self, it is not difficult to point out *theoretically* how to reach this aim. What has to be achieved is to expand the personal consciousness into that of the Self; to reach up, following the thread or ray (see diagram II) to the star; to unite the lower with the higher Self. But this, which is so easily expressed in words, is in reality a tremendous undertaking. It constitutes a magnificent endeavor, but certainly a long and arduous one, and not everybody is ready for it. But between the starting point in the lowlands of our ordinary consciousness and the shining peak of Self-realization there are intermediate phases, plateaus at various altitudes on which a man may rest or even make his abode, if his lack of strength precludes or his will does not choose a further ascent.

In favorable cases the ascent takes place to some extent spontaneously through a process of natural inner growth, fostered by the manifold experiences of life; but often the process is very slow. In all cases, however, it can be considerably accelerated by our deliberate conscious action and by the use of appropriate active techniques.

The intermediate stages imply new identifications. The men

and women who cannot reach their true Self in its pure essence can create a picture and an ideal of perfected personality adequate to their caliber, their stage of development and their psychological type, and therefore can make this ideal practicable in actual life.

For some it may be the ideal of the artist who realizes and expresses himself as the creator of beautiful forms, who makes art the most vital interest and the animating principle of his existence, pouring into it all his best energies. For others it may be the ideal of the seeker after Truth, the philosopher, the scientist. For yet others it is a more limited and personal ideal, that of the good father or mother.

These "ideal models" imply, as is evident, vital relationships with the outer world and other human beings, and hence a certain degree of extraversion. But there are people who are extraverted to an extreme degree and go so far as to project, as it were, the vital center of their personality outside themselves. A typical example of such projection is the ardent patriot who gives himself entirely to his beloved country, which becomes the center of his life and interest, almost his very self. All his thoughts and feelings are directed toward this cause for which he is willing to sacrifice even his life. Another illustration (a frequent case in the past) is that of the woman who identifies herself with the man she loves, lives for him and is absorbed in him. The ancient Hindu wife not only made her husband her human master, but worshipped him also as her spiritual teacher, her Guru—almost as her God.

This outward projection of one's own center, this excentricity (in the etymological sense of the word) should not be underrated. While it does not represent the most direct way or the highest achievement, it may, despite appearances, constitute for the time being a satisfactory form of indirect self-realization. In the best instances the individual does not really lose himself in the external object, but frees himself in that way from selfish interests and personal limitations; he realizes himself *through* the external ideal or being. The latter thus becomes an indirect but true link, a point of connection between the personal man and his higher Self, which is reflected and symbolized in that object:

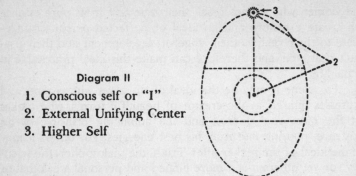

Diagram II

1. Conscious self or "I"
2. External Unifying Center
3. Higher Self

4. Psychosynthesis: the Formation or Reconstruction of the Personality Around the New Center.

When the unifying center has been found or created, we are in a position to build around it a new personality — coherent, organized, and unified.

This is the actual *psychosynthesis*, which also has several stages. The first essential is to decide the plan of action, to formulate the "inner program." We must visualize the purpose to be achieved — that is, the new personality to be developed — and have a clear realization of the various tasks it entails.

Some people have a distinct vision of their aim from the outset. They are capable of forming a clear picture of themselves as they can and intend to become. This picture should be realistic and "authentic", that is, in line with the natural development of the given individual and therefore capable — at least in some measure — of realization, and should not be a neurotic, unreal "idealized image" in the sense of Karen Horney (32). A genuine "ideal model" has a dynamic creative power; it facilitates the task by eliminating uncertainties and mistakes; it concentrates the energies and utilizes the great suggestive and creative power of images.

Other individuals of a more plastic psychological constitution, who live spontaneously, following indications and intuitions rather than definite plans, find it difficult to formulate such a program, to build according to a pattern; they may even positively dislike such a method. Their tendency is to let themselves be led by the Spirit within or by the will of God, leaving Him to choose what they should become. They feel that they can best reach the goal by eliminating, as much as possible, the obstacles and resistances inherent in their personality; by widening the channel of communication with the higher Self through aspiration and devotion and then letting the creative power of the Spirit act, trusting and obeying it. Some take a similar attitude but express it in a different way; they speak of tuning in with the cosmic order, with the universal harmony, of letting Life act in and through them (the Wu-Wei of Taoists).

Both methods are effective, and each is appropriate to the corresponding type. But it is well to know, to appreciate and to use both to some extent in order to avoid the limitations and the exaggerations of each by correcting and enriching the one with elements taken from the other.

Thus, those who follow the first method should be careful to avoid making their "ideal picture" too rigid; they should be ready to modify or to enlarge it —and even to change it altogether as later experiences, fresh outlooks or new clarifications indicate and demand this change.

On the other hand, those who follow the second method should guard against becoming too passive and negative, accepting as intuitions and higher inspirations certain promptings which are, in reality, determined by unconscious forces, wishes and desires. Moreover, they must develop the ability to stand steady during the inevitable phases of inner aridity and darkness, when conscious communion with the spiritual Center is interrupted, and the personality feels itself abandoned.

The "ideal models" or images that one can create are many, but they can be divided into two principal groups. The first is formed of images representing harmonious development, an all-round personal or spiritual perfection. This kind of ideal is aimed at chiefly by introverts. The second group represents specialized efficiency. The purpose here is the utmost development of an ability or quality corresponding to the particular line of self-expression and the social role or roles which the individual has chosen. This is the ideal of the artist, the teacher, the advocate of a good cause, etc. Such models are generally preferred by extraverts.

Once the choice of the ideal form has been made, *practical psychosynthesis, the actual construction of the new personality, begins.* This work may be divided into three principal parts:

1. *Utilization* of the available energies. These are (a) the forces released by the analysis and disintegration of the unconscious complexes; (b) the tendencies latent, and until now neglected, which exist on the various psychological levels. Such utilization demands the transmutation of many of these unconscious forces. Their inherent plasticity and mutability makes this possible. In fact, such transmutation is a process that is continually taking place within us. Just as heat is changed into motion and electric energy, and *vice versa*, our emotions and impulses are transformed into physical actions or into imaginative and intellectual activities. Conversely, ideas stir up emotions or are transformed into plans and hence into actions.

Instances of such transformations have been observed and recognized by many people. When the Latin poet says, "*Facit indignatio versus*" (Indignation produces my poems) he shows that he has realized how an emotional wave of indignation, if denied a natural outlet through external action, can be transformed into poetic activity. Again, when Heine writes, *Aus meinen grossen Schmerzen mach' ich die kleinen Lieder* (Out of my great suffering I produce my little songs) he indicates that his pain has been sublimated into poetry, and thus transfigured into beauty.

Important teachings and examples concerning the doctrine and practice of this transformation of the inner energies can be found in the yoga of the Hindu, in Christian mysticism and asceticism and in works on spiritual alchemy, while some points have been contributed by psychoanalysis. We therefore possess sufficient elements for the formation of a science of psychological energies (*psychodynamics*), and of reliable and adequate techniques by which to bring about the desired changes in ourselves and in others.

2. *Development* of the aspects of the personality which are either deficient or inadequate for the purpose we desire to attain. This development can be carried out in two ways: by means of evocation, autosuggestion, creative affirmation; or by the methodical training of the undeveloped functions (such as memory, imagination, will) — a training analogous to that used in physical culture or in developing technical skills such as singing or playing an instrument.

3. *Coordination and subordination* of the various psychological energies and functions, the creation of a firm organization of the personality. This ordering presents interesting and suggestive analogies with that of a modern state, with the various groupings of the citizens into communities, social classes, professions and trades, and the different grades of town, district and state officials.

*   *   *   *   *

Such is, in brief outline, the process by which psychosynthesis is accomplished. But it should be made clear that all the various stages and methods mentioned above are closely interrelated and need not be followed in a strict succession of distinct periods or phases. A living human being is not a building, for which the foundations must be laid, then the walls erected and, finally, the roof added. The carrying out of the vast inner program of psychosynthesis may be started from various points and angles at the same time, and the different methods and activities can be wisely alternated through shorter or longer cycles, according to circumstances and inner conditions.

All this may at first appear rather formidable, but there is no reason for doubt or discouragement. The help of a competent therapist or teacher obviously makes the task much easier; on the other hand, one may also reach a satisfactory result by one's own unaided efforts and through one's own trials and errors. Having absorbed the preliminary instruction on the psychological principles and laws involved, and having learned the various psychosynthetic techniques to be followed, the rest is a question of practice, experience, intelligence, and intuition, which increase according to the need and to the steadfastness of the endeavor. In this way the new regenerated personality is formed, and a new and higher life begins, the *true life*, for which the preceding one can be considered as a mere preparation, almost a gestation.

If we now consider psychosynthesis as a whole, with all its implications and developments, we see that it should not be looked upon as a particular psychological doctrine, nor as a single technical procedure.

It is first and foremost a dynamic, even a dramatic conception of our psychological life, which it portrays as a constant interplay and conflict between the many different and contrasting forces and a unifying center which ever tends to control, harmonize and utilize them.

Moreover, psychosynthesis utilizes many techniques of psychological action, aiming first at the development and perfection of the personality, and then at its harmonious co-ordination and increasing unification with the Self. These phases may be called respectively "personal" and "spiritual" psychosynthesis. According to the various fields of activity in which it is used, and the different purposes which it may serve, psychosynthesis is or may become:

1. A method of psychological development and Self-realization for those who refuse to remain the slaves of their own inner phantasms or of external influences, who refuse to submit passively to the play of psychological forces which is going on within them, and who are determined to become the master of their own lives.

2. A method of treatment for psychological and psychosomatic disturbances when the cause of the trouble is a violent and complicated conflict between groups of conscious and unconscious forces, or when it is due to those deep-seated and tormenting crises (not generally understood or rightly judged by the patient himself) which often precede a phase of Self-realization.

3. A method of integral education which tends not only to favor the development of the various abilities of the child or of the adolescent, but also helps him to discover and realize his true spiritual nature and to build under its guidance an harmonious, radiant and efficient personality.

Psychosynthesis may also be considered as *the individual expression of a wider principle, of a general law of inter-individual and cosmic synthesis.* Indeed, the isolated individual does not exist; every person has intimate relationships with other individuals which make them all interdependent. Moreover, each and all are included in and part of the spiritual super-individual Reality.

Thus, inverting the analogy of man being a combination of many elements which are more or less coordinated, each man may be considered as an element or cell of a human group; this group, in its turn, forms associations with vaster and more complex groups, from the family group to town and district groups and to social classes; from workers' unions and employers' associations to the great national groups, and from these to the entire human family.

Between these individuals and groups arise problems and conflicts which are curiously similar to those we have found existing within each individual. Their solution (interindividual psychosynthesis) should therefore be pursued along the same lines and by similar methods as for the achievement of individual psychosynthesis. A detailed study of this parallelism might prove very illuminating and help us to discover the profound significance and real value of the many efforts towards organization and synthesis, both of a practical and of a psychological nature, which are increasingly being attempted between the various national, social, economic, scientific and religious groups.

From a still wider and more comprehensive point of view, universal life itself appears to us as a struggle between multiplicity and unity—a labor and an aspiration towards union. We seem to sense that—whether we conceive it as a divine Being or as cosmic energy—the Spirit working upon and within all creation is shaping it into order, harmony, and beauty, uniting all beings (some willing but the majority as yet blind and rebellious) with each other through links of love, achieving—slowly and silently, but powerfully and irresistibly—*the Supreme Synthesis.*

REFFRENCES

1. Abraham, K.: *Selected Papers on Psychoanalysis,* New York, Basic Books, 1953.
2. Adler, A.: *The Pattern of Life,* New York, Cosmopolitan Book Co., 1931.
3. Allendy, R.: *Le Problème de la Destinée,* Paris, Gallimard, 1927.
4. Allport, G.: *Becoming,* New Haven, Yale University Press, 1955.

5. Angyal, A.: *Foundations for a Science of Personality*, Cambridge, Harvard University Press, 1941.
6. Bach, G.R.: *Intensive Group Psychotherapy*, New York, Ronald Press, 1954.
7. Baruk, H.: *Psychiatrie Morale Expérimentale, Individuelle et Sociale*, Paris, Presses Universitaires, 1945.
8. Baudoin, C.: *Découverte de la Personne*, Paris, Presses Universitaires, 1940.
—— *Suggestion and Autosuggestion*, London, Allen and Unwin, 1920.
—— *La Force en Nous*, Neuchâtel, Delachaux & Niestlé.
—— *De l'Instinct à l'Esprit*, Paris, Desclée de Brohwer.
—— *Mobilisation de l'Energie*, Paris, Institut Pelman, 1931.
9. Berne, E.: *Transactional Analysis in Psychotherapy*, New York, Grove Press, 1961.
10. Bezzola, D.: *Des Procédés propres à réorganiser "La Synthèse Mentale" dans le traitement des névroses*, Revue de Psychiatrie, Cahors, Paris, 1908.
11. Bjerre, P.: *Von der Psychanalyse zur Psychosynthese*, Halle, 1925.
12. Binswanger, L.: *Grundformen und Erkenntniss Menschlicher Dasein*, Zurich, Niehaus, 1942.
13. Bucke, R.M.: *Cosmic Consciousness, a Study in the Evolution of the Human Mind*, New York, Dutton, 1923.
14. Cartwright, D. & Zander, A.F.: *Group Dynamics: Research and Theory*, Evanston, Ill., Row Peterson, 1953.
15. Caruso, I.A.: *Psychoanalyse und Synthese der Existenz*, Wien, Seelsorger Verlag, Herder, 1952.
—— *Tiefen psychologie und Daseinswerte*, Wien, Seelsorger Verlag, Herder, 1948.
16. De Jonge,: *Quelques principes et exemples de psychosynthèse*, II. Tagung der Kommission für Psychotherapie der Schweiz, Bern, Gesellsch. f. Psychiatrie, 1937
17. Desoille, R.: *Le Rêve Eveillé en Psychothérapie*, Paris, Presses Universitaires, 1945.
18. Ellis, A. & Harper, R.A.: *A Guide to Rational Living*, New York, Prentice-Hall, 1961.
—— *Reason and Emotion in Psychotherapy*, New York, Lyle Stuart, 1962.
19. Ferenczi, S.: *Further Contributions to the Theory and Technique of Psychoanalysis*, New York, Liveright, 1926.
20. Frankl, V.E.: *The Doctor and the Soul: An Introduction to Logotherapy*, New York, Knopf, 1955.
—— *From Death-Camp to Existentialism: a Psychiatrist's Path to a New Therapy*, Boston, Beacon Press, 1959.
21. Freud, S.: *The Standard Edition of the Complete Psychological Works of Sigmund Freud*, New York, Macmillan, 1953.
22. Fromm, E.: *Escape from Freedom*, New York, Farrar and Rinehart, 1941.
23. Geley, G.: *From the Unconscious to the Conscious*, New York, Harper, 1921.
24. Goldstein, K.: *The Organism*, New York, American Book Co., 1939.
25. Hall, Calvin S.: *Theories of Personality*, New York, Wiley, 1957.
26. Hall, Winslow W.: *Observed Illuminates*, London, Daniel, 1926.
27. Happich, C.: *Anleitung zur Meditation*, Darmstadt, Rother, 3rd ed., 1948.
28. Harding, M.E.: *Psychic Energy: Its Source and Goal*, New York, Pantheon Books, 1948.

29. Hauser, R. & H.: *The Fraternal Society*, London, Bodley Head, 1962.
30. Heiler, F.: *Das Gebet. Eine Religionsgeschichtliche und Religionspsychologische Untersuchung*, Munchen, Reinhardt, 1918.
31. Hesnard, A.: *Freud dans la Société d'après-guerre*, Genève, Mont Blanc, 1946.
32. Horney, Karen: *Our Inner Conflicts*, New York, Norton, 1945.
33. James, W.: *The Varieties of Religious Experience*, New York, Longmans, Green, 1902.
34. Janet, P.: *L'automatisme Psychologique*, Paris, Alcan, 1889.
35. Jung, C.G.: *Collected Works*, Bollingen Series, New York, Pantheon Books, 1953-54.
36. Keyserling, H.A.: *Creative Understanding*, New York, Harper, 1929.
37. Klein, Melanie, et al.: *Developments in Psychoanalysis*, New York, Hillary House, 1952.
38. Kretschmer, W., Jr.: *Selbsterkenntniss und Willensbildung im ärztlichen Raume*, Stuttgart, G. Thieme, 1958.
39. Laforgue, R.: *Psychopathologie de l'Echec*, Paris, Payot, 1941.
40. Lepp, I.: *Clartés et Ténèbres de l'Ame — Essai de Psychosynthèse*, Paris, Ed. Aubier, 1957.
41. Lewin, K.: *A Dynamic Theory of Personality*, New York, McGraw Hill, 1935.
42. Lodge, O.: *Raymond or Life and Death*, New York, Doran (now Doubleday), 1916.
43. Maeder, A.: *Die Richtung in Seelenleben*, Zurich, Rascher, 1928.
—— *Heilung und Entwicklung im Seelenleben*, Zurich, Bacher, 1918.
—— *Psychoanalyse und Synthese*, Schwerin i.M., Bahn, 1927.
44. Martin, P.W.: *Experiment in Depth*, New York, Pantheon Books, 1955.
45. Maslow, A.H.: *Motivation and Personality*, New York, Harper, 1954.
—— *Toward a Psychology of Being*, Princeton, N. J., Van Nostrand, 1962.
46. Mayo, E.: *Some Notes on the Psychology of Pierre Janet*, Cambridge, Harvard University Press, 1948.
47. McDougall, W.: *The Energies of Men. A Study of the Fundamentals of Dynamic Psychology*, London, Methuen, 1932.
48. Mead, Margaret: *Male and Female*, New York, Morrow, 1949.
49. Moreno, J.L.: *Psycho-drama*, New York, Beacon House, 1946.
50. Munroe, R.L.: *Schools of Psychoanalytic Thought*, New York, The Dryden Press, 1955.
51. Murphy, Gardner: *Personality*, New York, Harper, 1947.
52. Myers, F.W.H.: *Human Personality and its Survival*, New York, Longmans, Green, 1920.
53. Neutra, W.: *Seelenmechanik und Hysterie*, Leipzig, Vogel, 1920.
54. Osty, E.: *La Connaissance Supranormale*, New York, Sutton, 1923.
55. Ouspensky, P.D.: *Tertium Organum*, New York, Knopf, 1931.
56. Perls, F.S., Hefferline, R.F. & Goodman, P.: *Gestalt Therapy: Excitement and Growth in the Human Personality*, New York, The Julian Press, 1951.
57. Progoff, I.: *The Death and Rebirth of Psychology*, New York, Julian Press, 1956.

58. Rank, O.: *Will Therapy and Truth and Reality,* New York, A. Knopf, 1945.
59. Reothlisberger, F.S., Fritz, Jules, & Dickson, W.J.: *Management and the Worker,* Cambridge, Harvard University Press, 1939.
60. Rhine, J.B.: *New Frontiers of the Mind,* New York, Farrar & Rinehart, 1937.
61. Richet, C.R.: *Treatise on Metaphysics,* New York, Macmillan, 1923.
62. Schmitz, O.: *Psychoanalyse und Yoga,* Darmstadt, Reichl, 1923.
63. Schultz, J.H.: *Das Autogene Training,* Leipzig, Thieme, 1934.
64. Slavson, S.R. (Editor): *The Practice of Group Therapy,* New York, International Universities Press, 1945.
65. Smuts, J.C.: *Holism and Evolution,* New York, Macmillan, 1926.
66. Sorokin, P.A., et al: *Forms and Techniques of Altruistic and Spiritual Growth,* Boston, Beacon Press, 1954.
—— *The Ways and Power of Love,* Boston, Beacon Press, 1954.
67. Stekel, W.: *Compulsion and Doubt,* New York, Liveright, 1949.
68. Stern, W.: *General Psychology from the Personalistic Standpoint,* New York, Macmillan, 1938.
69. Stocker, A.: *De la psychanalyse à la psychosynthèse,* Paris, Beauchesse, 1957.
70. Sullivan, H.S.: *The Interpersonal Theory of Psychiatry,* New York, Norton, 1953.
71. Swartley, W.M.: *A Comparative Survey of Some Active Techniques of Stimulating Whole Functioning.* Ms. Available from the librarian, Psychosynthesis Research Foundation.
72. Terman, L.M., et al.: *Genetic Studies of Genius,* Stanford University Press, 1926.
73. Tournier, P.: *Médecine de la Personne,* Neuchâtel, Delachaux & Niestlé, 1941
74. Trüb, H.: *Psychosynthese als Seelisch-Geister Heilungsprozess,* Zurich, Leipzig, Ed. Niehaus, 1936.
75. Underhill, E.: *Mysticism,* New York, Dutton, 1911.
76. Urban, H.J.: *"Uebernatur" und Medizin,* Innsbruck, Tyrolia, 1946.

CHAPTER II

Self-Realization and
Psychological Disturbances

The study of the psychopathological aspects of human nature has contributed a vast mass of observations, theories, and techniques for the diagnosis and treatment of psychiatric disorders. It has produced the widespread psychoanalytic movement and other aspects of dynamic psychology which have greatly enlarged and deepened our knowledge of the human psyche.

However, this pathological approach has, besides its assets, also a serious liability, and that is an exaggerated emphasis on the morbid manifestations and on the lower aspects of human nature and the consequent unwarranted generalized applications of the many findings of psychopathology to the psychology of normal human beings. This has produced a rather dreary and pessimistic picture of human nature and the tendency to consider its higher values and achievements as derived only from the lower drives, through processes of reaction formation, transformation, and sublimation. Moreover, many important realities and functions have been neglected or ignored: intuition, creativity, the will, and the very core of the human psyche—the Self.

These limitations have been realized in recent times by a growing number of investigators who have started a healthy reaction. Attention has been called to the neglected factors both in normal men and women and in those more highly developed, aptly termed by Goldstein (11) and Maslow (16) "self-actualizing" individuals. The importance and value of the ethical element and of the religious tendencies in human nature have been emphasized by Allport (2), Angyal (3), Baruk (5), Caruso (6), Frankl (8), Fromm (10), Jung (13), Maslow (16), May (15), Progoff (22), Rank (23), Sorokin (24 and 25), Urban (76), and others; this trend has recently been covered by the names of *ortho-psychology*, proposed by Maslow (19), and *ortho-genesis*, suggested by Ferrière (7) in Switzerland. It is a current of research which appears to be headed in the right direction, and although still in its initial stages promises to offer most valuable contributions to the knowledge of the *whole* human nature, and to the unfolding of its higher creative possibilities.

Yet, we think that also in this case some caution should be used, for all reactions have the tendency to go towards the other extreme, and one can already note evidence of such overcompensation in this field. Some representatives of the new current show a leaning towards reversion to the former conception of man as an already unified personality, which, unfortunately, is far from being the case. The drive towards integration has been rightly described and emphasized as a basic and normal urge of the human personality; but this is something quite different from the illusion of an *already* organically and harmoniously functioning personality.

A realistic observation of the flow of the psychological life in ourselves and in others shows clearly the existence of a number of differing and conflicting tendencies, which at times constitute the nuclei of semi-independent sub-personalities. Both psychoanalysis and the picture of human beings given by great novelists who were good intuitive psychologists point up these basic conflicts inherent in human nature.

The recognition that different drives and the various psychological functions are interrelated and interacting does not mean that they are integrated in a harmoniously functioning organism as are the biological functions in a healthy body. Even conflict constitutes a relation; and two armies fighting each other surely interact powerfully.

One kind of conflict which occurs frequently is that evidenced by ambivalence, and it explains many curious, contradictory manifestations of human beings. Another basic conflict is that between inertia, laziness, tendency to preservation, craving for security (which expresses itself in conformity) on the one hand, and the tendency towards growth, self-assertion and adventure on the other. Still another source of conflict is that of the awakening of new drives or needs which oppose pre-existing ones; this occurs on two chief occasions: first, the tumultuous awakening of new tendencies at the time of adolescence, and second, the awakening of religious aspirations and new spiritual interests, particularly in middle age. It is this last type of conflict which is the primary concern of this chapter.

It therefore appears that "organic unity" is *a goal* and not a present reality—a goal which can be visioned, approached, and up to a certain point achieved. It is in the most favorable cases the fruit of spontaneous growth and maturation; in others it is the well-earned reward of self-training, education or therapy, through the use of a variety of techniques, in order to help and hasten the process. In the exposition which follows, we shall try to describe the various stages of self-realization, and to point out the difficulties and the emotional and mental disturbances which often—although not necessarily—occur during the process.

First of all, it is well to have a clear idea of what self-realization is. The term has been used to indicate two kinds of growth in awareness, of expansion of consciousness, which, although more or less related, are different in their nature and have quite different manifestations. The meaning most frequently given to self-realization is that of psychological growth and maturation, of the awakening and manifestation of latent potentialities of the human being—for instance, ethical, esthetic, and religious experiences and activities. These correspond to the characteristics Maslow (18) ascribes to *self-actualization,* and it would perhaps be well to use this term in order to distinguish it from the second kind of self-realization. This is the *realization of the Self,* the experience and awareness of the synthesizing spiritual Center. It is not the realization of the personal conscious self or "I", which should be considered merely as the reflection of the spiritual Self, its projection, in the field of the personality.

Self-actualization may be achieved at different levels and does not necessarily include what can be called the spiritual level.

On the other hand, an individual may have genuine spiritual experiences without being at all integrated, i.e., without having developed a well-organized, harmonious personality. This has been clearly shown by Jung (15, p. 155) who calls our attention to the fact that the developing of the personality is not an absolute prerogative of the man of genius, and that he may have genius without either having personality or being a personality. Spiritual awakening and spiritual realization are something different from conscious awareness of the Self. They include various kinds of awareness of superconscious *contents,* either descending into the field of consciousness or found in the process of ascending to superconscious levels and thus having what Maslow (18) calls a "peak experience." The distinction between the personal conscious self, the superconscious, and the spiritual Self is indicated in our discussion of the psychological constitution of man and in its accompanying diagram in the preceding chapter, but it is appropriate here to comment that, in the diagram, the superconscious constitutes the higher section or aspect of the person of which the ego or self (the point in the middle of the circle) is not normally aware. But at times the conscious self rises or is raised to that higher region where it has specific experiences and states of awareness of various kinds which can be called "spiritual" in the widest sense. At other times it happens that some contents of the superconscious "descend" and penetrate into the area of the normal consciousness of the ego, producing what is called "inspiration." This interplay has great importance and value, both for fostering creativity and for achieving psychosynthesis.

We are using the word "spiritual" in its broader connotation which includes, therefore, not only the specific religious experience, but all the states of awareness, all the functions and activities which have as common denominator the possessing of *values* higher than the average, values such as the ethical, the esthetic, the heroic, the humanitarian, and the altruistic. We include under the general heading of "spiritual development" then, all experiences connected with awareness of the contents of the superconscious, which may or may not include the experience of the Self. It should also be pointed out that the reaching up into the realm of the superconscious and its exploration, while approaching the consciousness of the Self, may sometimes even constitute an obstacle to full Self-realization, to the reaching of the summit where the personal-I awareness blends into awareness of the spiritual Self. One can become so fascinated by the wonders of the superconscious realm, so absorbed in it, so identified with some of its special aspects or manifestations as to lose or paralyze the urge to reach the summit of Self-realization.

In the following analysis of the vicissitudes and incidents which occur during the process of spiritual development, we shall consider both the successive stages of self-actualization and the achievement of full Self-realization.[a]

Man's spiritual development is a long and arduous journey, an adventure through strange lands full of surprises, difficulties and even dangers. It involves a drastic transmutation of the "normal" elements of the personality, an awakening of potentialities hitherto dormant, a raising of consciousness to new realms, and a functioning along a new inner dimension.

We should not be surprised, therefore, to find that so great a change, so fundamental a transformation, is marked by several critical stages, which are not infrequently accompanied by various nervous, emotional and mental troubles. These may present to the objective clinical observation of the therapist the same symptoms as those due to more usual causes, but they have in reality quite another significance and function, and need very different treatment.

The incidence of disturbances having a spiritual origin is

---

[a]Maslow has well recognized that self-actualization should not be considered as a state in which all conflicts have been eliminated and full unity is achieved once and forever. His exposition of this important point is so lucid and cogent that it deserves to be quoted in full:

This paper is the first of a projected series, "Critique of Self-Actualization," whose long-term aim is the further exploration of the full reach of human nature, but whose immediate, pedagogical aim is to correct the widespread misunderstanding of self-actualization as a static, unreal, "perfect" state in which all human problems are transcended, and in which people "live happily forever after" in a superhuman state of serenity or ecstasy....

To make this fact clearer, I could describe self-actualization as a development of personality which frees the person from the deficiency problems of growth, and from the neurotic (or infantile, or fantasy, or unnecessary, or "unreal") problems of life, so that he is able to face, endure and grapple with the "real" problems of life (the intrinsically and ultimately human problems, the unavoidable, the "existential" problems to which there is no perfect solution). That is, it is not an absence of problems but a moving from transitional or unreal problems to real problems.(Maslow, 18, p. 24.)

rapidly increasing nowadays, in step with the growing number of people who, consciously or unconsciously, are groping their way towards a fuller life. Moreover, the heightened development and complexity of the personality of modern man and his more critical mind have rendered spiritual development a more difficult and complicated process. In the past a moral conversion, a simple whole-hearted devotion to a teacher or savior, a loving surrender to God, were often sufficient to open the gates leading to a higher level of consciousness and a sense of inner union and fulfillment. Now, however, the more varied and conflicting aspects of modern man's personality are involved and need to be transmuted and harmonized with each other: his fundamental drives, his emotions and feelings, his creative imagination, his inquiring mind, his assertive will, and also his interpersonal and social relations.

For these reasons a general outline of the disturbances which can arise at the various stages of spiritual realization and some indications pertaining to their proper treatment will, we believe, serve a useful purpose. We might, for the sake of clarity, tabulate four critical stages:

1. Crises preceding the spiritual awakening.
2. Crises caused by the spiritual awakening.
3. Reactions to the spiritual awakening.
4. Phases of the process of transmutation.

We have used the symbolic expression "awakening" because it clearly suggests the perception, the becoming aware of a new area of experience, the opening of the hitherto closed eyes to an inner reality previously ignored.

1. Crises Preceding the Spiritual Awakening

In order to understand thoroughly the strange experiences that often precede the awakening, we must review some of the psychological characteristics of the "ordinary" human being.

One may say of him that he "lets himself live" rather than that he lives. He takes life as it comes and does not worry about the problems of its meaning, its worth or its purpose; he devotes himself to the satisfaction of his personal desires; he seeks enjoyment of the senses and endeavors to become rich and satisfy his ambitions. If he is more mature, he subordinates his personal satisfaction to the fulfillment of the various family and social duties assigned to him, without taking the trouble to understand on what bases those duties rest or from what source they spring. Possibly he regards himself as "religious" and as a believer in God, but his religion is outward and conventional, and when he has conformed to the injunctions of his church and shared in its rites he feels that he has done all that is required of him. In short, he believes implicitly that the only reality is that of the physical world which he can see and touch and therefore he is strongly attached to earthly goods, to which he attributes a positive value; thus he practically considers this life an end in itself. His belief in a future "heaven," if he conceives of one, is altogether theoretical and academic, as is proved by the fact that he takes the greatest pains to postpone as long as possible his departure for its joys.

But it may happen that this "ordinary man" becomes both surprised and disturbed by a change—sudden or slow—in his inner life. This may take place after a series of disappointments; not infrequently after some emotional shock, such as the loss of a loved relative or a very dear friend. But sometimes it occurs without any apparent cause, and in the full enjoyment of health and prosperity. The change begins often with a sense of dissatisfaction, of "lack," but not the lack of anything material and definite; it is something vague and elusive that he is unable to describe.

To this is added, by degrees, a sense of the unreality and emptiness of ordinary life; all personal affairs, which formerly absorbed so much of his attention and interest, seem to retreat, psychologically, into the background; they lose their importance and value. New problems arise. The individual begins to inquire into the origin and the purpose of life; to ask what is the reason for so many things he formerly took for granted; to question, for instance, the meaning of his own sufferings and those of others, and what justification there may be for so many inequalities in the destinies of men.

When a man has reached this point, he is apt to misunderstand and misinterpret his condition. Many who do not comprehend the significance of these new states of mind look upon them as abnormal fancies and vagaries. Alarmed at the possibility of mental unbalance, they strive to combat them in various ways, making frantic efforts to re-attach themselves to the "reality" of ordinary life that seems to be slipping from them. Often they throw themselves with increased ardor into a whirl of external activities, seeking ever new occupations, new stimuli and new sensations. By these and other means they may succeed for a time in alleviating their disturbed condition, but they are unable to get rid of it entirely. It continues to ferment in the depths of their being, undermining the foundations of their ordinary existence, whence it is liable to break forth again, perhaps after a long time, with renewed intensity. The state of uneasiness and agitation becomes more and more painful and the sense of inward emptiness more intolerable. The individual feels distracted; most of what constituted his life now seems to him to have vanished like a dream, while no new light has yet come. Indeed, he is as yet ignorant of the existence of such a light, or else he cannot believe that it may ever illuminate him.

It frequently happens that this state of inner disturbance is followed by a moral crisis. His conscience awakens or becomes more sensitive; a new sense of responsibility appears and the individual is oppressed by a heavy sense of guilt and remorse. He judges himself with severity and becomes a prey to profound discouragement. At this point it is not unusual for him to entertain ideas of suicide. To the man himself it seems as if physical annihilation were the only logical conclusion to his inner breakdown and disintegration.

The foregoing description constitutes merely a general outline of such experiences. In reality individuals differ widely in their inner experiences and reactions. There are many who never reach this acute stage, while others arrive at it almost in one bound. Some are more harassed by intellectual doubts and metaphysical problems; in others the emotional depression or the moral crisis is the most pronounced feature.

These various manifestations of the crisis bear a close relationship to some of the symptoms regarded as characteristic of psychoneuroses and borderline schizophrenic states. In some cases the stress and strain of the crisis also produce physical symptoms, such as nervous tension, insomnia and various other troubles (digestive, circulatory, glandular).

The differential diagnosis is generally not difficult. The

symptoms observed isolatedly may be identical; but an accurate analysis of their genesis, and a consideration of the patient's personality in its entirety and (most important of all) the recognition of his actual existential problem, reveal the difference in nature and level of the pathogenic conflicts. In ordinary cases, these occur between the "normal" drives, between these drives and the conscious ego, or between the ego and the outer world (particularly human beings closely related, such as parents, mate or children). In the cases which we are considering, the conflicts are produced by the new awakening tendencies, aspirations, and interests of a moral, religious, or spiritual character, as previously mentioned; and it is not difficult to ascertain their presence once their reality and validity are admitted rather than being explained away as mere phantasies, or as the internalizations of social tabus. In a general way they can be considered as the result of crises in the development, in the *growth* of the patient's personality.

There is this possible complication: the presence in the same patient of symptoms deriving, in varying proportions, from both sources; but in these cases too, the differential criterion consists in discovering the different sources.

2. Crises Caused by the Spiritual Awakening

The opening of the channel between the conscious and the superconscious levels, between the ego and the Self, and the flood of light, joy and energy which follows, often produce a wonderful release. The preceding conflicts and sufferings, with the psychological and physical symptoms which they generated, vanish sometimes with amazing suddenness, thus confirming the fact that they were not due to any physical cause but were the direct outcome of the inner strife. In such cases the spiritual awakening amounts to a real cure.

But in some cases, not infrequent, the personality is inadequate in one or more respects and therefore unable to rightly assimilate the inflow of light and strength. This happens, for instance, when the intellect is not balanced, or the emotions and the imagination are uncontrolled; when the nervous system is too sensitive; or when the inrush of spiritual energy is overwhelming in its suddenness and intensity.

An incapacity of the mind to stand the illumination, or a tendency to egotism or conceit, may cause the experience to be wrongly interpreted, and there results, so to speak, a "confusion of levels." The distinction between absolute and relative truths, between the Self and the "I", is blurred and the inflowing spiritual energies may have the unfortunate effect of feeding and inflating the personal ego.

The author encountered a striking instance of such a harmful effect in the Psychiatric Hospital at Ancona. One of the inmates, a simple little man, formerly a photographer, quietly and persistently declared that he was God. Around this central idea he had constructed an assortment of fantastic delusions about heavenly hosts at his command; at the same time he was as peaceful, kind and obliging a person as one could imagine, always ready to be of service to the doctors and patients. He was so reliable and competent that he had been entrusted with the preparation of medicines and even the keys of the pharmacy. His only lapse in behavior in this capacity was an occasional appropriation of sugar in order to give pleasure to some of the other inmates.

Doctors with materialistic views would be likely to regard this patient as simply affected by paranoid delusions; but this mere diagnostic label offers little or no help in understanding the true nature and causes of such disturbances. It seems worthwhile, therefore, to explore the possibility of a more profound interpretation of this man's illusory conviction.

The inner experience of the spiritual Self, and its intimate association with and penetration of the personal self, gives to those who have it a sense of greatness and internal expansion, the conviction of participating in some way in the divine nature. In the religious tradition and spiritual doctrines of every epoch one finds numerous attestations on this subject — some of them expressed in daring terms. In the Bible there is the explicit sentence "I have said, Ye are gods; and all of you are children of the most High." St. Augustine declares: "When the soul loves something it becomes like unto it; if it should love terrestrial things it becomes terrestrial, but if it should love God (we may ask) does it not become God?" The most extreme expression of the identity of the human spirit in its pure and real essence with the Supreme Spirit is contained in the central teaching of the Vedanta philosophy:

"Tat Twam Asi" (Thou art That) and *"Aham evam param Brahman"* (In truth I am the Supreme Brahman).

In whatever way one may conceive the relationship between the individual Self and the universal Self, be they regarded as identical or similar, distinct or united, it is most important to recognize clearly, and to retain ever present in theory and in practice, the difference that exists between the Self in its essential nature—that which has been called the "Fount," the "Center," the "deeper Being," the "Apex" of ourselves—and the small ordinary personality, the little "self" or ego, of which we are normally conscious. The disregard of this vital distinction leads to absurd and dangerous consequences.

The distinction gives the key to an understanding of the mental state of the patient referred to, and of other less extreme forms of self-exaltation and self-glorification. The fatal error of all who fall victim to these illusions is to attribute to their *personal* ego or "self" the qualities and powers of the Self. In philosophical terms, it is a case of confusion between an absolute and a relative truth, between the metaphysical and the empirical levels of reality; in religious terms, between God and the "soul."

Our illustration represents an extreme case, but instances of such confusion, more or less pronounced, are not uncommon among people dazzled by contact with truths which are too powerful for their mental capacities to grasp and assimilate. The reader will doubtless be able to record instances of similar self-deception which are found in a number of fanatical followers of various cults.

Once the delusion has become established it is a waste of time to antagonize and to ridicule the patient's aberration; it will merely arouse his opposition and resentment. The better way is to sympathize and, while admitting the ultimate truth of his belief, point out the nature of his error and help him learn how to make the necessary distinctions.

In other cases the sudden influx of energies produces an emotional upheaval which expresses itself in uncontrolled, unbalanced and disordered behavior. Shouting and crying, singing and outbursts of various kinds characterize this form of response. If the individual is active and aggressive he may be easily impelled by the excitement of the inner awakening to play the role of prophet or savior; he may found a new sect and start a campaign of spectacular proselytism.

In some sensitive individuals there is an awakening of para-psychological perceptions. They have visions, which they believe to be of exalted beings; they may hear voices, or begin to write automatically, accepting the messages at their face value and obeying them unreservedly. The quality of such messages is very varied. Sometimes they contain fine teachings, but they should always be examined with much discrimination and sound judgment, and without being influenced by their uncommon origin or by any claim by their alleged transmitter. No validity should be attributed to messages containing definite orders and commanding blind obedience, and to those tending to exalt the personality of the recipient.

3. Reactions to the Spiritual Awakening

The reactions accompanying this phase are manifold and often occur a certain time after the awakening. As has been said, a harmonious inner awakening is characterized by a sense of joy and mental illumination that brings with it an insight into the meaning and purpose of life; it dispels many doubts, offers the solution of many problems, and gives a sense of security. At the same time there wells up a realization that life is one, and an outpouring of love flows through the awakening invididual towards his fellow beings and the whole of creation. The former personality, with its sharp angles and disagreeable traits, seems to have receded into the background and a new loving and lovable individual smiles at us and the whole world, full of eagerness to please, to serve, and to share his newly acquired spiritual riches, the abundance of which seems almost too much for him to contain.

Such an exalted state lasts for varying periods, but it is bound to cease. The personal self was only temporarily overpowered but not permanently transformed. The inflow of light and love is rhythmical as is everything in the universe. After a while it diminishes or ceases and the flood is followed by the ebb.

Necessarily this is a very painful experience and is apt in some cases to produce strong reactions and cause serious troubles. The personal ego re-awakens and asserts itself with renewed force. All the rocks and rubbish, which had been covered and concealed at high tide, emerge again. The man, whose moral conscience has now become more refined and exacting, whose thirst for perfection has become more intense, judges with greater severity and condemns his personality with a new vehemence; he is apt to harbor the false belief of having fallen lower than he was before. Sometimes it even happens that lower propensities and drives, hitherto lying dormant in the unconscious, are vitalized by the inrush of higher energy, or stirred into a fury of opposition by the consecration of the awakening man—a fact which constitutes a challenge and a menace to their uncontrolled expression.

At times the reaction becomes intensified to the extent of causing the individual even to deny the value and reality of his recent experience. Doubts and criticism enter his mind and he is tempted to regard the whole thing as an illusion, a fantasy or an emotional intoxication. He becomes bitter and sarcastic, ridicules himself and others, and even turns his back on his higher ideals and aspirations. Yet, try as he may, he *cannot* return to his old state; he has seen the vision, and its beauty and power to attract remain with him in spite of his efforts to suppress it. He cannot accept everyday life as before, or be satisfied with it. A "divine homesickness" haunts him and leaves him no peace. Sometimes the reaction presents a more pathological aspect and produces a state of depression and even despair, with suicidal impulses. This state bears a close resemblance to psychotic depression or "melancholia" which is characterized by an acute sense of unworthiness, a systematic self-depreciation, and self-accusation; the impression of going through hell, which may become so vivid as to produce the delusion that one is irretrievably damned; a keen and painful sense of intellectual incompetence; a loss of will power and self-control, indecision and an incapacity and distaste for action. But in the case of those who have had an inner awakening or a measure of spiritual realization the troubles should not be considered as a mere pathological condition; they have specific psychological causes. One of these has been indicated by both Plato and St. John of the Cross with the same analogy.

Plato, in the famous allegory contained in the Seventh Book of his *Republic,* compares unenlightened men to prisoners in a dark cave or den, and says:

> At first, when any of them is liberated and compelled suddenly to stand up and turn his neck around and walk towards the light, he will suffer sharp pains; the glare will distress him, and he will be unable to see the realities of which, in his former state, he had seen the shadows.

St. John of the Cross uses words curiously similar in speaking of the condition called "the dark night of the soul":

> The self is in the dark because it is blinded by a light greater than it can bear. The more clear the light, the more does it blind the eyes of the owl, and the stronger the sun's rays, the more it blinds the visual organs, overcoming them by reason of their weakness, depriving them of the power of seeing. . . . As eyes weakened and clouded suffer pain when the clear light beats upon them, so the soul, by reason of its impurity, suffers exceedingly when the Divine Light really shines upon it. And when the rays of this pure Light shine upon the soul in order to expel impurities, the soul perceives itself to be so unclean and miserable that it seems as if God has set Himself against it and itself were set against God. (Quoted by Underhill, 26, p. 453.)

Before proceeding further it seems appropriate to point out that crises, less total and drastic, but in many ways similar to those taking place before and after the "awakening," occur in two main types of creative individuals — artists and scientists.

Artists have often complained of periods of aridity, frustration, inability to work. At such times they feel depressed and restless and may be affected by many of the psychological symptoms mentioned above (pp. 40-42). They are apt to make vain attempts at escape or evasion of that painful condition by means such as alcohol or drugs. But when they have reached the depth of despondency or desperation there may come a sudden flow of inspiration inaugurating a period of renewed and intense productive activity.

Often the work of art appears as a virtually finished product elaborated without conscious awareness at some unconscious level or region of the artist's inner being. As Murray (21, p. 107) has stated in his brilliant essay, *Vicissitudes of Creativity*, speaking of the requirements of creation, "there must be sufficient *permeability* (flexibility) of boundaries, boundaries between categories as well as boundaries between different spheres of interest and—most important for certain classes of creation—sufficient permeability between conscious and unconscious processes. . . . Too much permeability is insanity, too little is ultraconventional rationality."

The "frustrations" which harass the scientist at various stages of research and the role they play "in sending the energy inward to richer sources of inspiration" have been ably described by Progoff (22, pp. 223-232).

The proper treatment in this type of crisis consists in conveying to the sufferer an understanding of its true nature and in explaining the only effective way of overcoming it. It should be made clear to him that the exalted state he has experienced could not, by its very nature, last forever and that reaction was inevitable. It is as though he had made a superb flight to the sunlit mountain top, realized its glory and the beauty of the panorama spread below, but had been brought back reluctantly to his starting point with the rueful recognition that the steep path leading to the heights must be climbed step by step. The recognition that this descent or "fall" is a natural happening affords emotional and mental relief and encourages the subject to undertake the arduous task confronting him on the path to Self-realization.

4. Phases of the Process of Transmutation

We now have to deal with the stage in which it has been recognized that the necessary conditions to be fulfilled and the price to be paid for the high achievement of Self-realization are a drastic transmutation and regeneration of the personality. It is a long and many-sided process, which includes phases of active removal of the obstacles to the inflow and operation of super-conscious energies; phases of development of the higher functions which have lain dormant or undeveloped; phases in which the ego must let the higher Self work, enduring the pressure and the inevitable pain of the process.

It is a most eventful period, full of changes, of alternations between light and darkness, between joy and suffering. The energies and the attention of the individual are often so engrossed in this task that his power of coping with the problems and activities of normal life may be impaired. Observed from the outside and gauged in terms of ordinary efficiency he seems to have deteriorated and to be less capable than before. He is not spared unfair judgment on the part of well-meaning but unenlightened friends or physicians, and he is often the target of pungent and sarcastic remarks about his "fine" spiritual ideals and aspirations making him weak and ineffective in practical life. This sort of criticism is felt as very painful, and its influence may arouse doubts and discouragement.

This trial constitutes one of the tests on the path of Self-realization; it teaches a lesson in overcoming personal sensitiveness, and is an occasion for the development of inner independence and self-reliance, without resentment. It should be accepted cheerfully, or at least serenely, and used as an opportunity for developing inner strength. If, on the other hand, the people in the individual's environment are enlightened and understanding, they can help a great deal and spare him much unnecessary friction and suffering.

In reality this is a period of transition; a passing out of the old condition, without having yet firmly reached the new; an intermediate stage in which, as it has been aptly said, one is like a caterpillar undergoing the process of transformation into the winged butterfly. The insect must pass through the stage of the chrysalis, a condition of disintegration and helplessness. But the individual generally does not have the protection of a cocoon in which to undergo the process of transformation in seclusion and peace. He must—and this is particularly so nowadays—remain where he is in life and continue to perform his family, professional, and social duties as well as he can, as though nothing had happened or was still going on. His problem is similar to that which confronts engineers in the reconstruction of a railway station without interrupting the traffic even for an hour. It is not surprising then that this difficult and complicated task, this "double life," is likely to produce a variety of psychological troubles, such as exhaustion, insomnia, emotional depression, aridity, mental agitation, and restlessness. These in turn can easily produce all kinds of physical symptoms and disorders.

Sometimes the trouble is caused, or at least aggravated, by an excessive personal effort to hasten the higher realization by the forceful inhibition and repression of the sexual and aggressive drives—an attempt which only serves to produce an intensification of the conflict with resultant tension and neurotic symptoms. Such an attitude often is the outcome of moral and religious conceptions too rigid and dualistic—which engender condemnation of the natural drives, viewed as "bad" or "sinful." Then there are people who have abandoned *consciously* that attitude, but who are still *unconsciously* conditioned to some extent by it and manifest either ambivalence in this respect, or oscillation between the two extreme attitudes—that is, *sup*pression, and the uncontrolled *ex*pression of all drives. The latter, while cathartic, is by no means an acceptable solution, from either the ethical standpoint or the medical, because it inevitably produces new conflicts—between the various basic drives, or between these drives and the restrictions imposed not only by the conventions of the social order, but also by the demands of interpersonal relations, and *right* social integration and adjustment.

The solution lies, rather, along the lines of a harmonious integration of all drives into the total personality, first through the proper subordination and coordination, and then through the transformation and sublimation of the excessive or unused quota of energy.

The achievement of this integration is not only not impeded but can be greatly facilitated by the activation of the superconscious functions, by the realization of the Self, because those larger and higher interests act as a magnet which draws up the "libido" or psychic energy invested in the "lower" drives. Moreover, when one of the specific functions of the Self, the will, is recognized and utilized, it too can contribute effectively, by means of its regulating and controlling power, to the harmonious integration, to the bio-psychosynthesis of the *whole* human being.

A different and, in a sense, opposite difficulty confronts the individual during the periods in which the flow of superconscious energies is easy and abundant. If not wisely controlled it may be scattered in feverish excitement and activity. Or, on the contrary, it may be kept too much in abeyance and unexpressed, so that it accumulates and its high pressure may injure the nervous system, just as too much electric current may burn out a fuse. The appropriate remedy is to use the inflowing energies constructively and harmoniously in the work of inner regeneration, in creative expression and in fruitful service, in such ways as the individual's capacities, conditions, and opportunities may determine.

The subject of this chapter has made it necessary to stress the darker and more painful side of spiritual development, but it should not be inferred that those who are on the path of Self-realization are more likely to be affected by psychological disturbances than ordinary men and women. The stage of most intense suffering often does not occur. The following points should, therefore, be made clear:

1. In many individuals such development is being accomplished in a much more gradual and harmonious way than that which has been described, so that the inner difficulties are overcome and the different stages passed through without causing severe reaction or producing definite symptoms.

2. The neurotic symptoms and the emotional disorders of the average man or woman are often more serious and intense, more difficult for them to bear and for doctors to cure, than those connected with Self-realization. They are mostly due to violent conflicts between the various aspects of the personality, or to unreasonable rebellion against circumstances and people. Some of these conflicts may be explicable in terms of Freud's (9) interpretation (which is by no means valid for all), some in accordance with those of Adler (1), Frankl (8), Horney (12), Jung (14), and others. It is often difficult to cure them satisfactorily because—the higher psychological levels and functions of these patients being not yet activated—there is little to which one can appeal to induce them to make the necessary sacrifices or submit to the discipline required in order to bring about the needed adjustments.

3. The nervous, emotional, and mental problems arising on

the way of Self-realization, however serious they may appear, are merely temporary reactions, by-products, so to speak, of an organic process of inner growth and regeneration. Therefore, they either disappear spontaneously when the crisis which has produced them is over, or they yield more easily to proper treatment.

4. The sufferings caused by periods of depression, by the ebbing of the inner life, are abundantly compensated for by periods of renewed inflow of superconscious energies and by the anticipation of the release and enhancement of the whole personality produced by Self-realization. This vision is a most powerful inspiration, an unfailing comfort, and a constant source of strength and courage. One should therefore make a special point of recalling that vision as vividly and as frequently as possible, and one of the greatest services we can render to those struggling along the way is to help them to keep the vision of the goal ever present before the inner eye.

Thus one can anticipate, and have an increasing foretaste of, the state of consciousness of the Self-realized individual. It is a state of consciousness characterized by joy, serenity, inner security, a sense of calm power, clear understanding, and radiant love. In its highest aspects it is the realization of essential Being, of communion and identification with the Universal Life.[b]

Implications for Diagnosis and Treatment

Considering the question more strictly from the medical and psychological standpoint, we should realize that, while the troubles that accompany the various phases of Self-realization may be outwardly very similar to, and sometimes appear identical with, those which affect ordinary patients, their causes and significance are very different, and the treatment should correspondingly be different. In other words, the existential situation in the two groups not only is not the same, but it is, in a sense, opposite.

---

[b]Some of the characteristics of Self-actualization and Self-fulfillment have been very well described by Prof. A. H. Maslow in his paper, *Cognition of Being in the Peak Experiences*—Presidential Address, Division of Personality and Social Psychology, American Psychological Association, Chicago, Ill., Sept. 1, 1956.

The psychological symptoms of ordinary patients have generally a *regressive* character. These patients have not been able to accomplish some of the necessary inner and outer adjustments that constitute the normal development of the personality. In many cases they have not succeeded in freeing themselves from emotional attachment to their parents, which persists into later life in the form of childish dependence on them or on other individuals who have become their substitutes. Sometimes an unwillingness to meet the requirements of ordinary family and social life, or an inability to cope with its difficulties, make them unconsciously seek refuge in illness or invalidism. In other cases the cause is an emotional shock or bereavement that they cannot or will not accept, which may lead to reactive depression or other neurotic symptoms. In all these cases we find, as a common characteristic, some conflict or conflicts, between various conscious and unconscious aspects of the personality, or between the personality and its environment.

The difficulties produced by the stress and strife in the various stages towards Self-realization have, on the contrary, a specifically *progressive* character. They are due to the stirring of superconscious potentialities, to the strong "call from above," to the pull of the Self, and are specifically determined by the ensuing maladjustment and conflicts with the "middle" and "lower" aspects of the personality. This crisis has been described in striking terms by Jung:

> To be "normal" is a splendid ideal for the unsuccessful, for all those who have not yet found an adaptation. But for people who have far more ability than the average, for whom it was never hard to gain successes and to accomplish their share of the world's work—for them restriction to the normal signifies the bed of Procrustes, unbearable boredom, infernal sterility and hopelessness. As a consequence there are many people who become neurotic because they are only normal, as there are people who are neurotic because they cannot become normal. (Jung, 13, p. 55.)

It is obvious that psychotherapeutic treatment appropriate to the two diverse kinds of patients must correspondingly be altogether different.

The therapeutic problem concerning the former group is that of helping the patient to reach the normal state of the average man or woman by means of the elimination of repressions and inhibitions, of fears and childish dependence; to find his way out of his self-centeredness, his emotionally distorted outlook, into an objective, sane and rational consideration of normal life, into a recognition of its duties and obligations, and a right appreciation of other individuals. The contrasting, partly undeveloped, uncoordinated conscious and unconscious trends and functions have to be harmonized and integrated in a *personal psychosynthesis*.

The specific therapeutic task for the latter group, instead, is that of arriving at a harmonious adjustment by means of the proper assimilation of the inflowing superconscious energies and of their integration with the pre-existing aspects of the personality; that is, of accomplishing not only a personal but also a *spiritual psychosynthesis*.

From this it is apparent that the treatment suitable for the first group of patients proves not only unsatisfactory, but may be definitely harmful for those of the second group. The lot of the latter is doubly hard if they are being treated by a therapist who neither understands nor appreciates the superconscious functions, who ignores or denies the reality of the Self and the possibility of Self-realization. He may either ridicule the patient's uncertain higher aspirations as mere fancies, or interpret them in a materialistic way, and the patient may be persuaded that he is doing the right thing in trying to harden the shell of his personality, and close it against the insistent knocking of the superconscious Self. This, of course, can aggravate the condition, intensify the struggle and retard the right solution.

On the other hand, a therapist who is himself spiritually inclined, or has at least an understanding of and a sympathetic attitude towards the higher achievements and realities, can be of great help to the individual when, as is often the case, the latter is still in the first stage, that of dissatisfaction, restlessness, and unconscious groping. If he has lost interest in life, if everyday existence holds no attractions for him and he has not yet had a glimpse of the higher reality, if he is looking for relief in wrong directions, wandering up and down blind alleys—then the revelation of the true cause of his trouble and the indication of the real unhoped-for solution, of the happy outcome of the crisis, can greatly help to bring about the inner awakening which in itself constitutes the principal part of the cure.

The second stage, that of emotional excitement or elation—when the individual is carried away by an excessive enthusiasm and cherishes the illusion of having arrived at a permanent attainment—calls for a gentle warning that his blessed state is, of necessity, but temporary; and he should be given a description of the vicissitudes of the way ahead of him. This will prepare him for the onset of the inevitable reaction in the third stage, and enable him to avoid much suffering because it is foreseen, as are subsequent doubts and discouragement. When a patient under treatment during this reaction has not had the benefit of a warning of this sort, the therapist can give much help by assuring him that his present condition is *temporary* and not in any sense permanent or hopeless as he seems compelled to believe. The therapist should insistently declare that the rewarding outcome of the crisis justifies the anguish—however intense—he is experiencing. Much relief and encouragement can be afforded him by quoting examples of those who have been in a similar plight and have come out of it.

In the fourth stage of the "incidents of ascent," during the process of transmutation—which is the longest and most complicated—the work of the therapist is correspondingly more complex. Some important aspects of the treatment are:

1. To enlighten the patient as to what is really going on within him, and help him to find the right attitude to take.

2. To teach him how, by the right use of the will, to wisely control and firmly master the drives emerging from the unconscious without repressing them through fear or condemnation.

3. To teach him the techniques of the transmutation and sublimation of sexual and aggressive energies. These techniques constitute the most apt and constructive solution of many psychological conflicts.

4. To help him in the proper recognition and assimilation of the energies inflowing from the Self and from super-conscious levels.

5. To help him express and utilize those energies in altruistic love and service. This is particularly valuable also for counteracting the tendency to excessive introversion and self-centeredness that often exists in this and other stages of self-development.

6. To guide him through the various phases of the reconstruction of his personality around a higher inner center, that is, in the achievement of his spiritual psychosynthesis.

At this point we should like to make it clear that the psychotherapeutic treatment we are describing does not by any means exclude an appropriate physical treatment, which can be combined with the former. But it is outside the scope of this chapter to deal with the physical means that can be used and which differ greatly according to the special requirements of each patient.

In some cases the treatment is complicated by the fact that there is an admixture of "regressive" and "progressive" symptoms. These are cases of irregular development. Such people may reach a high level with one part of their personality and yet be handicapped by certain infantile fixations or dominated by unconscious conflicts. One might say that a careful analysis shows that most of those who are engaged in the process of self-actualization are to be found with remnants of this kind; this is not surprising because the same can well be said also of so-called normal people who, as Maslow rightly states, live "in a state of mild and chronic psychopathology and fearfulness, of stunting and crippling and immaturity."(17, p. 1.)

From all that has been said it is apparent that, in order to deal in a satisfactory way with the psychological troubles incident to Self-actualization, a twofold competence is required—that of the professionally trained psychotherapist and that of the serious student of, or better still, the experienced traveller along the way to Self-realization. This twofold endowment is at present only rarely found; but, considering the growing number of individuals who require such treatment, it is becoming increasingly urgent that as many as possible of those who wish to serve humanity by administering to its greatest needs should be induced to qualify for the task.

It would also be of great benefit if the public were better informed about the general facts of the subject. At present, it frequently happens that ignorance, prejudice, and active opposition—particularly on the part of the patient's relatives—hamper the task of patient and therapist.

With a more enlightened approach by both the public and by psychotherapists, much unnecessary suffering can be avoided. Thus many earnest men and women will more easily and speedily reach the goal of their endeavor—the attainment of an ever increasing Self-realization.

REFERENCES

1. Adler, A.: *The Pattern of Life,* New York, Cosmopolitan Book Co., 1931.
2. Allport, G.: *Becoming,* New Haven, Yale University Press, 1955.
3. Angyal, A.: *Foundations of a Science of Personality,* Cambridge, Harvard University Press, 1941.
4. Assagioli, R.: *Dynamic Psychology and Psychosynthesis,* Monograph, New York, N.Y., Psychosynthesis Research Foundation, 1958.
5. Baruk, H.: *Psychiatrie Morale Expérimentale, Individuelle et Sociale,* Paris, Presses Universitaires, 1945.
6. Caruso, I.A.: *Psychoanalyse et Synthèse Personelle,* Paris, Desclée de Brouwer, 1959. Originally in German: *Psychoanalyse und Synthese der Existenz,* Wien, Herder, 1952.
7. Ferrière, A.: *L'Orthogenése Humaine ou l'Ascension vers l'Esprit,* Neuchâtel, Messeiller, 1959.
8. Frankl, V.E.: *The Doctor and the Soul: An Introduction to Logotherapy,* New York, Knopf, 1955.
9. Freud, S.: *The Standard Edition of the Complete Psychological Works of Sigmund Freud,* New York, Macmillan, 1953.
10. Fromm, E.: *Psychoanalysis and Religion,* New Haven, Yale University Press, 1950.
11. Goldstein, K.: *The Organism,* New York, American Book Co., 1939.
12. Horney, K.: *Our Inner Conflicts,* New York, Norton, 1945.
13. Jung, C.G.: *Modern Man in Search of a Soul,* New York, Harcourt Brace, 1933.
14. Jung, C.G.: *Collected Works,* Bollingen Series, New York, Pantheon Books, 1953-54.
15. Jung, C.G.: The Development of Personality. In C. Moustakas (Ed.), *The Self,* New York, Harper, 1956.
16. Maslow, A.H.: *Motivation and Personality,* New York, Harper, 1954.

17. Maslow, A. H.: *Cognition of Being in the Peak Experiences.* Monograph. Waltham, Mass., Dept. of Psychology, Brandeis University, 1956.
18. Maslow, A.H.: "Critique of Self-Actualization," *Journal of Individual Psychology,* 1959, 15, 24-32.
19. Maslow, A.H., and Sutich, A.J.: *Journal of Ortho-Psychology. Statement of Purpose.* Unpublished paper, 1958.
20. May, R.: *Man's Search for Himself,* New York, Norton, 1953.
21. Murray, H.A.: Vicissitudes of Creativity. In H. H. Anderson (Ed.), *Creativity and Its Cultivation,* New York, Harper, 1959.
22. Progoff I.: *Depth Psychology and Modern Man,* New York, Julian Press, 1959.
23. Rank, O.: *Will Therapy and Truth and Reality,* New York, Knopf, 1945.
24. Sorokin, P. A., et al.: *Forms and Techniques of Altruistic and Spiritual Growth.* Boston, Beacon Press, 1954 (a).
25. Sorokin, P.A.: *The Ways and Power of Love,* Boston, Beacon Press, 1954 (b).
26. Underhill, E.: *Mysticism,* London, Methuen, 1913.
27. Urban, H.J.: *"Uebernatur" und Medizin,* Innsbruck, Tyrolia, 1946.

Part Two

TECHNIQUES

METHODS AND TECHNIQUES EMPLOYED IN
PSYCHOSYNTHESIS | INTRODUCTION | GENERAL
ASSESSMENT AND EXPLORATION OF THE UNCONSCIOUS |
PERSONAL PSYCHOSYNTHESIS — TECHNIQUES | SPIRITUAL
PSYCHOSYNTHESIS — TECHNIQUES | INTERPERSONAL
PSYCHOSYNTHESIS — TECHNIQUES

METHODS AND TECHNIQUES EMPLOYED
IN PSYCHOSYNTHESIS*

I. Initial Techniques

Assessment and Analysis

1. Biography—Autobiography—Diary
2. Questionnaires
3. Associations: a) Free b) Stimulated c) Chain Associations
4. Dream Analysis
5. Tests (various)
6. Projective Techniques: a) Rorschach; b) Thematic Apperception Test (T.A.T.); c) Free drawing—Modelling—Musical Improvisation—Free Movements, etc.

**II. Evaluation—Discovery and Understanding
of the Existential Situation and Its Problems and Tasks**

III. Special Techniques

(Owing to the great difficulty of compiling a systematic classification of the techniques, they are given here in alphabetical order.)

Acceptance
Acting "AS IF"
Bibliotherapy

---

*This list is not final. Information about other techniques will be gratefully received.

Bio-Psychosynthesis (Physical training—
  Games—Sports—Rhythmic movements)
Catharsis
Chromotherapy
Concentration a) Inner b) In action
Creative expression
Disidentification
Graphotherapy
Humor (Smiling Wisdom)
Hypnosis
Imagination (Visualization, etc.)
  a) Reproductive b) Creative
Inspiration
Introspection
Intuition
Logotherapy
Meditation and Contemplation
Model (Ideal) a) of oneself b) outer models
  (Historical figures, etc.)
Music a) Listening b) Performing
Objective observation
Playful attitude
Proportion (Sense of)—Right emphasis
Psycho-shock
Relaxation
Repetition
Self-realization
Semantics
Silence (inner)
Substitution
Suggestion and Auto-suggestion a) Direct b) Indirect
Superconscious (Awareness of)
  a) Ways and Methods: aesthetic—ethical—devotional and
      mystical—heroic (through action)—illuminative—ritual.
  b) Utilization of superconscious energies
Symbols (use of)
Synthesis of the opposites
Transmutation and sublimation of psychological energies
  (sexual—combative, etc.)
Will: Stages: a) Goal, valuation, motivation b) Deliberation
              c) Decision d) Affirmation e) Planning
              d) Direction of the execution

IV. Combined Exercises

1. Directed day dreams (Rêve éveillé) — Symbolic Visualizations
2. Imaginative Training
3. Evocation and Cultivation of Higher Feelings (Peace — Joy — Love — Compassion)
4. Series (Grail legend — Dante's Divine Comedy, etc.)

V. Personal Influence

a) Through presence and example (catalytic)
b) Deliberate

VI. Group Techniques

1. Group Analysis
2. Psychodrama
3. Cooperative Group Activities

VII. Techniques Employed in Inter-Individual Psychosynthesis

(Several of the techniques listed above can be used for inter-individual psychosynthesis; for instance: Visualization — Imaginative training — Humor — the Group Techniques. Here are mentioned only those which are specific for interpersonal and social psychosynthesis.)

1. Comradeship — Friendship
2. Cooperation — Team work — Sharing
3. Empathy
4. Goodwill
5. Love (Altruistic)
6. Responsibility (Sense of)
7. Right Relations: a) Between the Individual and the Group
                                    b) Between Groups
8. Service
9. Understanding — Elimination of Prejudice.

INTRODUCTION

Some basic comments and general remarks as an introduction to the Techniques of Psychosynthesis

It is opportune, at the outset, to stress the necessity of relating the different techniques to the over-all purpose of psychosynthesis, so that we retain this purpose clearly in mind when we apply the techniques—which are only tools, and as tools can be modified. What is important are the principles and the basic purpose of the entire endeavor. The basic purpose of psychosynthesis is to release or, let us say, help to release, the energies of the Self. Prior to this the purpose is to help integrate, to synthesize, the individual around the personal self, and then later to effect the synthesis between the personal ego and the Self. Therefore, all the techniques should be subordinated to this basic goal; they are not a static collection of tools, but can be used and modified at will by therapists and educators, provided they keep in mind the basic purpose of the therapy.

There is an inevitable overlapping of techniques. For instance, bibliotherapy works partly through suggestion, but not only in that way, for it can also arouse the higher feelings, develop concentration, provide mental training, and so on. Another instance is musical therapy: its influence can be ascribed partly to suggestion, partly to the cultivation of higher feelings, and partly to inducing relaxation, according to the purpose for which it is used. Yet, although each technique is specific, a specific tool or means, this fact of overlapping does not really constitute a difficulty. We do not aim at a rigid separation or systematization of the techniques. We will enumerate and describe them separately for didactic purposes, and then indicate various combinations of several of them in *exercises,* each for a specific purpose.

The best procedure is to present the techniques in the approximate order of the steps that are indicated in the usual development of a psychosynthesis. (We refer here to the basic exposition given in Chapter One where not only the over-all picture is given but also the various stages for reaching a psychosynthesis.) Instead of detailing the techniques (approximately forty) we will present the various steps in the psychotherapeutic-psychosynthetic process, and then bring in those techniques which are appropriate to each step. As we shall see, the same exercise or the same technique may be used at more than one step, but each technique will be presented in detail at the step where it would be *first* used, and then if used at a later step suitable back reference will be made.

It is well to point out at the outset the difference existing between techniques and exercises and between both of them and methods.

A technique can be regarded as a specific psychological procedure used in order to produce a definite effect on some aspect or on some function of the psyche.

An exercise consists of the combination or association of various techniques in order to produce a more general effect. For instance, the rather simple exercise for evoking serenity (see p. 223) includes the use of a number of techniques such as relaxation, rhythmical breathing, mental concentration, visualization, creative imagination—all of them used and directed by the will.

A method is a combination of techniques and exercises used in a specific succession or alternation according to a definite program in order to achieve the therapeutic or educational aim considered necessary or valuable.

In psychosynthesis the emphasis is put on a holistic or integral conception of the treatment, which should always be kept in view and to which every method, exercise, and technique should be subordinated. The needs not only of each patient but also of the different phases of the treatment in each case are very different and sometimes opposite. Therefore, the use of a specific technique or exercise which may prove useful in one case or in one phase may be unsuitable or even harmful for other individuals or in different conditions. The following is a clear instance of this. The exercise for evoking serenity is obviously most useful in counteracting the excessive tension, emotional stress, and anxiety so widespread nowadays among not only nervous patients but also "normal" people. Indeed, it should constitute a daily practice of psychological hygiene in modern life. But it would be a great mistake to make it, or similar exercises, the central part of a treatment, neglecting the use of other and quite different procedures. If used opportunely, this exercise can eliminate obstacles to deep analysis (such as an *excessive* anxiety) and support the patient during the inevitable crises and upheavals produced by the analysis. But if it is used as a psychological "tranquilizer" it might produce a false sense of well-being and security, and therefore give the illusion of a cure; which would be only superficial and unreliable, because the real issues have remained unresolved.

A similar warning should be made concerning all other techniques and methods. For instance, the main contention of psychosynthesis is that no mere analytic treatment is sufficient to bring about true integration and growth, which require the use of active techniques and of the other helps indicated in this Manual.

In conclusion, we as therapists, while utilizing to the full all existing techniques, should bear constantly in mind that they, per se, are not enough, and that, as L.W. Dobb has warned, "technicians tend to fall in love with, and then be corrupted by, psychological weapons." (*Personal Problems and Psychological Frontiers*, p. 274)

However, in the case of psychosynthesis this danger can and, we hope, will be offset; first, by the very multiplicity and variety of the techniques which prevents giving undue importance to any one of them; second, by the steady cultivation and use of the synthetic spirit, by the constant endeavor to keep the entire picture in view, to relate always the part to the whole; last, by emphasizing in theory and in practice the central, decisive importance of the *human* factor, of the living interpersonal relation between the therapist and the patient.[a]

---

[a]*Note:* Most of the techniques and exercises described in this Manual can also be used for psychosynthetic self-realization and for educational purposes both by teachers and parents.

CHAPTER III

General Assessment and
Exploration of the Unconscious

The preliminary step in psychosynthesis, as indicated in *Dynamic Psychology and Psychosynthesis* (see Chapter I), is a thorough knowledge of the conscious and the unconscious aspects of one's personality.

Psychoanalysis with its emphasis on the unconscious generally starts with the exploration of the unconscious through its specific techniques—free associations, interpretation of dreams and so on—in order to release the forces repressed in the unconscious. In our opinion, it is advisable to start with an inventory and assessment of the *conscious aspect of the components of the personality,* not only to follow the general rule "from the known to the unknown," but because it is imperative for each man and woman who wants to live consciously to be well aware of those elements or components of their personality—not a dim, passive awareness, but a deliberate assessment, valuation, understanding and control of them.

Moreover, the distinction between conscious and unconscious components is much less sharp than psychoanalysis asserts. It is a *relative* distinction; there is a constant osmosis going on between the field or area of consciousness and that of the unconscious. Further, the strengthening of the conscious personality prepares it for easier assimilation of the unconscious aspects. There are real dangers in the premature irruption of unconscious forces in an unprepared and loosely knit personality.

The assessment requires on the part of the patient a certain degree of the attitude of the observer. In the first stage, the subject assumes this attitude unconsciously, obliged by the task itself or—during the sessions—aided by the therapist. Later, in the course of therapy, the attitude can and should be assumed more and more consciously, deliberately and fully. By "attitude of the observer" we mean an attitude analogous to that of the scientist observing an experiment through his instruments, or the attitude of a detective observing the scene of a crime and noticing the objects existing in the room where the crime happened.

This means that the patient begins to realize that his psychological experiences and functions can be looked at *objectively*. Also, it means a certain dis-identification of the self from the contents of the conscious personality. This develops an increasing self-awareness which is the chief characteristic of the personal "I" or self.

Therefore, while being used and developed in and through the work of assessment, this dis-identification serves also as a technique for acquiring pure self-awareness, the pure sense of self-identity (see p. 112). This—in a sense—means the "I", or point of self-awareness, observing one's foibles, one's abilities, difficulties and conflicts in as detached and unemotional a way as one can achieve, recognizing that, of course, we are bound to be emotionally concerned, since we are dealing with ourselves; but little by little we may acquire more of a scientific attitude, and emotion may become less of a disturbing and distorting element.

Let us remember that the assessment at this stage refers primarily to the past history, to the biography of the patient. By this he is enabled to see his own life history objectively, to consider its development and to recognize the chain of causes which have operated—and may still operate.

Biography

In order to get a preliminary picture of the patient on the one hand, and to orient him towards introspection, or self-observation, on the other, it is well to begin with a biography. Sometimes a verbal biography at the very start of the sessions will suffice temporarily, but in addition it is advisable to get a *written* biography from the patient. This has both practical and therapeutic advantages: *practical,* because it saves time, it saves sessions; *therapeutic,* because it helps the patient to make a review of his own life. When the patient first consults the therapist he usually gives various spontaneous disconnected biographical items. This provides a good opportunity to suggest to him that he make a written biography in chronological order, so that he will be helped to know himself better and to furnish useful information to the therapist.

There is a further important advantage of a *qualitative* nature. In writing both conscious and unconscious factors are active; therefore, it often happens that, while the subject starts writing down what he is consciously aware of, later on things come up which he had not thought of before and which sometimes surprise him. They emerge from unconscious levels; to speak metaphorically, "the unconscious takes hold of his hand." There is a wide range of emergence of unconscious contents, including occasionally the strange cases of automatic writing. There often is a surprising qualitative difference between oral and written expression; we find that people express different aspects of their personality in writing from those they express verbally.

Diary

Whenever possible the patient should be asked to keep a diary during the treatment. This is useful in two ways: it saves time in the sessions, because the therapist can read the diary rapidly; secondly, because of the different elements which come out in the process of writing; many patients are more outspoken when they write without the presence of the therapist. This written diary gives a psychological film of the dynamic development of the patient's psychological state, of his mind-stream—using mind in the larger sense. The patient can be asked to send in the diary either one or two days before the interview, or the same morning if it is not long, furnishing thus fresh material for the session.

The technique of writing is therapeutically useful in various ways: it serves 1) for the assessment, 2) as a means of self-expression and 3) as a technique of active training in concentration, attention and will.

A complete assessment includes the following points or parts:

1. *The origin of various personality traits.*
2. *The recognition of existing complexes.* There are complexes of which the patient is often painfully aware.
3. *The recognition of polarities, ambivalences and conflicts.*
4. *The recognition of the various "selves";* this in the sense given to them by William James. We may call them *sub-personalities.*
5. *The persistence of traits belonging to preceding psychological ages:* a) infantile, b) adolescent, c) juvenile.

A systematic questioning on these five points is made. The patient is asked, for instance, what traits he thinks he may have derived from his father and family, his mother and family. Questions on each of the five points can be asked by the therapist in the opening session or sessions, or—if the patient prefers writing because it is an easier way of expression for him, or if there are time limitations—he can be presented with a list of questions which he may then answer at home.

Origin of Traits

It is of value to the patient to know the sources of the psychological forces and qualities he is using. Therefore, the therapist should explain to the patient that there may be similarities between himself and his parents and ancestors, and that these similarities—or dis-similarities—have a bearing on the family situation; and further, that they constitute parts of his own psychological set-up. Very often patients come with some family problems—the relation to family, mother or the sibling. To know how alike, or how different, the family members are gives important clues.

The "origin of traits" means chiefly finding the characteristics of the parents and their similarities in the patient. It is such similarities of characteristics that can create a conflict between the patient and a parent, or cause them to become overly attached to each other.

But the patient should also recognize the traits that cannot be attributed to family sources. He should be asked where he sees obvious dis-similarities from the family members, or indirectly, in what way he feels apart from them or not understood, e.g., artistic tendencies in a patient who is a member of a "business family." Many such non-family traits or incompatibilities may be found existing in the general environment or in particular groups to which the patient belongs. Some traits, however, have a solely individual source; one finds clearly defined tendencies or traits which have no source in the family or the general surroundings at all. These lead to the inner, more individual side of the person.

The systematic questioning on this first point, of the origin of the traits, should bring about a clear picture covering more or less fully the following points:

1) Family influences
   a) from the father and his family
   b) from the mother and her family
   c) ancestral, from ancestors and in general from collective sources in the past
   d) from siblings
2) Group and Collective Sources of the present
   a) the present collective psyche of humanity as a whole
   b) race-characteristics
   c) national traits
   d) class or social traits
   e) psychological influences of any other groups to which one belongs
3) Individual characteristics not traceable to and different from family and group sources listed above.

Whenever possible, information on all these points should also be collected from the patient's family and friends.

Conscious Complexes

The second question, the recognition of existing and conscious complexes, requires first a definition of the term "complex." It is used here in the standard sense of being a conglomeration of psychological—to use a debatable word—"elements" which have developed a strong emotional charge, revealed under certain situations as typified in the inferiority complex.

The recognition of such complexes by patients is rendered easier because such terms as "inferiority complex," "father" and "mother complex" are so well known and current these days. So it is simple to quietly tell a patient that he has such a complex, and then follow up with the question: "Tell me what you know of its original beginning; from what circumstance was it derived, or from what condition? Was it in school, in the family situation, etc.?"

Everything that is conscious or attainable in the memory of the patient can be exhausted in this way before we need turn to the unconscious contents.

In general it could be said that every phobia is a complex, but this does not necessarily constitute a problem in the person's life. For instance—to take a simple example—there are some people who are identified with their complex of inferiority to such a degree that they do not fight it; they simply have no conflict, for they are convinced that they *are* inferior to others. The way that they have accepted consciously that they are inferior can be masochistic, in a psychological sense. Such persons may come to the therapist with some psychosomatic complaint or to get rid of a phobia, but when they are confronted with it they may feel guilt, despair, self-pity, etc., but without conflict. For this the word "character-disorder" has been used. This term with its static, permanent connotation gives a wrong impression, because as soon as the patient is made aware of the fact that he is a victim of a conflict and that there is a way out, he jumps at the opportunity, and it is of therapeutic value that he feels there is a solution to his problem. This illustrates false identification; the patient is identified with his complex but as soon as he sees that it is a complex, then in that recognition there is a beginning of dis-identification, and he can then be told that he can get rid of the complex through the techniques of psychosynthesis—thus instilling hope.

We have, of course, all kinds of sexual complexes, such as the complex of impotence; or, on the emotional level, women often have the complex of being ugly (the inferiority complex in its aesthetic aspect). Then there is the father complex in both its positive and negative manifestation—the urge to become like the father or the hatred of the father. Again, there is often a jealousy complex towards the next child, or towards the first and preferred child. In all these the characteristic is an intense emotional charge—either positive or negative; the "voltage" is characteristic of the complex, for the whole question is one of psychodynamics. Wherever there is a strong emotional voltage, enclosed in a series of ideas or one object, there is a complex.

Polarities, Ambivalences and Conflicts

Polarities and ambivalences have to be distinguished from conflicts. They are not the same thing. Conflict is a stage in which the patient has recognized his complexes as such, and wants to get rid of them but is unable to do so unaided. Ambivalence, in contrast, is vacillation between two extremes—not due to his effort to be rid of one of the extremes, but simply to his oscillation between the two. For instance: love and hate, inferiority and superiority, aggression and masochism, activity and passivity. These are polarities and ambivalences because they are spontaneous. A conflict exists only when there is an actual fight between different parts of the personality. Very often laziness, unwillingness to act or difficulty in doing so—for instance in writing—can be due to such a situation.

Sub-Personalities

At first glance it might appear difficult to the therapist to introduce the concept of sub-personalities to the "innocent" patient. But practice has shown that the concept is easily accepted by him if presented in some way similar to the following: "Have you noticed that you behave differently in your office, at home, in social interplay, in solitude, at church, or as a member of a political party?" In that way he is easily brought to recognize the differences and even the contradictions in his behavior. There are the two classical types: the he-man in the office and the milquetoast man in his family life, and vice-versa. Thus he can be led to the conscious recognition that, as a son, he acts differently than as a husband, or as a father. Of course, it should be explained to him that these differences are normal, because each one of us has different selves—according to the relationships we have with other people, surroundings, groups, etc., and it is well for us not to identify ourselves with any of these "selves," and to recognize that these are all roles that we play. And that although it seems paradoxical it is yet true that the less we are identified with a particular role the better we play it.

It is good to emphasize this "playing of roles." Actually the role is a point of arrival, not the starting point. The starting point is the complete immersion in each sub-personality, with degrees of awareness of the incongruity of the situation. The goal is the freed self, the I-consciousness, who can play *consciously* various roles.

William James dealt with this concept of sub-personalities— which he called "the various selves." The functions of an individual, in whom various psychological traits are not integrated, form what we consider to be sub-personalities. It is probably better to use the word "roles" instead of "functions," to avoid semantic confusion. The patient should be asked to describe himself in his various roles: as a son or daughter, as a husband or wife, as father or mother, as having a professional role of some kind; and in these roles to examine his corresponding attitudes toward subordinates, towards superiors, and towards his peers. Other subpersonalities, or roles, are those played in the different social groups, including his religious group or church, his political group or party, and other roles which he may have or may want to play in life.

The organization of the sub-personalities is very revealing and sometimes surprising, baffling or even frightening. One discovers how very different and often quite antagonistic traits are displayed in the different roles. These differences of traits which are organized around a role justify, in our opinion, the use of the word "sub-personality." Ordinary people shift from one to the other without clear awareness, and only a thin thread of memory connects them; but for all practical purposes they are different beings—they act differently, they show very different traits. Therefore, one should become clearly aware of these sub-personalities because this evokes a measure of understanding of the meaning of psychosynthesis, and how it is possible to synthesize these sub-personalities into a larger organic whole without repressing any of the useful traits.

Another advantage is that revealing the different roles, traits, etc., emphasizes the reality of the observing self. During and after this assessment of the sub-personalities one realizes that the observing self is none of them, but something or somebody different from each. This is a very important realization and another of the keys for the desired and future psychosynthesis. This is similar to the distinction that Jung made between "ego" and "persona" (only we speak of person*ae*—the plural—which is more realistic and nearer to facts) and what Paul Tournier in *The Meaning of Persons* called "Le Personnage," which would correspond to the series of roles, and "La Personne" which corresponds to the central inner Self. Charles Baudoin also makes this same distinction.

A definite confirmation of the existence of sub-personalities is found in psychiatric literature, and cases of alternating personalities or more than two distinct personalities are reported. In some cases even the thin thread of memory, mentioned above, which connects the sub-personalities is non-existent, and one sub-personality can ignore the others. A certain number of cases have been accurately studied; one by Pierre Janet, and William James dealt with this subject in his *Principles of Psychology*. But the most carefully studied case is that of Miss Beauchamp by Morton Prince. Morton Prince had a most objective mind and his report is photographic, with a bare minimum of interpretation—which is fortunate because it gives us an undistorted picture. The reading of his book, *Dissociation of a Personality*, is more fascinating and eventful than most novels. It describes the splitting of the subject's personality into two, then three, then into four; also the warfare between the personality and a sub-personality (one sub-personality was aware of the behavior of these sub-personalities, and described and interpreted the symbolism).

Also, Thigpen and Cleckley in *The Three Faces of Eve* present a case history of a woman with multiple personalities, and the book was made into a successful motion picture.

Such cases, however, are not too common but rarity does not prove anything, as the analogy of the comet shows. Comets despite their rarity have taught astronomers much, not only about comets but about the universe in general. These cases conform to the conception of the self as a projection of a higher Self, because in the case of multiple personality there is a splitting into three or four selves; but the case of Miss Beauchamp shows that the multiplicity is only temporary and that the "selves" can re-unite. This illustrates the empirical reality of a personal self, while the possibility of re-union confirms the existence of a unique higher Self behind the scenes.

It is our scientific duty to point out the parapsychological aspect of certain of these cases. There are some cases—like that of Velida, reported by Janet—in which there is no trace of parapsychological elements, and all can be explained by disassociation and later re-association. But in the case of Miss Beauchamp the sub-personality Sally was different from the others. Sally had a power which the others did not have, and she was excluded from the final re-association or synthesis. She agreed with Dr. Prince to retire—one does not know where.

A case studied and extensively reported by another Dr. Prince also presents evidence of parapsychological interest. (W. F. Prince, *The Doris Case of Multiple Personality*, The American Society for Psychic Research, 1916)

Traits Belonging to Preceding Psychological Ages

For this next step in the assessment the patient should be prepared by the therapist (through explanations of what this stage is meant to accomplish) to search himself for persisting traits belonging to preceding psychological ages: infantile, adolescent and juvenile. This self-examination can be made during the session—with time for reflection and with no pressure on the patient to answer immediately. It is worthwhile to have the patient find out for himself as much as possible what in his present feeling, thinking or behavior corresponds to those previous stages of psychological development. Of course, during further sessions, some of these traits come up spontaneously, and as they are important, the therapist should constantly be on the watch for them and whenever they are obvious or can be inferred, the attention of the patient should be called to them.

At this point of the procedure, however, the therapist should be conscious of the fact that the persistence of such traits is not only the characteristic of patients but of every adult in general, in various degrees. Some hobbies, for instance, are evidently of that character. Many men have a hobby of electric trains. First they buy a train with the pretext of giving it to their children—but then they play with it more than the children do. As a specific instance, one of the foremost baritones in Italy has spent large sums on his hobby and has a huge room, complete with rails and locomotives. This is an obvious and amusing persistence of infantile traits; and, of course, there are several other games which have the same character and in which some adults indulge. It must be pointed out that this is not necessarily reprehensible, that it is not a thing to be labeled as a morbid symptom or anything of that kind. On the contrary, it may have its proper place—but this point will be dealt with more fully when we speak of the psychosynthesis of the ages.

QUESTIONNAIRES

We now give four questionnaires which have proved useful in practice and adequate for a first rough psychological profile. They are very revealing. These four are variations of one basic questionnaire, modified by questions of growing complexity for four age groups: #1 for *Children* (6-12 years), #2 for *Adolescents* (13-17 years), #3 for *Young Adults* (18-26 years), with the latter serving, with slight modifications as #4 for *Adults* (over 26 years).

It is useful to present the same questions again after a month, six months or even a year. The examination of the differences in the answers provides a check on the progress of psychosynthesis.

Questionnaire 1

QUESTIONS ADDRESSED TO CHILDREN
(6 to 12 years) '

1. What man, woman or child (of the past or the present) do you admire most. Why?
2. What kind of books do you like most? Which books have given you the greatest pleasure? Which books did you not like? Have any books caused you harm? How?

3. a) Which poems do you like most? Why?

   b) Do you prefer pictures or statues? Which of these do you admire most? Why?

   c) Which public buildings, churches and monuments have attracted your attention most?

   d) Do you like music and the singing of patriotic and religious hymns? Which song and which piece of music do you like best?

   e) Which do you prefer: the theatre or the cinema? Which film has impressed you most? And which film gave you the greatest pleasure? Did any films have a bad effect on you? Which ones? *How* did they hurt you?

4. What games and sports interest you most? Do you also like, or prefer, to be an onlooker?

5. Would you like to have a great deal of money? If you had it what would you do with it?

6. Do you prefer to play with girls or with boys? Why?

7. Do you have many friends? Are you fond of them? Why?

8. Do you prefer to be alone or with other people? Do you like being with grown-ups?

9. Do you love your country?

10. Are you sorry for the poor and for those who suffer all over the world?

11. Do you think you are good or naughty? Why? How do you distinguish good from bad?

12. Are you more often happy or sad? Which things make you most unhappy? Can you stop yourself from being sad? How do you do it?

13. Which things are giving you the greatest pleasure now? And what other things do you think would give you great pleasure?

14. What do you want to do when you are grown-up? What do you intend to do then? Would you like to do what your father (or your mother) is doing? If not, why?

15. What do you like doing most and what kinds of studies do you prefer? In which are you most successful?

16. Do you prefer to be in the country, at the sea, or in town? Why?

17. Which interest you most: animals, plants, toys or machines?

18. Do you like going to school or would you prefer to study at home?

19. Are you satisfied with yourself? Do you wish to improve? Would you like advice in this respect?

20. Do you feel that your parents and your teachers understand you? Do you get on well with them? Also with your brothers and sisters?

Questionnaire 2

QUESTIONS ADDRESSED TO ADOLESCENTS
(13 to 17 years)

1. Who is your ideal man and who is your ideal woman? Which men and women (of the past and the present) do you admire and appreciate most? Why?

2. What kind of books do you like most? Which books have given you the greatest enjoyment and which have benefited you most? Which books have caused you harm? Why?

3. a) Which poems and novels do you like most? Why?

   b) Do you prefer pictures or statues? Which picture or statue do you admire most? Why?

   c) Which public buildings, churches and monuments have attracted your attention most?

   d) Do you like music and singing? Which song and which piece of music do you like best?

   e) Which do you prefer: the theater or the cinema? Which film has impressed you most? And which film gave you the greatest pleasure? Did any films have a bad effect on you? Which ones? How did they hurt you?

4. What importance do you attach to sport? Which games and sports do you prefer? Do you also like, or do you prefer, to be an onlooker?

5. What value has money for you? If you had a great deal of it, how would you spend it?

6. Do you prefer friends of your own age or those older than you? Do you prefer the company of your own sex or that of the other? Why?

7. What does friendship mean to you?

8. How much and how do you feel family affection and national, social, and human solidarity?

9. How do you distinguish good from evil?

10. Was your childhood sad or happy? What things cause you to suffer most? Have you any doubts that disturb you, and that you would like to have explained to you? What are they?

11. What things give you the greatest happiness? When are you most contented?

12. What value has life for you?

13. Are you religious? Do you believe in God, in a Spiritual Reality? What do you understand by it? What importance has it in your life?

14. Which studies and activities do you prefer? In which are you most successful?

15. Which profession or activity would you like to take up? Have you decided which one, or not? What would you *like* to do when you are grown-up? What do you *propose* to do then? Would you like to do what your father (or your mother) is doing? If not, why?

16. Do you prefer to be in the country, at the sea, or in town? Why?

17. What do you think of school?

18. Are you content with yourself? Would you like to be better? Would you like advice and help in this respect?

19. Do you feel that your elders understand you? What more do you feel they should be or do?

Questionnaire 3

QUESTIONS ADDRESSED TO YOUNG ADULTS
(18 to 26 years)

1. Whom do you consider as "ideal models"? Which men and women (of the past and the present) do you appreciate and admire most? Why?

2. Which are your favorite books and the ones you have most enjoyed and benefited from? Which books have caused you harm? In what way?

3. a) Which poems and novels do you like most? Why?

   b) Do you prefer pictures or statues? Which of these do you admire most? Why?

   c) Which public buildings, churches and monuments have attracted your attention most?

   d) Do you like music and singing? Which song and which piece of music do you like best?

   e) Which do you prefer: the theater or the cinema? Which film has impressed you most? And which film gave you the greatest pleasure? Did any films have a bad effect on you? Which ones? In what way did they hurt you?

4. What importance do you attach to sport? Which games and sports do you prefer? Do you also like, or do you prefer to be, an onlooker?

5. What is your attitude toward money? What significance has wealth or poverty for you? What, in your opinion, are the advantages or disadvantages of the one and the other?

6. What is your attitude toward love? What do you understand by it? What do you think of the opposite sex? What is your attitude toward marriage and children?

7. What significance and value has friendship for you?

8. Are you an individualist or do you feel family, national, social or human solidarity? Which of these do you feel most?

9. What is your attitude toward moral principles and demands? What ideas and feelings do you connect with duty?

10. What events and what inner conditions make or made you suffer most? Was your childhood happy or sad? What problems trouble you most?

11. What events and what inner conditions give, or have given you, the greatest joy? What ideas and what conditions give you the greatest satisfaction? What is your attitude toward joy and favorable circumstances? Do you think you can attain joy and happiness? By what means?

12. What is your attitude toward life? What significance, value and purpose has life for you? Are you inclined to be optimistic or pessimistic? Why?

13. What is your attitude toward religion? Do you believe in God, in a spiritual Reality? What do you understand by it? What importance has religion in your life?

14. What caused you to choose the subjects you are studying or the work you are doing?

15. Do you prefer to be in the country, at the sea, or in town? Why?

16. Which aspects of the inner life are prevalent in you and which do you like most (thinking, imagination, feeling, prayer, or contemplation)?

17. What has school given or not given you? Do you think it advisable to change the methods and programs used in education? Which of them? And how?

18. Are you satisfied with yourself? Do you think you can improve yourself? By what means? Would you like to receive advice in this respect?

19. What is your attitude toward the older generation, both generally and in regard to your family? Are there misunderstandings and conflicts? Of what kind? How do you think they could or should be overcome?

20. Have you any other ideas or suggestions and observations you would like to express regarding the problem of young people and their relationship to adults?

21. What do you think of the present political and economic conditions of the world?

22. How do you think it possible to arrive at a real and lasting peace between the peoples of the world?

23. What men, in your opinion, are today the most representative in the world?

24. Do you believe that we are actually at the end of an epoch and at the beginning of a new one? What, in your opinion, are the signs of this renewal? What characteristics (spiritual, cultural, social, practical) will the new epoch eventually have?

Please state: The place and date of your birth; the address where you are now living; the occupation of your parents and their place of birth.

Please mark with a star(*) those statements of yours which you think express the characteristics of young people at all times, and with a cross (+) those which you think correspond to the mentality of the youth of today.

Questionnaire 4

QUESTIONS ADDRESSED TO ADULTS
(over 26 years)

This questionnaire comprises the twenty-four questions given in the preceding one (#3). This serves a twofold purpose: for the assessment and also to help the adult relate more satisfactorily to younger people. It brings to the fore, in the most complete manner possible, the similarities and differences existing between adults and younger age groups.

To contribute towards and promote the reciprocal knowledge and understanding which are necessary for harmonious co-operation in solving the present difficult problems of the relationship between generations, it is suggested that adults (from the age of 26 on) replying to the questions should mark:

with a cross (+) the replies which they believe to represent the views prevailing in their own generation;

with a small circle (o) those replies which they believe to express their own views;

with an interrogation mark (?) those about which they are in doubt.

The Constitution of Man

At the beginning of treatment—parallel to the patient giving his spoken or written autobiography and answering the questionnaires—instructions on the psychological constitution of man should be given to him. This can be done by showing him the first pages of the monograph *Dynamic Psychology and Psychosynthesis,** including the diagram (page 6), taking care to explain and emphasize the terminology adopted. There are many words which are used by different writers with quite diverse meanings; for instance: soul, irrational, unconscious, individuality, personality. The word "self" is also most confusing. Allport, in *Personality: A Psychological Interpretation,* lists 50 different meanings attributed to the word "personality." Semantics is a new word for a very old realization—the ancient Chinese sages, especially Confucius, laid great emphasis on what they called "right designation."

In presenting the constitution of man to a patient we must also guard against the danger of "indoctrination." We must keep in mind that, after all, we are giving the conception of man according to psychosynthesis *as it has been developed up to the present time.* The patient must be made aware of the fact that it is only a working hypothesis that he is asked to accept. Everyone has some kind of a philosophy, and everyone has a kind of psychology which is generally very crude, hazy, and partly erroneous. There is a great advantage in presenting a picture of the constitution of man, provided the instruction is clearly indicated as a working-hypothesis for the treatment, without obligation on the patient's part to believe it as a fixed truth. Later, he may even find his own particular way of expressing his self-concept. But, for the practical purposes of the treatment, we must have a semantic understanding of the common frame of reference. With some patients— especially well-educated people—the monograph *Dynamic Psychology and Psychosynthesis* may be handed to them for study. To others we present the conception in simpler terms. But in all cases use is made of the visual picture, the diagram on page 6 of the monograph, for it has proved in practice to be very helpful.

---

*Incorporated as Part One, Chapter One, but available in booklet form from Psychosynthesis Research Foundation, New York, N.Y.

The Self

To many, who are confronted for the first time with psychosynthesis, the concept of two selves (a "personal self" and a "higher Self") seems to constitute an obstacle, but the higher Self, for instance, can—in the beginning of therapy—simply be presented as a hypothesis which will be verified or disproved later. With some we advise them not to concern themselves about it, particularly where we are dealing with only a *personal* psychosynthesis (as distinct from a spiritual psychosynthesis) and the Self, therefore, remains more or less in the background.

In cases where a patient is proceeding towards a subsequent spiritual psychosynthesis, we first point out that there is a sense of self-identity: "I am my self," but that this self-consciousness is generally hazy, because of its many identifications. Therefore a process of dis-identification[a] is useful in order to become aware of the self-identity. The discussion of the subject with the patient can well be halted at this point, postponing until a much later stage of the treatment the question of the higher unconscious or superconscious and the spiritual Self. Only where patients, when they first come to us, already have spiritual or religious problems do we enter more thoroughly into this question at this early stage of therapy. We use a pragmatic attitude and seek—essentially—to respond to the immediate interest of the patient, to meet him on the ground of his immediate major preoccupation. In this way we are sure to capture his interest and to create the needed rapport. So, in practice, there is no rigid system, but a responding to the actual need of the unique situation of each patient and at each stage of the patient's life.

To be more specific about the presentation of the higher Self: naturally, the same explanation is not suitable for all patients, but with only a little knowledge of a patient's background and mentality we can easily vary our description appropriately. To all who are religious we can say that it is the neutral psychological term used for the soul; for those who are agnostic we use their language: presenting the hypothesis that there is a higher center in man, and explaining that there is a mass of evidence of direct experience of many people—some in the West and more in

---

[a] A specific "Exercise in Dis-Identification" is given on pages 116-119.

the East—of becoming aware of superconscious contents and of the Self. For instance, we can quote from Bucke's *Cosmic Consciousness*, from Ouspensky's *Tertium Organum*, as well as general Eastern and Western (Platonic) philosophy. As a specific example, the patient can be told: "There is evidence of direct awareness, either through spontaneous illumination, or through exercises of concentration, that such realities exist. Later on, if you are interested and when the treatment requires it, we will explore the situation more deeply."

In such ways we adapt our presentation to the patient's mentality and terminology. We translate our neutral terminology—e.g., "Self" or "superconscious"—into his terminology.

Very often patients ask for specific clarification on the *quality* of the Self and of so-called higher experiences. In such cases we explain some of the main characteristics. The chief quality is the experience of synthesis or the realization of individuality and universality. The real distinguishing factor between the little self and the higher Self is that the little self is acutely aware of itself as a distinct separate individual, and a sense of solitude or of separation sometimes comes in the existential experience. In contrast, the experience of the spiritual Self is a sense of freedom, of expansion, of communication with other Selves and with reality, and there is the sense of Universality. It feels itself at the same time individual and universal.

The Self (with a capital S) is often somewhat misleadingly considered to be the central concept in psychosynthesis and the idea which really differentiates psychosynthesis from previous psychotherapeutic approaches. If this were the main idea, psychosynthesis would only attempt to develop the patient's ability to integrate his life around the spiritual Self. This, however, is only partly true; for on the *personal* level the psychosynthetic approach has something different to offer in psychotherapy, in education and in self-realization.

Because a good personal psychosynthesis is all that we can look for in many of our patients the idea which is of capital importance, and around which the entire personal psychosynthesis revolves, is that of a personal self, of a point of consciousness and self-awareness, coupled with its realization and the use of its directing will.

Will

We emphasize the will as being the function most intimate with the self. In this respect we may be accused of resurrecting the will of 19th Century psychology, but the latter was based essentially on the conscious aspect of personality and disregarded the unconscious forces which Freud, Jung, and others emphasized.

It is important in psychosynthesis to discriminate between the willing based on unconscious motivation and the true will of the personal self. We think that there is such a thing as the "unconscious will" of the higher Self which tends always to bring the personality in line with the over-all purpose of the spiritual Self. One of the purposes or goals of spiritual psychosynthesis is to make this "unconscious will" of the spiritual Self a conscious experience.

Later in this Manual a distinction between unconscious motive and fully self-conscious motivation will be drawn more clearly. (See *"The Technique for the Development of the Will."*)

We think it preferable to speak of a "superconscious will," meaning that it operates from a level at which the conscious personal self is not aware. Of course, everything of which that conscious self is not aware can be called "un-conscious," including the lower, middle, and higher part of the unconscious. But we think that whenever possible it is better to indicate the *level* of which we are speaking, and therefore use for the higher unconscious the word "superconscious," although in so doing we use it in a neutral, descriptive way.

Valuation

By the mere use of the word "super" we give it value, we assume that it is superior to the conscious personal self; and here is a problem which could best be called "The Inevitability of Valuation." Many psychologists who refuse to accept valuation are making valuation judgments all the time, although blissfully unconscious of it. Surely it is better to do it consciously and deliberately. For instance, the difference between ourselves and a tape-recorder is that while we speak we do not notice the ticking of the clock and other noises around us, because we do not value them as of importance or relevant. But, in contrast, a tape-recorder does not discriminate; for the microphone, intelligent sounds and senseless noises have the same value—it is a purely physical intensity which is registered. With us, there is continuously—and happily—this selective activity of attention, and this implies a judgment value.

In this respect it is interesting to note that in the last few years an increasing number of clinicians have started to talk about the problem of values in psychotherapy, of the relationship between the values of the therapist and the values of the patient, whether and when it is advisable for the therapist to divulge his own values, how he can help the patient to more mature values, and so on. The question of values is simply unavoidable, and we must face the problem.

The persisting resistance to and denial of values among many psychologists can be explained, we think, historically. In the 18th Century there were fixed sets of so-called objective values, ethical and religious, imposed from without by authority, often rigid and sometimes even inhuman. Inevitably, there resulted an uprising, a revolt against such authoritarian values and dogmatic theories, and so the pendulum has swung to the other extreme. Now it is time to try to find the middle path, to empirically endeavor to establish the *relative* values based on vital criteria. We insist on the adjective "relative" because, while there may be great ethical and spiritual principles, their values in the psychological sense can only be related to the individual, to his age, to his general condition and to his stage in therapy.

Assessment of the Higher Aspects

It is relevant at this point to take up the question of assessment as far as it concerns the higher unconscious, the superconscious—or, rather, the higher aspects of the personality. These can well be put within the category of "conception of the world," *"Weltanschauung"* or "philosophy of life." As Molière's character, M. Jourdain, says, he had been talking prose all his life and never knew it till his professor told him; so everybody—even primitive people—have some kind of view or conception of life, which can be called a philosophy of life. Sometimes they are conscious of it; sometimes it is implied but easily brought to awareness; we could call it pre-conscious in Freud's terminology. Sometimes, instead, it is quite unconscious and comes up only in the technique of exploration of the unconscious. Here again, we see there is no hard and fast division between conscious and unconscious. A philosophy of life includes inevitably a set of values, so we see that the consideration of values is inescapable. Therefore, in the assessment of the patient, the subject is very easily brought up—either from relevant answers to the questionnaire or through direct interrogation, using of course language appropriate to his cultural level and explaining that the questions are asked so that we may know where he stands on these common human problems and concerns. For instance, we can ask: "What, according to you, is the purpose and the meaning of life; individual, collective, universal?" "What are your ethical standards?" "What are your religious beliefs, if any?"

When the patient answers, the therapist must remain silent, be completely objective for the time being, making no comments, in order not to influence or repress the patient in any way. Comments on his answers will come in much later sessions, and we will touch on this when we take up the other stages of psychosynthesis. These initial questions are simply for the therapist's information, and we tell the patient so. We reassure him that we will not seek to influence him in any way, but that we need to know his beliefs and values because they are a vital part of his being and may have some bearing on his neuroses. In putting it in that way, we keep a patient free from many inhibitions and anxieties.

There is a specific test on this subject which we have found most revealing. We call it the "Cosmic Test"; that is, to bring the patient to face the immensity, the infinity in space and time of the universe. The reactions vary, but often there are two markedly opposite ones. One is a sense of crushing anxiety, almost despair—a dramatic realization of the smallness, helplessness of the little individual in this enormous cosmic reality and process. The other reaction is a sense of elation, of expansion of consciousness, a sense of reverence, sometimes even of worship and joyous participation in that larger reality, a sense of relief from the narrow limitations of the personal self, and a sharing, a communion in universal life. This latter response is not only revealing but also therapeutic, because in this setting the trouble of the neurotic personality takes its proper dimension. This therapeutic value we will discuss later for this cosmic test is part of a further technique used in a later stage of psychosynthesis. At this initial stage, however, it is simply a test in the assessment, later it becomes a technique for infusing a sense of right proportions into the world of the individual.

For this cosmic test any of the many fine astronomical photographs available are good, particularly some of the galaxies, of the island-universes, pointing out that they are composed of millions of suns and that these island-universes are numberless. But a more specific and effective means is that constituted by the small book by Kees Boeke, *Cosmic View — the Universe in 40 Jumps* (New York, John Day, 1957), published first in resumé in the UNESCO *Courier* of May 1957. (Incidentally, the *Courier* is a magazine which we strongly recommend because it has much material useful for psychosynthesis, especially for inter-individual psychosynthesis.)

Although the book was written essentially for children, the illustrations can well be used for adults. Kees Boeke was the founder and former director of the "Workplats" children's community at Bilthoven, Netherlands, a pioneer "comprehensive school" created in 1926.

It is suggested, when using this material as a test, to start with illustration No. 9, the Planet, thus emphasizing the larger picture, the place of our little planet in the Solar System, in the Milky Way, and in the Universe. The picture may be shown along with a brief reading of part of the description given by the author. When arriving at the last picture in the series the patient can be asked: "What is your personal reaction to this realization of the vastness of the Universe?" The reactions of the patient are sometimes truly dramatic, but of course we not only listen to what he says, but we watch his whole behavior, including the subtle emotional reactions.

Later, if Boeke's book is used in the technique of inducing a right sense of proportion, we show all the illustrations from No. 1 onwards, followed by the series showing man in relation to smaller and smaller objects. In other words, first man's relationship to the Macrocosm, and then to the microcosm. This procedure is very revealing, very simple and quick.

EXPLORATION OF
THE UNCONSCIOUS

Association Test

In the exploration of the unconscious we come to psychoanalytic techniques in the strict sense. The first technique used is that of word association—the patient's reactions to a series of word-stimuli. With modifications referred to below we have used Jung's "hundred words" which he used at the beginning of his psychoanalytical practice and about which he wrote in his book "Studien uber Assoziation" (see *Experimental Researches*—Collected Works of C. G. Jung, Vol. II, 1957). With some additions they have proved to be a very fruitful survey of the field of the unconscious, using "survey" in a similar sense as in the systematic drilling of territory for oil.

Through these probes with word-stimuli the chief complexes often emerge clearly, and—continuing the oil survey analogy—points are indicated where it is profitable to drill further and deeper.

In studying the patients' reactions we are concerned with what in German is called "Komplex-Merkmale," the signs of symptoms of complexes. The first and most telling symptom is the prolongation of the time of reaction, i.e., hesitation or even failure to answer. In Jung's studies he carefully recorded the length of the reaction time.

However, a short prolongation in reaction time is not always indicative, because it can be due to various causes; for instance, the reaction to abstract terms is habitually a little longer than the reaction to concrete and familiar words. The reaction to long words is often a little longer than the reaction to short words, and so on. Therefore, to be relevant to the purpose of analysis, the prolongation must be marked and therefore clearly observable without any need of measurement.

Other signs of a complex are, of course, emotional reactions with their psychosomatic symptoms—such as short nervous laughs or signs of embarrassment—and the inhibition of any reaction is yet more revealing. The association experiment is generally carried out in two sessions of 50 words each; but with some patients it may be advisable to use four sessions of 25 words each.

Immediately after having completed the test it is good to also follow Jung's procedure of repeating the experiment. In the second run through, there is psychoanalytical, diagnostic value if the reaction is different. The analysis of the reactions can be done either immediately, in the same session, or later on.

Over a period of time we experimented by adding to each of the fifty-word sessions ten more words in which were included three or four words bearing relationship to probable specific complexes or difficulties of the patient, surmised from the biography and other techniques of the general assessment. At the present time, the modification which we have found to be the most helpful has been the use, in succession, of a series of words (generally 20) chosen to elicit reactions consonant with the specific complex which we surmise to be present, or which will elicit further reactions that may indicate some other complex or other unconscious contents, some spiritual or — as is often the case — some noetic problem. This technique has proved very revelatory.

A general remark which is relevant here applies to most of the techniques mentioned in this Manual, but is of special importance at this particular stage of the treatment. It is whether the therapist should discuss the findings of the association test with the patient or not. To this question one cannot give a definite "yes" or "no," for it is a part of the techniques that must be left very fluid and must be adapted to each case individually. Sometimes the reactions can be analyzed without giving evidence to the patient of what we have found. Sometimes we do not even analyze in the same session; in other cases we discuss the findings with the patient and immediately enter into the depth psychology. The course adopted depends entirely on the individual characteristics of the patients. There are patients who have no idea of psychology and there are patients who have already gone through several psychoanalytic treatments. Therefore, this part of the technique must be correspondingly varied. It depends so much on the psychological type of the patient, on his cultural level, on his attitude towards these matters.

As a general rule it can be said that the patient should only be told that which seems really useful and desirable for the therapeutic purpose; and we should not indulge in the temptation of theoretical inquiry and theoretical research—which would be of no benefit to the patient and perhaps harmful, unduly prolonging the treatment or even sidetracking it. Therefore, the explanations and interpretations which we share with the patient are mainly those necessary for the next technique and stage in the treatment.

Dreams

One of the best known and most widely used techniques for the exploration of the unconscious, extensively adopted by Freud and his followers, is that of dreams. While we will not enter here into a discussion of Freud's system of interpretation, we would point out that although dreams do give access to the unconscious of the subject, we have often found that they give access only to one part of it. In many subjects only one part of the unconscious is able or cares to express itself through dreams.

There are many kinds of dreams: of very different type, quality and meaning. (We have made a classification of dreams which we hope to include in a later book.) In our practice we ask patients to recount their dreams, and we give them the needed instructions for the analysis of them, but we definitely point out the fact that dream-interpretation is only *one* of the techniques and not the chief one.

Projective Techniques

Now let us consider briefly the *expressive techniques*, which include free drawing, free movement, clay modelling, etc., and some of the *projective techniques* such as the Thematic Apperception Test, the Rorschach, the drawing of the Tree, the Szondi Test and others.

Most of these projective techniques are called tests, which shows that they have been developed more for diagnostic purposes, and for the purposes of differential psychology (i.e., establishing psychological types, etc.), than for directly therapeutic purposes. The two ways of using them overlap, but they are mainly diagnostic tests and therefore more generally used by psychologists with a "laboratory-mentality" than with a "therapy-mentality." Free drawing, clay modelling, and movement, being active techniques, are more truly expressive techniques, which also have purposes other than testing. Of course, they can and do give insight into the working of the unconscious. We will deal with them more fully later in their particular frame of reference.

TAT

A comment on the TAT is appropriate at this point, because it is so widely used. We have used it, but have found that it does not evoke the superconscious levels; the TAT pictures are chosen with a view to drawing out the standard, well-known complexes, but not the higher drives or problems, or any repressed *higher* unconscious material. Therefore in practice we generally use other pictures chosen with the purpose of evoking such higher material. While we have a relatively small number of pictures which can be used with almost all patients, we often used special pictures for a particular patient for a special purpose. Because, as we have stated earlier, in therapy we have no statistical preoccupation, nor aim at exact comparisons, we use what we find of immediate usefulness in a specific case or specific phase of the treatment. Thus, here again the aim is to remain flexible and adaptable to individual needs. Therefore a small number of standard pictures are sufficient, but we strongly advise the therapist to choose others which he considers specifically relevant to the particular needs of his various cases.

As to the actual procedure in the therapy: it is preferable to keep instructions to the patient deliberately vague, asking him for instance, "What does this picture suggest to you?" "What does it evoke in you? Let your imagination have free play." In this way we do not directly ask for a personal reaction, because to ask for a definite story—as in the TAT—might inhibit a patient with little imagination. We thus attempt to strike a happy medium between the composition of a story and a personal reaction; but in effect, some patients react personally, almost violently, whereas others enter into a kind of day-dreaming about the material. Both responses are revealing.

Initiated Symbol Projection

Initiated Symbol Projection, developed and used by Dr. Hanscarl Leuner, is both a psycho-diagnostic and psychotherapeutic technique. Briefly it consists in placing the patient in a comfortable chair or on a couch, asking him to close his eyes, inducing him to relax by one or other methods. Then the patient is asked to visualize a standard series of twelve symbolic situations presented verbally by the therapist. A description of these basic symbols and an introductory discussion of the significance and interpretation of patients' reactions to them is given in the paper *Initiated Symbol Projection* by Dr. William M. Swartley. This paper — based on unpublished manuscripts by Hanscarl Leuner which unfortunately, at the time of writing, have not yet been translated from German into English — is given in the Appendix, p. 287; and is also available as a separate pamphlet from the Psychosynthesis Research Foundation, New York.

The results, both diagnostically and therapeutically, so far obtained indicate that Initiated Symbol Projection is a valuable technique in the process of psychosynthesis.

Free Drawing

Another fruitful technique for the exploration of the unconscious is that of free drawing. This is not surprising. As a matter of fact, originally writing was drawing. The first writing was ideographic; it was through pictures; and the unconscious, which in certain respects has primitive and archaic traits, uses more easily — one might say more happily — picture language, which can be called the use of symbols. It is well known that every abstract word is a symbol of something concrete. For instance, anima (soul) comes from the Greek animos — wind. Spirit is also spoken of as "breath"; and Diaus, Deus, the name for God, means "shining." Therefore it is not surprising that free drawing entices — so to speak — the unconscious, which expresses itself freely through it. Also this technique has a double use, attracting unconscious contents to the surface of consciousness and also functioning as an active method for psychosynthesis. But at this point we will refer only to the first function, that of bringing to the surface unconscious contents.

To elicit free drawing we tell the patient to procure paper or a notebook of a rather large size and a set of colored pencils. We ask him to sit down in front of the paper, with all the pencils ready to hand; then just to begin playing, to draw lines of different colors automatically, "letting it happen" in a free, relaxed, playful mood, seeing with eager curiosity what will happen. We emphasize the fact that we are looking for nothing artistic, nothing which has any aesthetic value, because usually the immediate objection he makes is: "But I am not able to draw!" and we answer: "So much the better. Any academic training in drawing or any practice in aesthetic drawing would be a drawback and would have almost to be un-learned. So, the fact that you are 'virgin soil' in this connection is favorable; it is an advantage and not a drawback."

So we advise the patient not to think out in advance what he is going to draw, because this would prevent a free flow of unconscious material. On the other hand, if he finds himself beginning to be almost impelled in an automatic manner, having very little control over his hand, it may be wise to tell him to stop—if we have, for example, an individual who tends toward dissociation. However, before stopping him, we should try to tell him to become wide awake, not to fall into hypnosis or semi-hypnosis, and to look carefully at what his hand has done; because we believe that independent activity of the unconscious is, up to a certain point, a normal state.

Hypnosis

Another technique for the exploration of the unconscious, which chronologically in the history of analysis was the first one used, is hypnosis. It is common knowledge that it was through hypnosis that first Breuer then Freud found the origin of certain neurotic symptoms, which started the research and practice of psychoanalysis. In hypnosis the waking consciousness is abolished; therefore, the unconscious can freely emerge; but this technique has serious inconveniences. It tends unduly to dissociate the patient, to make him too passive and dependent upon the therapist-hypnotizer, and very extensively responsive to his suggestions, even if they are unconscious ones. Moreover, hypnosis, in our opinion and subject to the exceptions mentioned below, is not necessary. Allied in a sense to hypnosis is narco-analysis, which has been and is being used as a kind of shortcut. This too has similar drawbacks to hypnosis. Therefore we do not adopt actively those methods, but we utilize and even encourage light hypnoidal states, occurring in deep relaxation, in which unconscious material spontaneously emerges.

In parenthesis, we should mention that we do not consider that hypnosis should be completely excluded in all psychotherapy. It is clearly apparent from experience that it can be usefully applied for anesthesia, in dental practice and in minor surgical operations, especially when the heart condition or other physical conditions are against the use of the ordinary means of anesthesia or when those means can be applied only in minimum quantities.

In such and similar cases, we think that the use of hypnosis is not only justified, but proves to be of real help. The same can be said concerning the elimination of disturbing symptoms such as continuous vomiting during the early gestation period or compulsive hiccups.

Dangers and Drawbacks

We must indicate the possible dangers of the exploration of the unconscious. The first and foremost is the release of drives and emotions which were locked in the unconscious and which can flood the conscious ego before it is ready and prepared and competent to contain, control and utilize them. It is the situation of the "apprentice sorcerer." Let us remember in this respect that Adler has rightly pointed out that a neurosis is often a defense mechanism or structure for keeping within safe bounds destructive, menacing, and otherwise overpowering drives. Therefore, when we try to undo this defense mechanism we must be ready to help the patient to deal with the unleashed energies. This is a very important point. We think that cases of suicide or of the development of psychotic states can be due to the premature and uncontrolled release of explosive drives and emotions from the unconscious.

A second drawback—less serious but also important—is that of increasing the dissociation, of emphasizing the multiplicity, and the trend to retrogression to primitive stages; a losing of the self in the great sea of the unconscious.

A third drawback can be an excessive preoccupation with oneself, an excessive interest in the unconscious, resulting in excessive introversion, in a morbid self-analysis.

Another, a fourth danger, is that of exaltation. The inflow of potent psychological forces can give to the subject a sense of grandeur, of power, of the personal self that is being built up. To use the witty terminology of Jung—it is psychic inflation. He describes it at length in his book, *Die Beziehungen zwischen dem Ich und dem Unbewussten* (translated into English as "The Relations between the Ego and the Unconscious," see *Two Essays in Analytical Psychology*[a], Part One, "The Effects of the Unconscious upon the Conscious").

The frequent cases of spontaneous irruption and the overflowing of unconscious aspects into the conscious personality confirm the dangers we have mentioned above. These happen in so-called "mania," which is marked by uncontrolled exuberance and incoherent ideas flowing in the stream of consciousness, and in its contrary, depression, in which negative contents of the unconscious fill the field of consciousness. This also happens in a different way in schizophrenic disorders.

Apart from these psychotic conditions, the dangers are greater in all who are psychic, sensitive or mediumistic, in whom this blending of conscious and unconscious is much more extensive than is normally the case. This also applies to artists who, in a sense, depend on the inspiration of the unconscious for creativity, and also to some of the mystics of a more passive and negative type.

Fractional Analysis

Precautions have to be taken, and psychosynthesis has a definite way of preventing some of these pathological reactions to the exploration of the unconscious.

Such dangers can be successively offset by what we call "fractional analysis," i.e., not starting first with the analysis of the unconscious, but with the *conscious* assessment, with the consolidation of the conscious personality, and, moreover, with the establishing of the positive rapport between the therapist and the

---

[a]Collected Works of C.G. Jung, Vol. 7 (1953)

patient. This is the reason why, as already described in the preceding pages, we begin with the exploration of the conscious. Then the exploration of the unconscious is carried out "by installments," so to speak, i.e., part of a session is given to a particular exploratory technique, and then it is stopped and other techniques dealing with the conscious aspect are used. So, the quantity of analysis, of exploration of the unconscious, is relatively limited during the treatment, and care is taken that the varied quota or amount or voltage of energies released from the unconscious into the conscious is immediately dealt with—cautiously; it is controlled, transmuted or utilized through expression.

Another point is that we do not aim at a thorough, complete, exhaustive exploration of the unconscious. We have not found it necessary for therapeutic and psychosynthetic purposes to look almost pedantically into every little corner of the unconscious, dust it free from every last bit of—let us call it—dirt or impurity. We think we can—as normal people generally do—put up with a certain amount of unanalyzed unconscious material, as long as it remains more or less quiet and does not interfere with normal life and normal activities. We do not aim at perfection in this respect, and this explains the paradox of the shorter time which psychosynthesis takes, compared with the classical psychoanalysis. Therefore, as we have found in practice, we can go as far as this: after a certain amount of analysis, sufficient for the immediate situation of the patient, we end it for the time being; and if something has remained in the unconscious which is really disturbing it will give notice through resistances and through other symptoms in the course of the proceeding treatment. Then, when the unconscious again takes up the offensive, when it throws up resistance or symptoms, then we undertake another period of analysis to remove that difficulty or block. This sequence is repeated as circumstances necessitate, even towards the end of the therapy. We take the practical view: when the unconscious disturbs, it has to be dealt with; if it keeps quiet, we do not make a systematic offensive against it.

CHAPTER **IV**

Personal Psychosynthesis — Techniques

CATHARSIS

We now turn to a group of techniques which help to dispose of the excessive energies released by the exploration of the unconscious, and which also serve in handling the excess of emotional energy which many people have in their psychological make-up, or which may be aroused by some external stimulus, situation or person. Catharsis, of course, has been much emphasized and used in psychoanalytic treatment, as demonstrated in the famous case of Anna A. described by Breuer and Freud in the classical *Studien über Hysterie* ("Studies in Hysteria"). The latter shows an important fact: that it was not the mere fact of bringing to consciousness an unconscious content which produced the healing, i.e., the elimination of the symptoms, but it was the emotional discharge which accompanied it.

Live It Again

This basic technique is very simple. It consists in asking the patient to live again, as realistically as possible, the scene or situation which aroused the emotional disturbance, letting the emotion have a free psychosomatic discharge. The process can be repeated several times, until the intensity of the emotional upheaval gradually decreases and finally exhausts itself.

The applicability and limitations of this technique are easy to understand. Its maximum usefulness is in cases of a well-defined traumatic experience, or when there is also protracted emotional tension in the patient's situation. However, it is merely a relief which can eliminate some symptoms, but it cannot be considered in any way as a cure. It does not eliminate the causes, which produced the symptoms and made possible the accumulation of the emotional charge.

The most favorable condition for the performance of this technique is provided when the patient is stretched on a couch in a state of relaxation, the eyes closed; then he is asked to recollect the event, not as an objective event as seen by a spectator, but as a participator or as a living actor. It is of importance to really re-live the experience, to recall fully, encouraging the free flow of the emotions instead of trying to control them, as perhaps the patient had done at the original time of the experience.

Here we should take into consideration the fact that the process can be very complex—technically speaking. It is actually a process of identification, re-living the scene which may be composed of feeling, hearing, and visualization, all at the same time. Therefore, we do not specifically suggest that the patient recall the visual image or the re-hearing of sounds, etc. We only tell him: "Imagine that you are actually in that situation again—that you are again *living* the experience." According to whether the patient is a visual or an auditory type he will naturally emphasize the one or the other, but that is not important. The importance lies in putting himself into the given situation; and to suggest either auditory or visual images would divert his attention from the actual identification with that event.

This same technique—of living in imagination an event or situation and letting the accompanying emotion have a free outlet—can be also applied to *future* events of which the person may be afraid, the expectation of which evokes anxiety. But as this technique is part of a more complete exercise for this purpose we will describe the exercise in full at the proper time in our exposition.

Verbal Expression

Another cathartic technique, often spontaneously used by patients, is that of verbal expression. It is well known that when a person, for instance, has been in danger, say in a train or airplane accident, he has an almost compulsive tendency to relate the event in a dramatic way, with great display of emotion, and to retell it several times. This is a self-therapeutic process because, after a certain number of times, the emotion is discharged—a little each time the experience is retold.

As we can expect, other elements may come in which are not of a therapeutic nature; as an example, the subject can utilize the incident for displaying self-importance, to attract the attention of others, to put himself at the center of the stage. But this does not prevent the actual discharge of emotion taking place; even the satisfaction of attracting the interest of others to oneself is therapeutic on that level. This is what happens with some patients sometimes in sessions; they repeat over and over again similar complaints, similar incidents and similar troubles. Sometimes this is valuable, but sometimes it has to be stopped, particularly in the case of hypochondriac patients, who use it to gain attention. In the latter cases it is not a real emotional discharge, and often they do not show the psychosomatic symptoms of the expulsion of the emotion; it is the urge—in an introvert attitude of masochistic self-complacency—to arouse pity and interest. The psychological effect is different because the inner attitude is different.

Writing

Another technique for giving release to emotions in a therapeutic way is that of writing. For instance, when there is a strong resentment against somebody, either justified or not, the therapist may suggest to the patient: "Sit down and write a letter to that person giving free expression to all your resentments, your indignation, stating your rights—holding nothing back. Then either give it to me or burn it."

This technique is more helpful than it may appear, because it involves the interesting mechanism of *symbolic satisfaction*. The unconscious is satisfied by this symbolic act of retaliation in writing. This should always be remembered because it is useful in many ways to relieve emotional tension.

Diary

Another way to utilize writing as an emotional discharge is by keeping a diary. Some criticism—which in our opinion is unjust—has been made against diaries; it considers them only suitable for sentimental and idle people and as encouraging excessive introversion; this is not necessarily so. It is a fact that many strong and active men have kept diaries. Of course, a diary has various kinds of usefulness; but here we mention only the advantage it provides of a constant release of the emotions aroused by current situations.

The fact that emotion is released and is, in a certain sense, "accumulated" in the diary, brings up the problem of the effect that such writings may have on others. To put it bluntly, these effects can be really psychologically poisonous. Because of this, a great responsibility is involved in making public or giving to others writings which carry such powerful emotional charges. We have an historical example of this in Goethe's novel *Die Leiden des jungen Werther*. As is well known, the youthful Goethe went through a violently romantic phase and fell in love with a married woman whom he could not hope to marry. After the break-up of the affair and his renunciation he went through a period of great depression and harbored ideas of suicide; but having literary talent, he poured into his novel all his emotional anguish and his unfulfilled desire. The tragic result was that several young men, after reading *Werther*, committed suicide. It is not necessary to emphasize the deduction that can and should be made from this example. Also, it is by no means an isolated case.

It is good, therefore, to suggest to a patient that he keep a diary, and to encourage him to show it to the therapist by pointing out to him the advantages we mentioned earlier: the saving of time in the sessions, and giving a more complete picture because he may otherwise forget relevant things that come to his mind between sessions. Furthermore, there is the fact that in writing one expresses different sides of the personality; some people are freer, less inhibited in writing than in speaking about delicate subjects face to face with the therapist.

The patient is asked to keep the diary in loose-leaf form so that he can give the latest newly written pages to the therapist at the beginning of each session. If the diary is not too long it can be read through rapidly in a few minutes and the material may be used immediately for that session. If it is too long it can be read later and the information used for the next session.

Muscular Discharge

Another method of catharsis which really comes under the category of transmutation but which, because of its simplicity, we will take up here, is that of muscular discharge. This is particularly helpful in dealing with the aggressive drives; and can also have a symbolic meaning which satisfies the unconscious.

In many cases of neurotic disturbances varied forms of this technique can be applied with good results provided the patient is able (or can be enabled by the therapist) to adopt an attitude of awareness towards his selected actions, to develop a sense of detachment and of being the witness of himself, so that he performs the acts deliberately, and whenever possible with a sense of humor. This, in reality, constitutes an "exercise," which combines several techniques, but we will nevertheless give a typical example.

A young man, the son of a bank director, at the age of about 16 had developed two sets of symptoms. One was sudden fits of rage in which he broke furniture in his home. The other was a phobia of going out of the house and of walking in the streets alone. This latter symptom particularly disturbed him; he was angry because he had the phobia but he could not overcome it.

We started therapy in the following way. He had said that perhaps at the very onset of his fits of rage he might be able to do something to check them, but that after that first stage he was impotent and could not control his rage at all. So we told him to prepare beforehand some objects to break or material to destroy—he chose some old telephone directories. When he felt the first symptoms of his next fit of rage coming on, he ran for the telephone directories and tried to tear them to pieces, taking many pages at a time so as to demand greater muscular exertion; and at the same time he tried to see the funny side of his action and to remember that he was doing it in order to release his anger. He repeated this performance several times with successive fits of anger, with very good results. He broke no more furniture, and after a few times he began to laugh towards the close of his destructive bouts — as he said, he found them ludicrous. At the same time the phobia of going out alone (which might have been a form of unconscious self-punishment caused by a feeling of guilt) subsided and was finally eliminated.

In this case there was no deep analysis made, because it was not necessary to make the patient aware of the conflict. To the therapist it was obvious that it was the standard conflict between the drive to independence and the inhibition of the same drive, caused by an authoritarian father. Of course, the therapist spoke to the parents and tried to induce them to change their conduct, but whether they did so or not, certainly the therapeutic effect of the technique on the son was very rapid.

Drawbacks of the Technique

Concluding this part on catharsis we should point out a possible drawback — or even danger — of these techniques, especially of the one first mentioned, re-living. On some people a re-living of a dramatic or traumatic scene may have an effect contrary to the one aimed at. A kind of feed-back effect and a recharging of the emotional tension may occur instead of the discharge. This depends on the psychological type of the patient and on his attitude. It is, however, relatively easy to detect when this is happening, and then either the technique has to be abandoned, or it has to be altered and adapted to the individual. And, of course, the patient should be made aware of what has occurred and the adaptation made.

In most of these cases it will be advisable to postpone this technique to a time when the personality is sufficiently organized and self-conscious, because at an earlier stage the personal self may not be strong enough for such "deep-digging" analysis and for the assimilation and regulation of the emotional forces released by the cathartic process.

CRITICAL ANALYSIS

Another cathartic technique is that of critical analysis. The rationale behind this technique has been already indicated in Chapter One, pp. 22-24; that is, criticism and analysis tend to control to some degree—and in certain cases to even paralyze—emotions and feelings.

The degree of control exercised by the mind over the emotions is relative; it varies in effectiveness with the individual and the various psychological types, but in every case there is a certain amount of influence by the mind and this can be increased through conscious deliberate use and training. The patient can and should be encouraged to use his mind, through observation and discrimination, to bring clearly into his awareness the irrational aspect of his drives and emotions, and also the possible drawbacks and harmfulness to himself and others of their uncontrolled manifestation. The sense of responsibility resulting from such recognition—or even the mere fear of harmful consequences of uncontrolled emotional expression—arouses an opposing emotion through which a primary drive or emotion is often conveniently neutralized, in part if not wholly so.

Procedure

This could be described as *impersonal observation* which, in its turn, is made possible by a certain degree of dis-identification. Therefore some practice of the latter is helpful, for in some cases critical analysis may even be considered as a constituent part of the technique of dis-identification.

In introducing this technique to the patient it is advisable to make him clearly aware of two basic points or possibilities. First, that to act on the spur of an impulse, a drive or an intense emotion can very often produce undesirable effects which one afterwards regrets. Secondly, therefore, he should learn—by repeated experiment and effort—to "insert" between impulse and action a stage of reflection, of mental consideration of a situation, and of critical analysis of his impulse, trying to realize its origin, its source.

Then, if he finds that its source is not "high" and is conducive to action that is undesirable and may have regrettable consequences, he must proceed with the aid of this clear mental anticipation of its possible effects, to consciously control the impulse, *but control it without suppression*. It is essential to make sure that the patient has clearly understood the instructions and grasps the idea and purpose of this period of mental reflection and assessment, and any questions on his part should be carefully answered. The reference to "control without suppression" is fundamental; it is the core of the technique. The very important difference, to be grasped by the patient and not only by the therapist, is that suppression tends to push the drive back again into the unconscious, whereas control implies neither fear nor condemnation but mastery and regulation. In other words, control allows for expression, but expression in some harmless or useful way. Control ensures a "lull" or the time necessary to proceed with the further task of utilizing the energy of the drive or emotion. (The utilization by re-direction or transmutation of that energy is the purpose of a technique which is taken up later.) Control is not an end in itself but a means of storing energies in a harmless way until they can be disposed of in a useful or creative way.

The whole process has four stages:

First, these techniques bring forth an awareness of drives, feelings and emotions hitherto kept unconscious;

Second, the control and "storage" of their energies;

Third, their transformation and sublimation, in order,

Fourth, to finally express them effectively and constructively.

So, we would again stress here that psychosynthesis is not anti-analytical and that it includes and even demands a full recognition of unconscious motives and feelings; but in addition to this, psychosynthesis supplies techniques whereby the released energies can either be expressed directly—but in a regulated way—or transformed into higher energies.

Indications and Applications

The use of this technique is clearly indicated whenever there is an excess of emotional affective energies and of undesirable drives. Therefore, this technique is useful not only for the surplus of such forces, released by the exploration of the unconscious, but also for the exuberant forces which are constitutional and belong to the psychological type of the individual, as well as for those waves of emotion and stimuli or urges which come from collective impacts and influences, both conscious and unconscious. We refer to mob-psychology and to the constant suggestion exercised by newspapers, radio, TV, advertising, etc. These constitute a real danger, a constant source of emotional excitement which is very harmful and really constitutes one of the worst aspects of present-day civilization. Therefore, the scope of this technique of critical analysis is very great and its usefulness, even its necessity, is evident.

Limitations

As with every technique, this one can be used in an exaggerated or inopportune way. It may constitute a handicap or inhibition to action. It can develop an over-critical attitude, and foster criticism of other people. Therefore it must be adapted to real need and be used in strictly regulated and directed ways. The technique would be contra-indicated with those individuals who are over-intellectualized, and particularly those who are basically extremely critical, for it would only intensify their unbalanced condition.

In order to minimize and offset some of the drawbacks of this technique, it is well to warn patients—particularly emotional types—not to make critical analysis a vehicle or screen for aggressive drives directed to others. This is very important, because their line of least resistance would be to express their drives in such a way that criticism would be at the service of the drives.

Another limitation of critical analysis is this: there are many idealists who are so taken by their ideal of perfection that they almost become prisoners of it and demand perfection of themselves and, even more often, of others; they criticize and emphasize everything which falls short of this ideal of perfection, which eventually can arouse a sense of frustration, anxiety, despondency or, again, excessive criticism. They do not realize that between present conditions and the ideal goal there can and inevitably always will exist many intermediate steps, and that it is sufficient if they are able to take—or help others to take—the next step. It could be called the attitude of right relativity, of wise compromise between the ideal and present reality.

Examining the question in a still wider framework, we may say that the tension arising from the *vision of the future* in opposition to *present conditions* can be creative only if it is considered and utilized as a stimulus to action, and as something good and inevitable. An analogy may make this clearer. Our sight should always be ahead of our feet; it is bad when, as too often happens, the vision is limited to the ground beneath our feet; just as, if one keeps the eyes steadily fixed on the far away mountain top, one can stumble and fall on the way. The eye has the faculty of rapidly changing its focus and point of interest from the step immediately ahead, through all the intermediate ones up to the mountain top, the goal—and vice-versa. In the same way our mental eye, our personal consciousness, should embrace the whole range from the immediate to the far off, and focus on that point or distance which is the most useful at any given time and in any particular situation.

In practice there are two main methods which can be used: the first would be the reduction of the ideal to a more realistic and attainable one. This is the method that is usually advised. It presents, however, a certain degree of danger, which is the leveling off of the high ideal and therefore the reduction of the point of tension, and sometimes a prostitution of what was originally an idealistic goal to some now "pedestrian" materialistic aim. Therefore, the second way is preferable: to help the individual to define his ideal, no matter how high it is, but at the same time to help him to arrive at some sub-goal or sub-ideal that is more realizable, which the patient defines and crystallizes, and then eventually materializes. This can be done in a succession of steps. If, to start with, we make these steps small, close enough and easily attainable, there results in the patient a feeling of success and achievement, which has a very important reinforcing value, and to some extent eliminates and reduces the frustration. This attainment of a visioned goal will be dealt with in further detail later.

SELF-IDENTIFICATION

Purpose

The conscious and purposeful use of self-identification—or dis-identification—is basic in psychosynthesis. It proceeds from a dynamic center on which the whole process of synthesizing the psychological multiplicity into an organic unit is based. It offers a very effective means of controlling the various elements of the personality. This is based on a fundamental psychological principle, which was given in Chapter One and is repeated here because of its central importance: *"We are dominated by everything with which our self is identified. We can dominate and control everything from which we dis-identify ourselves."* (p. 22)

Rationale

The rationale of this technique is the curious fact that everybody has some kind of self-identification—and yet very few people have ever stopped to ask themselves what it really means, what it implies, how it can be more consciously experienced and what are its effects. Self-identification is a rather ambiguous term, and we must distinguish three different meanings.

The first meaning—which is the one currently and generally accepted—is that of the individual identifying himself with that which gives him the greatest sense of being, of aliveness, with that which constitutes his greatest value, and to which he gives the most importance. This type of self-identification can be the predominant function or focus of consciousness and, on the other hand, the main function or role played in life. For instance: a girl who enters beauty contests identifies herself with her body and its beauty. There lies her focus and her point of self-identification, and she bends every effort to its improvement and conservation. A successful athlete also has his point of self-identification in the physical body, but in terms of his muscular strength and control. Others identify themselves with the emotional life, their so-called love-life. A smaller group—that of the intellectuals—identify themselves with their minds or brain power and consider themselves to be fundamentally thinkers or—in right or wrong self-estimation—geniuses.

In others the self-identification with a role is more evident. Many women find their self-identification in wifehood, and even more so in motherhood—they consider themselves, function and live only as the mother. This kind of self-identification does not give the experience of the pure self. The latter, the "I-hood" or the sense of personal identity is closely bound to, and almost merged in, the focus of valuation or the role. This has very severe consequences:

First, the individual does not really know or realize himself.

Second, the identification with one part of his personality excludes or diminishes greatly the ability of self-identification with all the other parts of his personality, and therefore constitutes a stumbling block in psychosynthesis.

Third, and this applies to both "role" and "predominant function" types of self-identification, the life process itself renders their continuance impossible; e.g., the aging of beautiful women; the loss of athletic strength; the disruption of the mother role through the maturity or death of her children. All these may produce very serious crises; the individual feels himself or herself lost, and this is a tragedy in many lives, which in not a few cases may lead to the extreme self-denial of suicide.

The second meaning which can be given to "self-identification" is the inner experience of pure self-awareness, independent of any content or function of the ego in the sense of personality. Curiously, it is a subject which has been neglected, and the explanation is that the experience of pure *self-identity*—or in other words, of the self, the I-consciousness, devoid of any content—does not arise spontaneously but is the result of a definite inner experimentation. Those who have tried have been able to reach a state of pure I-consciousness, self-identity, realization of oneself as a living center of awareness. This is well known to psychologists in the East, because they are interested in the experience, value it, and therefore use the techniques appropriate to achieving it.

The third meaning of "self-identification" is that of the realization of the higher or spiritual Self. This experience requires a further technique or techniques. It is different from the other experience of pure self already described—but it is not completely separate from it. Let us remember what was given in Chapter One, page 20, i.e., that there are not in reality two independent selves. There is one Self—but there are very different and distinct levels of self-realization. Therefore, between the self-identity of the ordinary or normal level of functioning and the full spiritual Self-realization there are intermediate stages or levels, ever wider, clearer, fuller.

The first experience of the self, the personal self, as a point of pure self-consciousness, is extremely important. No one experiences it spontaneously, and this explains the strange phenomenon that many people are apt to deny the very essence of their being.

Since we are speaking of the essence of Being, it is very important to point out that this is of course a central idea in existential analysis; many existential writers talk and write about Being, and the meaning of the word varies from writer to writer; and very often with the same writer the meaning shifts from Being as a totality of the personality plus some kind of spiritual center, to Being as a center for the personality, to Being as a spiritual center, something that may be referred to as the "essence of Being."

It is important to achieve clarity on these points and to experiment with the specific techniques for the achievement of the experience itself, not only by patients but also by therapists—which includes psychiatrists, psychologists, psychiatric social workers—because no one who has not had the experience can really help other people to have the experience themselves.

The experience of the point of self-awareness on the personality level is the first step toward the experience of the Self, or in existential terms, the essence of Being. To some extent it has some relationship to what Erik Erickson refers to as the search for self-identity. This problem of finding one's self, experiencing one's self, and from the center of oneself directing one's life, is a problem basic to our times where a great tendency towards conformity is present.

This has been stressed by many of the existentialist psychologists, particularly those whom we could call spiritual existentialists. Rollo May in his book *Man's Search for Himself* has pointed out this central quest; as also have Viktor Frankl and others. Therefore we emphasize the necessity for therapists to experiment with the techniques of "self-identification," not only on themselves but also with their patients, in order to discover not only some of the applications of the technique but also some of the difficulties that certain patients may experience—particularly certain borderline-psychotics in whom the sense of self-identity is very loose and yet who may particularly benefit from this quest.

Procedure

The procedure for achieving self-identity in the sense of the pure self-consciousness at the personal level, is an indirect one. The self is there all the time, what is lacking is a direct awareness of its presence. Therefore, the technique consists in eliminating all the partial self-identifications. The procedure can be summarized in one word, which was much used formerly in psychology but which recently has been more or less neglected, i.e., *introspection*. It means, as its terminology clearly indicates, directing the mind's eye, or the observing function, upon the world of psychological facts, of psychological events, of which we can be aware.

Through introspection we acquire a more focussed and clear awareness of what William James called the mind-stream, ceaselessly flowing within ourselves. It could also be called the attitude of the observer, the inner observer. It is an attitude quite similar, even identical, to that of the natural scientist who objectively, patiently and persistently observes the natural phenomena occurring around him, be it a Fabre, observing the behavior and habits of ants, or an astronomer patiently observing a star through a telescope. If we turn our ability to observe inwards we realize that there is actually an inner world of phenomena, at least as manifold and varied as the outer world, and that through the development of observation it becomes more and more definite to the observer.

The first field of observation is that of the *sensations*, produced by bodily conditions. These can be the sensations determined by the activity of the five senses, or the more obscure and undefined kinesthetic sensations of the organism. The observation, the calm dispassionate, objective observation of the flow of these sensations makes us realize how fleeting or impermanent many of them are and how easily they alternate (and sometimes one is substituted by its contrary). This gives us the certainty—let us say scientifically demonstrates—that the self is not the body, is not the sum of the sensations which it produces and projects, so to speak, into the field of our conscious awareness.

The second field of inner observation or introspection is the kaleidoscopic realm of *emotions* and *feelings*. It is much more difficult to observe objectively and in a detached way these contents of our consciousness, because our attention is apt to be carried away by the waves of the iridescent flood of our emotional states. But with patience, practice and a true scientific attitude and objectivity we can train ourselves to observe our own emotions and feelings in a detached way.

After a certain period of practice we come to the realization that the emotions and feelings also are not a necessary part of the self, of our self, because they too are changeable, mutable, fleeting and sometimes show ambivalence. Here the use of the previous technique of Critical Analysis is relevant.

The third field of observation is that of *mental activity*, of the mental contents. This, in a certain respect, is easy to observe, because it does not have the pull which emotions and feelings have on our attention. On the other hand it is more difficult because it is more subtle, the distinction between the self and the mind being at first less evident. Yet, here too the same criterion applies: mental activity is too varied, fleeting, changeable; sometimes it shows no continuity and can be compared with a restless ape, jumping from branch to branch. But the very fact that the self can observe, take notice and exercise its powers of observation on the mental activity proves the difference between the self and the mind.

In respect to mental activity, we can observe that it is linked with emotional activity in varying degrees, from the purely mental, abstract, mathematical thoughts—almost devoid of emotional content or overtones and undertones unless it involves the pure joy sometimes felt by highly developed mathematicians—to the emotionally loaded and derived rationalization, where, although the activity appears to be essentially mental, it is to a great extent motivated from emotional levels. So, although it may not, at times, be possible to distinguish and differentiate between the mental and emotional aspects of the thought processes, the important point to remember for this particular exercise is that there is within an observer who observes this succession of emotional and mental states, and that this observer is to some extent detached from them.

There is, as a matter of fact, a constant interplay between sensation, emotion and mental activity — and the distinction we have made is only a question of emphasis, of focussing the attention of the observer. The important point to be emphasized is the difference between these three interrelated fields of psychological activity and the observer as such. This objective observation produces naturally, spontaneously and inevitably a sense of dis-identification from any and all of those psychological contents and activities. By contrast the stability, the permanency of the observer is realized. Then the observer becomes aware that he can not only passively observe but also influence in various degrees the spontaneous flow, the succession of the various psychological states. Therefore, he feels himself different, is dis-identified from those contents.

Thus, one has to actively discriminate between the contents of the field of consciousness and its center — that which creates it, the self. The technique to be used is that of successive dis-identifications from the various groups or layers of contents — physical, emotional and mental, adapting the technique in terminology and language to the cultural level of the patient. The general formula of the technique is given in the following Exercise in Dis-identification.

EXERCISE IN DIS-IDENTIFICATION

The first step is to affirm with conviction and to become *aware* of the fact: "I *have* a body, but *I am not* my body." That seems evident. This body is something material and changeable (it has been stated that within a few years all the cells of the body are renewed). Nevertheless, we mistakenly identify ourselves all the time with our body and attribute to the "I" our physical sensations. For instance, we say "I am tired," which is nothing less than a psychological heresy; the "I" cannot be tired; *the body* is tired and transmits to the "I" a sensation of fatigue—which is something very different. This distinction is of great practical importance, because every time we identify ourselves with a physical sensation we enslave ourselves to the body.

The first step is comparatively easy; but the second step is much less so. It is the realization: "I *have* an emotional life, but *I am not* my emotions or my feelings." When someone says: "I am irritated," "I am content," or "I am dissatisfied," it is also a case of false identification of the "I" with those psychological states which are changeable and often contradictory. To say "*I* am irritated" is to commit an error of psychological grammar. Let us say instead: "There is *in* me a state of irritation."

The third step consists in realizing: "I *have* an intellect, but *I am not* that intellect." Ordinarily we identify ourselves with our thoughts, but when we analyze them, when we observe ourselves while we think, we notice that the intellect works like an *instrument*. We can look at the logical or illogical connections, at the working of the mind, observing it from above, as it were. This indicates that *we are not our thoughts*. They also are changeable: one day we think one thing, the following day we may think the opposite. We get ample proof of *not being* our thoughts when we try to control and to direct them. When we want to think of something abstract or boring, our mental instrument often refuses to obey us; every student who has to learn something that is annoying has that experience. If the mind is rebellious and undisciplined it means that the "I" is *not* the mind.

These facts give us evidence that the body, the feelings and the mind are *instruments* of experience, perception and action—instruments that are changeable and impermanent, but which can be dominated, disciplined, deliberately used by the "I", while the nature of the "I" is something entirely different.

The "I" is simple, unchanging, constant and *self*-conscious. The experience of the "I" can be formulated as follows: "I am I, *a centre of pure consciousness*." To state this with conviction does not mean one has yet reached the *experience* of the "I", but it is the way which leads to it. And it is the key to, and the beginning of, the mastery of our psychological processes.

This exercise can also be done in group formation. To do it in this way is in certain respects easier, because of the aid which comes from direction and reciprocal stimulation. The stimulus received and the results obtained will encourage the participants to continue to do the exercise regularly, each one by himself. It should become a daily psycho-spiritual health measure. One should begin the day by "entering into oneself." *To enter into oneself:* let us ponder on the deep significance of these words. Generally, we live "outside" ourselves; we are everywhere except in the "I"! We are constantly attracted, distracted, dispersed by countless sensations, impressions, preoccupations, memories of the past, projects for the future; we are everywhere except in our self-consciousness, in the consciousness of that which we are in reality.

The exercise can be done as follows (when it is performed by a group, the one who directs the exercise naturally speaks in the first person, but each one can apply to himself what is said):

I put my body into a comfortable and relaxed position with closed eyes. This done, I affirm: "I *have* a body but *I am not* my body. My body may find itself in different conditions of health or sickness; it may be rested or tired, but that has nothing to do with my self, my real 'I'. My body is my precious instrument of experience and of action in the outer world, but it is *only* an instrument. I treat it well; I seek to keep it in good health, but it is *not* myself. I *have* a body, but *I am not* my body.

"I *have* emotions, but *I am not* my emotions. These emotions are countless, contradictory, changing, and yet I know that I always remain I, *my-self*, in times of hope or of despair, in joy or in pain, in a state of irritation or of calm. Since I can observe, understand and judge my emotions, and then increasingly dominate, direct and utilize them, it is evident that *they are not myself*. I *have* emotions, but *I am not* my emotions.

"I *have* desires, but *I am not* my desires, aroused by drives, physical and emotional, and by outer influences. Desires too are changeable and contradictory, with alternations of attraction and repulsion. I *have* desires but they *are not* myself.

"I *have* an intellect, but *I am not* my intellect. It is more or less developed and active; it is undisciplined but teachable; it is an organ of knowledge in regard to the outer world as well as the inner; but *it is not myself*. I *have* an intellect, but *I am not* my intellect.

"After this dis-identification of the 'I' from its contents of consciousness (sensations, emotions, desires and thoughts) *I recognize and affirm that I am a Centre of pure self-consciousness.* I am a Centre of *Will,* capable of mastering, directing and using all my psychological processes and my physical body."

*　*　*　*　*

When one has practiced the exercise for some time, it can be modified by a swift dynamic use of the first three stages of dis-identification, leading to a deeper consideration of the fourth stage of self-identification, coupled with an inner dialogue along the following lines:

> "What am I then? What remains after discarding from my self-identity the physical, emotional and mental contents of my personality, of my ego? It is the essence of myself — a center of pure self-consciousness and self-realization. It is the permanent factor in the ever varying flow of my personal life. It is that which gives me the sense of being, of permanence, of inner security. I recognize and I affirm myself as a center of pure self-consciousness. I realize that this center not only has a static self-awareness but also a dynamic power: it is capable of observing, mastering, directing and using all the psychological processes and the physical body. I am a center of awareness and of power."

In therapy the technique of self-identification should be used as early as possible, because its use by the patient facilitates and fosters the use of all the other techniques of psychosynthesis. Generally, it is introduced in an early session; first, a preliminary description and explanation is given to the patient, anticipating and answering his questions. Second, it has been found effective for the therapist to do the full exercise, speaking it aloud, ignoring the presence of the patient. This eliminates possible adverse reaction of subconscious or personal emotivity on the part of the patient. This is the most superficial psychological reason; the deeper reason is that as the therapist goes through the exercise in a concentrated intense manner, the "feel" and reality of the technique is subtly conveyed to the patient. To intensify the concentration it is helpful for the therapist to close his eyes, really forgetting the patient for the time being.

As the technique of self-identification is a basic technique not only for therapy but for education and personality integration, it can be considered also as a defense mechanism against the constant stream of influences, inner and outer, which try to capture the ego and demand identification. This technique can also be considered as a matter of everyday psychological and spiritual hygiene; and in therapy it is needed even more. Therefore, we advise the patient to use it as frequently as he feels is possible; once a day is sufficient, but that is a minimum. As mentioned above, it should precede the use of the other techniques because it helps the patient to use them more effectively.

Indications and Applications

The exercise is suited to all cases except people at such a primitive level that they are not able to really grasp the technique, or when they are in such an emotional turmoil and distracted state that temporarily they are unfit to use it.

The type of patients for whom the exercise is particularly indicated includes all those who are over-emotional, and all those who are either strongly identified with a particular affective state or linked with an idea or plan or type of action—which may be of a higher or low order—which keeps the patient almost in a state of obsession. This includes fanatics of all kinds. Similarly, another group is those who identify themselves completely with a role, be it the mother-role or father-role or a professional role, so as to be completely possessed by it and thus have almost no individual life of their own. The effect and results of the exercise are and should be of a liberating nature; and in fact those who use the technique successfully say that they obtain a sense of freedom, a sense of enhanced being, and a spontaneous control of the psychological contents with which they were previously completely identified.

The exercise is also useful for over-intellectualized people who tend to identify their focus of consciousness wholly with their mental processes—particularly if they are sophisticated and pride themselves highly on their mental abilities, and thus remain, so to speak, stuck on that level. Because those sophisticated intellectuals are the hardest nut to crack in therapy, it may be of therapeutic value for them to be able to experience that the center of themselves is *not* their mental processes.

The same technique can be used in connection with the various roles one plays in life. As we have already mentioned such roles are developed sub-personalities, in which emotional and mental contents are combined. The technique is the recollection and affirmation that: "I have, I must play and I quite willingly play, as well as possible, my roles in life; be it that of the son, of the father, of the husband, of the executive, of the artist or any other. But I am not only the son, the father, the artist; these are roles, specific but partial roles, which I, myself, am playing, agree to play, watch and observe myself playing. Therefore *I* am not any of them; I am self-identified, and I am the director of the acting, not only the actor."

This reminds us particularly of certain statements of Paul Tournier who in his book *The Meaning of Persons* emphasized the essential difference between the inner "Person" and the various "Personages" which this inner "Person" plays under the differing circumstances of life. However, we make a further distinction between the "person" as described by Tournier, and the pure self-identification. There are, in a sense, three different self-identifications: one with the "Personages," a second with the "Person," and the third a point of pure self-awareness.

To make this point clearer: the last and perhaps most obstinate identification is with that which we consider to be our inner person, that which persists more or less during all the various roles we play, that which is also a person in the etymological sense of Persona (Mask) as the ultimate mask of the self. This "Persona" or "person" has to be discarded in the sense of our no longer being identified with it and limited by it. This is important, because every identification with it tends to make us static and crystallized. It is a kind of image or pattern or model of which we are apt to become prisoners. This "person," even the relatively most intimate one, is in reality in process of constant change, of flow. There is a continuous intake of experiences which modify it and an output of energies from it. So it too is changeable, fluid, impermanent and therefore cannot be the pure self-identity which persists unchanged throughout all that flow.

This Exercise in Dis-identification enhances a sense of selfhood, a sense of being; and one finds it is really one of the essential techniques which enables one to experience what existential analysts have talked about so much—and provided so few techniques for reaching!—viz. the sense of identity, the sense of being, the sense of a center within oneself, the center of an essence within oneself. When this center has been experienced—which can come through the application of this exercise in self-identification—then it is possible to synthesize the different aspects from which one has dis-identified oneself. In other words, one becomes a self who uses the body, the feeling-apparatus and the mental abilities as tools, as instruments, in the same way as a car is the extension of a driver, but with the driver in control. This is analogous to the engineering concept of the man-machine complex, that man and machine make a unit and have to be considered as such. In the same way the self and its mechanism (and by mechanism we imply not only the physical body, but also the feeling-nature and the mental processes) can form a unity, and yet the self can always be aware that it is something over and above each constituent part of this whole.

Limitations and Contra-Indications

This technique has few general limitations and particular contra-indications. Specifically, this technique may not be indicated, or should be used with care, in the case of patients who are ever too prone to self-observation and self-analysis, with patients who are or become too much interested in the observation of their inner world—which may prove more pleasing and less strenuous than active participation in the outer life. In those cases, however, one could say that there is a subtle form of identification with the phenomena observed, or at least a strong link of the self with them. Therefore, the exercise should not be used except with the clear warning to the patient that its use must be *specific,* and must be limited to offsetting a subtle form of identification with his inner world. He must not over-emphasize it nor use it too frequently in comparison with the other techniques.

Among some patients, particularly Americans, there is a great deal of resistance to the idea of dis-identifying oneself from one's body, feelings, and thoughts; and a deep fear of becoming split into different parts by so doing. However, on the contrary, many patients like the idea of fully experiencing a center within themselves, a center from which they can find the strength and the wisdom to withstand the stresses of modern life. Life in America, in some of the big cities, is particularly strenuous, so that the motivation for doing this exercise is enhanced.

It may be alleged that there is an inconsistency between the emphasis on achieving a synthesis of all functions at all levels around a central self, and an exercise which emphasizes dis-identification from some of the parts; in other words, that the specific identification with one part of our personality excludes the inclusion of all other parts in the total personality, and therefore runs contrary to a synthesis of the whole. If patients were identified with the whole of the personality this objection might be valid, but each of them is identified with only one facet, one part—their pet idea or their strong emotions, or their paramount role—and it is that which constitutes a strong block to their psychosynthesis. Therefore, first we have to free them from this partial, one-sided, obsessive identification in order to proceed towards the synthesis.

Borderline Cases and Psychotics

Under the limitations and contra-indications of this technique it is important to consider certain dangers which may be present in cases such as borderline-psychotics, particularly when there is a condition of "de-personalization," e.g., when a patient has the feeling that his body does not belong to him. Then the added emphasis on "I am not the body" may further widen the split and run contrary to the fundamental idea of bio-psychosynthesis. For this reason, in order to offset such possible drawbacks, the emphasis should be put on the last stage in the technique which is the realization that one is a self. ("I recognize and affirm that I am a center of pure self-consciousness. I am a center of will, capable of mastering, directing and using all my psychological processes and my physical body.") In this way, dis-identification comes in as a by-product of this realization. The goal and results of the exercise are self-identification, and this should be emphasized in its presentation to the patients.

In borderline cases great care is essential before considering attempting a psychosynthesis. In general, such patients cannot be treated in the usual procedure of a regular psychosynthesis with the active cooperation of the patient in using the techniques. A psychotherapeutic technique of general validity, but which concerns particularly borderline cases and even psychotics, is that it is advisable to try to agree as much as possible with them, to accept as much as possible what they say or feel, and try only to show them the real meaning and purpose of what they say, i.e., to show it to them from a positive angle. For instance: if a patient says "I feel I have no body, I feel there are no emotions in me," we reply "Well, this is partially true; of course you are not your body, and in this sense you have had an insight that generally people do not have—only, you take it in a negative way instead of in a positive one. Practically speaking, you do have a body for while you deny having it you are actually using it in expressing your feelings through your larynx. Therefore, you see, this feeling of yours is just a subjective sensation. Of course you have a body, as everyone else, only you have had a sudden insight that you are not your body. Therefore, take it in the sense that philosophically you are right, but pragmatically wrong."

This type of approach has proved successful in many cases; the key thought is not to immediately label the patient's assertions as a morbid symptom, but to seize on the morsel of truth which is really contained in his remarks—only misinterpreted and taken negatively by him—and proceed to reinterpret and expand it.

There is very often an amazing intuitive insight in certain psychotics, which has been twisted by misinterpretation, and often used against themselves or others. A typical example of this is a man who stated he was God. He had a vivid insight of an ultimate wonderful truth, only it was too big for him, and he made the fatal mistake of identifying his empirical personality with this divine Self-realization.

Summation and Combination with Other Techniques

This technique can be considered as a preliminary exercise helping towards a more effective use of all the other techniques.

As we have shown, in following out this exercise there are necessary steps of partial dis-identification. It is therefore a combination or rather a fusion of the techniques of self-identification and dis-identification. In some cases it is even necessary to invert the order of the two, or to make them two phases of the one exercise, *beginning* with the self-identification, and adding the dis-identification as a necessary means to self-identification.

This exercise might be compared with the technique of critical analysis since one observes the passing emotional states. But there is this difference: critical analysis includes the active use of the mind and of the judging function in valuation, and in actively doing this we are identified with our critical function. Therefore, the technique of critical analysis is different in aim and procedure from the technique of self-identification.

In connection with its combination with other techniques we may well consider the test that Dr. Bugental of Los Angeles, U.S.A., has proposed, and which he calls "Who Am I?" In this very simple test he gives the patient a piece of paper and a pencil and asks him to write what comes into his mind in response to the question "Who am I?" Then he repeats the question a second time, and asks the patient to again write answers; and finally for a third time. Following this he uses a procedure of inquiry. Many of the individuals who were asked this question "Who am I?" gave a self-reference, related to their predominant role, be it a role of a mother or of a woman or wife; or for a man, his professional role; and it was the successive asking of the same question which sometimes elicited deeper answers on the part of the patient.

Two other techniques can be combined in order to help the stage of dis-identification. These are "Humor" and "Play." Their helpfulness is to some degree self-evident from their titles.

TECHNIQUE FOR THE DEVELOPMENT OF THE WILL

A somewhat fuller introduction is called for in considering the Technique of the Will than applies in the case of the other techniques, because the will can be truly called the unknown and neglected factor in modern psychology, psychotherapy, and in education.

Without attempting to analyze the causes of this surprising state of affairs—such as the reactions to the former over-emphasis of the inhibition aspect of the will or the many resistances encountered to the training of the will—we would draw attention to the paradox that the very fact of the central position of the will has been the cause of it being ignored; i.e., the will is the function which is most directly related to the self. Rank has gone so far as to say that "the human being experiences his individuality in terms of his will, and this means that his personal existence is identical with his capacity to express his will in the world" (*Death and Rebirth of Psychology*, by Ira Progoff, p. 210). Also, as we found in discussing the earlier techniques, the individual generally is not aware of his self, and consequently he is just as unaware of the direct function of the self, the will.

There are commonly two very one-sided conceptions of the will. The first is that of checking or inhibiting by sheer force, analogous to the taming of wild beasts. The second concept is that of pushing by force, analogous to a man trying to move his automobile by pushing it from behind. Because of its aptness, this analogy of a man and his automobile will be used to illustrate various points of our discussion of the will.

In reality an analysis of the will reveals various phases or stages, which we will deal with presently, but in general our aim and interest—for the practical purposes of the development and the training of the will—is in the complete, effective, successful, volitional act, and use of the will, i.e., the total will in action.

It is not necessary, therefore, to have an exact conception or theory of the will in order to train it, nor to discuss which of the various phases of the will is more essential or specifically of the essence of will. The purpose of developing the will is self-evident, because the will is needed first to decide upon and then to persist in, to take the needed time and trouble in, the use of any other technique—and, of course, for the whole work of psychosynthesis. There is, however, a prior and more immediate purpose of the technique: that is, the *will to train the will*. Those patients who say that they have no will, do in reality have some will for it is a direct function of the self, but a function that is largely latent. Such people have to learn to use their small "capital," their modicum of will, in order to strengthen and build it up to where it becomes a valuable asset—at least sufficient for each particular stage of the psychosynthesis, although there is no limit to the usefulness of an increasingly potent will.

The Stages of the Will

As said above we are concerned with training the complete will in *all* its phases, or to be more theoretically exact, attaining complete volition.

1. *The first stage* in the use of the will includes:

        a. goal—purpose—intention
        b. valuation
        c. motivation

As we are dealing with conscious will the element of purpose or aim is the first essential, for without a conscious aim there can be no pure will. After having decided on the aim comes the intention to attain it, and the evocation of motivation.

At this point it is necessary to clear up beforehand any erroneous conception that might possibly develop to the effect that psychosynthesis is returning to the old nineteenth century conception of the will, which overlooked the important unconscious motivating factors. However, since psychosynthesis evolved out of psychoanalysis, it is quite obvious that no such exclusion is intended and that the writer is fully aware of the very complex motivating factors which operate below the level of awareness. Therefore, the training of the will should be preceded by the exploration of the unconscious, which includes as one of its most important and useful aspects the uncovering of unconscious motives and of the rationalization of the same, in order to make them acceptable to the conscious ego. This is one of the most valuable aspects of psychoanalysis and we take it fully into account in the process of psychosynthesis.

Therefore, the consideration of motivation is for the most part the uncovering of unconscious drives; but after they have been recognized we must not fall into the mistake of 18th century psychology of condemning or suppressing those drives. The function of the will is to utilize them and insure their cooperation in the attaining of the chosen purpose.

Motivation inevitably implies valuation; and, as we mentioned earlier, valuation is unavoidable and in this regard even essential. True valuation implies a scale of values, which in its turn is the expression of a concept or philosophy of life and of the world (Weltanschauung). Every person has such a concept or philosophy but generally it has not been formulated; it is hazy and often self-contradictory. Incidentally, the clarification, the becoming aware of the position and attitude of the self towards the world, is, in the writer's opinion, the most fruitful aspect of Existential Analysis. It is evident that the purpose or aim towards which the will is to be directed must have an intense positive valuation, or what Lewin called "a positive valence."

2. Following valuation comes the stage of deliberation, consideration, weighing. In any particular situation it might seem that there is not much to deliberate, and that the choice should inevitably go to the highest conceivable aim or purpose; but the matter is not so simple. The purpose or aim must be not only of high value but it must also be attainable. We can visualize very high aims, but which, realistically, we recognize are unattainable—at least under existing psychological and environmental conditions. Therefore, the deliberation or consideration which will bring us to the next point (of decision or choice) cannot be made automatically by choosing the highest aim, for one must take into consideration the various conditions and circumstances. Although an alternative aim may be less high, it may for some reasons be more urgent; so wisdom is needed in the deliberation and consideration of the many factors in any given situation, for each is always unique.

3. *The third stage* in the use of the will is that of *decision*. This is a difficult stage because it involves choice, and goes counter to the strong tendency existing in the human being "to have his cake and eat it too." In psychoanalytical terms, it could be called the following of the pleasure-principle—which is irrational. The making of a deliberate choice implies instead the use of the reality-principle, which is a principle of relativity, the principle that one cannot have all, but must choose between alternatives. In the older psychological writings on the will this point was expressed in a negative terminology of renunciation; but for theoretical and especially for practical purposes it is much better to place the emphasis on positive terms of *preference*. When we choose, when we make a decision, it means that we prefer some-

thing which we consider to be more desirable and attainable than the other alternatives which we discard. The difficulty in making the voluntary decision is that the individual, either clearly or obscurely, realizes that decision involves responsibility, that decision is an act of freedom which inevitably involves responsibility. In recent times the curious escape from freedom by individuals and by communities has been clearly pointed out by Erich Fromm, among others; i.e., the escape from responsibility at the cost of giving up the most precious human gift, that of free will.

In this connection it is hardly necessary to recall that indecision is one of the outstanding symptoms of all patients in a state of depression, but we will take up this point later when dealing with the limitations to the training of the will.

4. *The fourth stage* in the act of willing, which should closely follow decision, is *affirmation*. Effective affirmation involves several factors: the first is faith—not simply "belief" but a living dynamic faith, even more, an assured conviction. If this is lacking, affirmation can yet be made on the basis of a willingness or decision to "attempt," to take risks, in a spirit of courageous adventure

The act of affirmation consists of a command or declaration made to oneself. It is the use of the imperative tense, through such words as the Latin "Fiat" or "let it be." The intensity or "psychological voltage" of the affirmation determines the degree and the extent of its effectiveness.

In many cases it is necessary to repeat, or rather to renew, the affirmation at intervals, in order to enhance its potency and overcome opposing factors. It is well to be aware of the fact that affirmation sometimes provokes contrary reactions; this should be explained to the patient so that they do not surprise or cause discouragement, and can be calmly resisted while they last and then overcome in appropriate ways, among which is the above mentioned renewal of the affirmation.

5. *The fifth stage* in volition is *planning*, the organizing of activity according to a clearly outlined program. This requires a pre-visualization of the various steps or stages which will have to be realized between the starting point and the ultimate goal or realization of the purpose. In some cases the ultimate goal will, of

course, be distant but there will be several intermediary aims which will lead successively to it; so it is necessary to have a clear, wise, well-organized program of the succession of partial tasks or achievements.

There are two opposite mistakes to be avoided. One is keeping the attention and the direction of the will so exclusively focussed on the final aim that it causes the patient to become impractical; and the other and more common mistake is that of becoming so interested in and over-valuing the secondary aims and the means to their attainment that one loses sight of the ultimate aim, or places undue emphasis on the means.

6. *The sixth stage* of the volitional act is *direction of the execution*. Here are needed two of the outstanding qualities of the whole will: firstly, the dynamic power of the will, one-pointed driving energy; and secondly, persistence or endurance. Of course, the perfect will would combine the maximum of dynamic power and the maximum of persistence or endurance; but typologically we find that some people have more of one quality than the other. Also, some tasks chiefly require the dynamic aspect, while other tasks of less strenuous but more protracted nature call for the patience and persistence aspects of the will. Therefore, it is a subjective question not only of which quality of the will is prevalent in the person, but also which is more needed for the particular task or aim. Obviously, in the training of the will, we will have to put the accent on the one which is relatively less developed.

The way in which the dynamic will manifests itself is through assertion and command, by "fiat." In contrast the persistence aspect of the will is needed for one of the most effective techniques of the will, i.e., keeping a clear mental picture or image steady in the focus of attention. The power of sustained images is enormous, a subject we will take up when dealing with the technique of visualization and imagination.

Another quality needed for this final stage of execution is that of maintaining direction, that is, *one-pointedness*. Also required is "inhibition," in the sense of excluding and discarding all obstacles which would interfere with the application of the will in execution.

Procedure in Training the Will

As mentioned earlier the first aim in the training of the will is to increase the patient's individual "capital" or active quota of the will itself. In other words, to train the will to will more effectively. The first step in this procedure consists in mobilizing the energy of the existing drives in the patient, and directing those energies to the aim of developing the will.

1. Mobilizing the Energies

The first indispensable condition for acquiring a strong will is the earnest resolve to devote to its attainment whatever time, energy and means are necessary. When this is presented to the patient he may object and say, "in order to do so, I would need a firm and decided will, and it is just that which I lack." This objection is not tenable, for all have at least some will and although it may only exist in an embryonic state, still it is sufficient for a beginning to be made.

To ensure success, it is of paramount importance that there be proper preparation to create the initial urge and impetus. This preparation should arouse a strong emotional desire to develop the will, transforming itself into a firm decision to do all that is necessary for the attainment of that end. In order to reach this state of mind, the following exercise will be found helpful, and we give it in a form in which it can be presented to a patient, or experimentally used by the therapist himself.

Exercise I — Part A

Put yourself into a comfortable position, muscles relaxed.

1. Picture to yourself as vividly as possible all the unfortunate consequences to yourself and to others which have actually occurred—and those which might occur in the future—as a result of your inadequate will. Examine them carefully one by one, formulating them clearly; then *make a list of them in writing.* Allow the feelings which these recollections and forecasts arouse in you to affect you intensely: shame, dissatisfaction with yourself, shrinking from a repetition of such conduct and the urgent desire to change this state of affairs.

2. Picture to yourself as vividly as possible all the advantages which the training of your will can bring to you, all the benefits and satisfactions which will come from it to yourself and to others. Examine them carefully, one by one: formulate these ideas with clarity, and write them down. Allow the feelings aroused by these thoughts to have full sway: the joy of the possibilities that open up before you, the intense desire to realize them, and the strong impulse to begin at once.

3. Picture yourself as vividly as possible as being possessed of a strong persistent will; see yourself walking with a firm and decided step, acting in various situations with decision, focussed intention, concentration of effort, persistence, and self-control; resisting any attempt at intimidation. See yourself successfully attaining the desired ends. In particular, select similar situations to those in which you previously failed to exert a sufficiently strong and persistent will, and then see yourself acting with the desired qualities.

Exercise I — Part B

Use selected reading material, specially chosen to cultivate and reinforce the feelings and determination aroused by Part A of the exercise. It must consist of literature that is encouraging, optimistic and dynamic in character, that stimulates self-reliance and incites to action. But in order to benefit fully from such a course of reading, it must be performed in a special way: read slowly, with undivided attention, marking the passages which impress you, and copying those that are most striking and which seem specially appropriate to your case. It is well to re-read those passages several times, absorbing their full meaning. Best suited for this purpose are biographies of outstanding personalities who have demonstrated the best qualities of a strong but constructive will, or other books which aim directly at awakening the desired inner energies. After having engaged in such reading for some time you will begin to feel a growing desire, and you will even be anxious, to set about the work. This is the right moment for deciding, with all the firmness you can muster, that you will devote all the time, energy and means which are necessary to the development of your will.

A word of warning: do not talk about this matter with others, not even with the laudable intention of inducing them to follow your example. Talking tends to disperse the energies needed and accumulated for action. Your purpose, if made known to others, easily provokes sceptical or cynical remarks which may inject doubt or discouragement. *Work in silence.* This cannot be stressed too much.

The above exercise with its two parts constitutes one technique or rather method, having the aim of mobilizing other drives to enhance the quota of energy of will already available.

Exercise II — The Performing of Useless Exercises

This technique is the performing of actions which have no utility whatever in themselves, and are performed for the sole purpose of training the will. They can be compared to muscular exercises in gymnastics which have no economic or other utility except the developing of the muscles and the enhancing of neuro-muscular coordination and physical well-being in general. This technique was first presented by William James in his book *Talks to Teachers* (New York, Henry Holt, 1912): "Keep the faculty of effort alive in you by a little gratuitous exercise every day. That is, be systematically heroic in little unnecessary points; do every day or two something for no other reason than its difficulty, so that, when the hour of dire need draws nigh, it may find you not unnerved and untrained to stand the test. Asceticism of this sort is like the insurance which a man pays on his house and goods. The tax does him no good at the time, and possibly may never bring him a return. But, if fire does come, his having paid it, it will be his salvation from ruin. So with the man who has daily inured himself to habits of concentrated attention, energetic volition, and self-denial in unnecessary things. He will stand like a tower when everything rocks around him, and his softer fellow-mortals are winnowed like chaff in the blast." (pp. 75-76)

The same procedure was practiced and developed by E. Boyd Barrett and explained in his book *Strength of Will* (New York, Harper, 1931).

III. Exercises of the Will in Daily Life

Another group of exercises to develop the will can be derived from the countless opportunities that present themselves in daily life, with its various duties and occupations. Most of our activities can be helpful in this way, because through our purposes, our inner attitude, and the way in which we accomplish them, they can become definite exercises of the will. For instance, the mere fact of rising in the morning at a definite time can be such a drill, if for that purpose we rise ten or fifteen minutes earlier than usual. Also, getting dressed in the morning can be used as such an opportunity, if we accomplish the various necessary movements with attention and precision, rapidly yet not hurriedly. Here is a very important precious ability to develop in daily life: to learn how to "make haste slowly." Modern life with its stress and strain tends to create in us the habit of hurry, even when the occasion does not require it—a result of "mass suggestion."

To make haste slowly is not easy, but it is possible; and it paves the way for efficiency and productiveness, without tension and without exhaustion. It is not easy because it requires of us that we be almost dual: the one who acts, and the one who simultaneously looks on as the observer; yet simply to try to do this constitutes a good way of developing the will.

Also, during the rest of the day—be it at the office or in professional work, or attending to domestic duties—one can do numerous exercises for the development of will which, at the same time, may enable one to unfold certain needed qualities. For instance, learning serenity or "self-recollectedness" during one's daily work, no matter how tedious the task may be; or to control emotion and acts of impatience when confronted with minor difficulties and annoyances, such as finding oneself in a crowded train, or waiting for the opening of a door, or when noticing the mistakes or faults of a dependent, or experiencing the injustice of a superior.

Further, when we return home, we have opportunity for similar valuable exercises: controlling the impulse to give vent to our bad temper—perhaps caused by various vexations, pre-occupations or business worries—bearing serenely whatever comes our way and trying to adjust any disharmonies in the home. At the table, an exercise just as useful for health as for the will is to control the desire or impulse to eat quickly, while thinking of business, etc. We should compel ourselves to masticate well and enjoy our meal with a relaxed and calm mind. In the evening we have other occasions for training, such as to resist the allurements of people or things that tend to divert us from our chosen tasks.

Whether away at business or in the home, wherever possible, we must resolutely cease working when tired, controlling the desire to hurry just to get a job finished. Rather we should give ourselves wise rest and recreation; a short rest taken in time, at the outset of fatigue is of greater value than a long rest necessitated by exhaustion. Short and frequent rest periods have been applied in industry and have resulted in increased output by workers.

During these rest periods, a few muscular exercises or relaxation by means of closing the eyes for a few minutes will suffice. For mental fatigue, physical exercises are generally the most beneficial, though each individual can find out by practice what suits him best. One of the advantages of such short and frequent interruptions is that one does not lose interest in, nor the impetus for, the work in hand, and at the same time one overcomes fatigue and nervous tension. An ordered rhythm in our activities generates harmony in our being; and harmony is a universal law of life.

A good exercise is to retire at a fixed hour, resolutely interrupting one's reading or an interesting conversation. It is difficult, especially at first, to do all these exercises well, and to attempt them all at once would easily lead to discouragement. Therefore, it is advisable to begin with only a few, spread over the day; and when success has been achieved with these, to increase their number, varying, alternating the exercises and performing them cheerfully and with interest, scoring successes and failures, setting oneself records, and trying to meet them in a competitive sporting attitude. Thus the danger is avoided of making life too rigid and mechanical; and we make interesting and colorful what otherwise would be tiresome duties; also all with whom we are associated become our cooperators (without their knowing it!). For instance, a dogmatic superior or an exacting partner becomes, as it were, the mental parallel bars on which our will—the will to right human relations—can develop its force and proficiency. Delay in being served with a meal gives us the opportunity to exercise patience and serenity, as well as the chance to read a good book while waiting. Talkative friends or time-wasters give us the chance to control speech; they teach us the art of courteous but firm refusal to engage in unnecessary conversations. To be able to say "no" is a difficult but very useful discipline.

Exercise IV — Physical Exercises in the Training of the Will

These constitute a very effective technique when used with the specific intention and purpose of developing the will; for as the French writer, Gillet, has expressed it, "gymnastics are the elementary school of the will . . . and serve as a model for that of the mind." In reality, every physical movement is an act of will, a command given to the body, and the deliberate repetition of such acts—with attention, effort and endurance—exercise and invigorate the will. Organic sensations are thus aroused: the consciousness of physical vigor, a more rapid circulation, a sense of warmth and agility of the limbs, and their ready obedience; all produce a sense of moral strength, of decision, of mastery that raises the tone of the will and develops its energy. However, we repeat, to extract from such exercises the utmost benefit, it is necessary that they be performed with the exclusive aim, or at least with the principal objective, of training the will.

Such exercises must be performed with measured precision, and with attention. They must not be too violent or too enervating; every single movement or group of movements must be executed with liveliness and decision. Exercises or sports best fitted for this purpose are not the ones of a violent or exciting nature, but rather those that call for endurance, calmness, dexterity and courage, permitting interruption, and variety of movement.

Many outdoor sports—such as golf, tennis, skating, walking, and climbing—are particularly suited for the training of the will; but where they are not possible, suitable selected physical exercises can always be carried out in the privacy of one's room.

2. Comments on the Exercises

A difficulty that may arise is that most individuals who have very little will to start with may simply do an exercise once or twice and then give it up. It may prove very difficult to motivate patients towards a consistent application because we have the "situation of circularity"—that in order to effectively do the exercises to develop the will, one has to have some will with which to start.

In these cases the techniques brought out so well by Baudoin appear to be suitable in seeking to engage the cooperation of other drives, which may provide a stronger incentive than the pure will. Those drives, of course, may not necessarily be of a high order, which is an example of the utilization of so-called "lower" or "primitive" drives and incentives for a higher purpose. Pride, vanity, the desire to please when there is a positive transference, self-aggrandizement, etc., can be mobilized for this purpose. Also even simpler incentives such as praise or objective prizes are very effective. We have found the best incentive to be that which utilizes the "ludic" instinct or the drive to play, the sporting attitude of a contest with oneself. This demands a certain proficiency in dis-identification, for in it the self "plays" with its sub-personalities and drives, treating it as a kind of game, not taking the matter too seriously, trying to win the game as would a good sportsman. To become interested in the game itself gives a drive which, being interesting and amusing, does not arouse the resistance or active opposition which a more forceful attitude of the imposition of the will would call forth.

Not to arouse resistances or rebellion in the unconscious, or in other constituents of the personality, is a general caution applicable in the use of all techniques, but particularly in the use of techniques for the development of the will. One method of guarding against arousing such resistance is to advise the patient not to use a technique too seriously, nor in a way which is pedantic or annoying to the unconscious. Instead, the aim must be to win the cooperation of the unconscious through amusing and interesting it—and that is the specific attitude of play. Parenthetically, this factor is even more important for teachers to remember, who are using psychosynthesis in education.

A playful attitude detracts in no way from the effectiveness of a technique but eliminates the counter-currents of resistance and rebellion.

3. Problems of Practical Application

The fundamental problem in the practical application of this training and use of the will is how to achieve an equilibrium between the different aspects or stages of the will which we have described above.

The first thing to aim for is insight or awareness on the part of the patient of the existing situation. Then follows the therapist's indication to the patient, and the acceptance by him, of the plan of action for achieving the desired equilibrium or harmonization; followed by teaching him the specific techniques—and in the right succession—so that he may reach his aim. The plan of action and the specific techniques differ for the various stages of the will, and in some cases are almost opposite.

The first stage—of clear purpose—is with many patients very often weak. Also we frequently find a strong personal will at the disposal of the most intense, predominant drive; and this occurs so frequently that it may explain and perhaps justify in some measure the curious lack of recognition of the very existence of a personal will, because so often it is disguised, masked by a dominant drive.

In modern psychology the attempt is made to eliminate the necessity of including even the concept of will, and to regard decisions as the result of opposing forces of mostly an emotional nature. This is the standard deterministic concept of the parallelogram of forces, so to speak, and it is the Freudian conception. However, the concept is not consistent with human experience; and in the training of the will we have the proof that the will can be distinguished and disassociated from, and even opposed to, the drives.

The model or analogy of a parallelogram of forces is too crude. In fact, the will or the willing self—besides being a genuine, independent energy contending with the drives—is or can be the organizer or coordinator of the drives, using them in a sense from another level or dimension. The will, therefore, can be, when freed, a supra-ordinate force—if it does not let itself be dragged down to the level of the contending drives.

The technique to be used in cases where the weakest phase of the will is that of conscious purpose and deliberation, is to first make the patient aware of his lack and its drawbacks, and to help him to consciously evaluate his situation, to gain a clear conception of life and a standard of values. On the basis of this we help him to find or choose an aim, and then deliberate with him on ways of attaining it.

Regarding the third stage of decision, if in spite of the satisfactory development of the first phase, the patient finds difficulty in deciding, we must analyze the cause of this inability. This may be due to an unwillingness to face alternatives or to indicate a preference for any one of them, which, of course, implies giving up or rejecting the other alternatives. The latter may be difficult for a patient with a strong will who does not accept any kind of renunciation and wants and wills to have all the alternatives. This is typical of the strong will of egotistical individuals; so in those cases we have an over-development of the driving will and the under-development of the deliberation and decision involved in such renunciation.

The fifth phase, of planning and organizing, is also one in which there may be a lack or under-development in people otherwise able to make quick decisions or use the dynamic will. Sometimes they are too sure of themselves, and at other times they are impatient with the slow—necessarily slow—careful planning, which implies consideration of all the elements of a situation and a sense of proportion and wisdom. They tend to put a plan into operation before it has been really thought out in detail; or, even worse, they rush almost madly to their goal without considering obstacles, timing, realistic assessment of the situation, consideration of other peoples' reactions, etc. These people often fail through the reactions they imprudently arouse in others. The application is clear: training them to the recognition of the value and necessity of this phase through the active cooperation of the therapist.

In other words, during the sessions we take up a goal that the patient has selected for himself, and then help him to think through all the different steps that would be wise for him to take in order to achieve that goal. To give a rather common instance: a young untrained girl comes for consultation and says in effect "I will become a movie actress, I will leave my family and go to Hollywood." Of course, one does not reject her aim but in effect says, "All right, let us plan it; let us see what your aim involves. You wish to succeed in this goal, so let us lay the needed plans to attain it." If we respond to her in a cooperative, permissive way, she will soon realize just what her goal and drive imply and how many difficult steps there are to be surmounted. That is a very simple example, but others that are more subtle and less obvious often arise in practice.

Considering the sixth phase of the *direction of the execution*, we have seen that it requires several important qualities of the will, such as clear and persistent visualization of the goal, one-pointedness, dynamic power, persistence, self-limitation. Each of these components may be insufficient for a successful execution. By "self-limitation" is meant the willingness and ability to eliminate, at least for the time being or for a sufficient period of time, other goals, and other plans, not letting oneself be sidetracked by too much attention or valuation of the means—both in the sense of not making the means an end in themselves, and of attachment to one or other of the means to the exclusion of others.

Therefore, the dynamic will can be used to develop persistence if this is originally lacking or insufficient, and vice versa; persistence can be used in applying the techniques which in turn arouse and feed the power of the will. As an example of this latter technique is the one mentioned previously, the vivid realization of the advantages of a strong will and of the disadvantages of a weak will. If one persistently practices this realization the dynamism of the will is enhanced.

A special word of caution, regarding this stage of decision, is called for in patients who are in a depressed state, and this we will refer to at greater length under Limitations and Contra-Indications.

Indications and Applications

The general applications of this technique of the will to the very many cases in which the will is weak or insufficient are obvious and need no explanation—but the fact of the technique of the will *not* being generally applied does need emphasis!

The specific indications and applications are based on the analysis of the will already existent and active in the patient or subject because—as we have seen—the will has various phases, and it is quite possible, and often occurs in practice, that one phase may be more developed or even overdeveloped and another one weak or almost absent. So the first necessity is to ascertain which of the five phases of the will need most or particular training. There are people whose will is rapid and decisive, but they do not have the persistence or quality to carry through. There are others for whom the phase of decision is the most difficult, even though once a decision is made the other aspects of their will are ádequate and sufficiently developed. Therefore, a differential training of the will is called for and a recognition of which of its components needs special development.

Limitations and Contra-Indications

These are very important and deserve full consideration. There are many people who have an over-developed personal will—generally directed towards self-assertion and the domination of other people; and these could be called the "Adlerian cases" because Adler so well described their type, although in our opinion he exaggerated and over-emphasized in the sense of making it a general blanket interpretation and explanation. Nevertheless, typical Adlerian cases are not rare to find, and in these cases any further development of the personal will is contra-indicated.

Apart from these "Adlerian cases," some phase of the will may be found to be overdeveloped in certain patients. Especially dangerous is the overdevelopment of the dynamic aspect of the will, which can have injurious and even destructive effects, especially on others. Therefore, it is important to consider how to minimize and offset these dangers and drawbacks. There are three ways:

First—that of equilibrizing, i.e., cultivating an equal, harmonious development of all the phases of the will, as mentioned above.

Second—and more important—is that of developing other functions in the individual which would check and balance the will-function. We allude chiefly to the feeling-function in its higher aspects, that is, development of humanitarian love, compassion, loving understanding of others, and the ethical sense, the sense of responsibility concerning the effect one has upon other people. The highest expression of this is harmlessness.

The *third* and highest way, which partially includes the second method, is the awakening and functioning of the *spiritual will*, connected with the realization of the spiritual Self. This checks and utilizes the personal will in not only a harmless but also a constructive way, and frees the personal will from the exploitation (to which it is often subject) by a prevalent drive. In the ordinary man, the will is the slave of one or several personal drives. Here the first necessity is to achieve a dis-identification of the personal self from those drives, and then the dedication of the personal will to the spiritual will; or inversely the spiritual will, the spiritual Self, takes possession of and utilizes the personal will.

There is a difference, not always recognized, between the fully awakened spiritual will and the obedience of the personal will to a higher feeling. For many patients, at a particular stage of the treatment, the latter may be the line of least resistance; i.e., there is a transfer of the emotional energy motivating the will from a lower to a higher level, yet still remaining an emotional motivating force, although with more constructive aims. But, of course, the first (establishing of a direct relation to the spiritual will, to the Self) is the goal of psychosynthesis. This means the developing of a constructive, strong, persevering and wise will—in essence, a fusion of what we consider to be some of the fundamental energies in the human being, viz. the energy of will and the energy of love, so that we eventually have in operation a "loving will."

The word "fusion" used above could be substituted by "organically coordinated functioning"; i.e., that is a *functional* fusion and not real fusion in a literal sense. Here the biological analogy is illuminating: there is no material fusion of organs or apparatus of the body—they remain anatomically and physiologically distinct—but their fusion is a functional unity, directed by what could be called a very able interlocked directorate with the summit in the central nervous system, which operates through the other nervous centers and the endocrine glands.

There is a definite limitation in regard to the third phase of decision in the training and use of the will. As is well known, indecision is one of the most frequent symptoms of people who are in a depressed state, "at the low ebb of psychological tension" to use Janet's point of view. In all such cases, it would be a therapeutic error to urge them to make decisions, because that would evoke in them a strong anxiety, for they are really for the time being unable to make decisions for themselves. To press them towards decision making would give them a sense of failure and frustration which would tend to increase their depressive condition and the usual sense of inferiority characterizing such cases. With such patients—and while the depressive condition continues—it is really a duty to relieve them as much as possible from making decisions. The best way is to explain to them that this stage of depression is temporary and that they should postpone any important decisions until after the cessation of the depression. This is very important because in that state such people often make decisions which they afterwards regret—such as selling property or stock at a low price owing to panic or pessimism.

The other alternative is to make decisions *with them,* not for them—giving them what they lack, and going through the other stages with them, especially that of deliberation, and then supplying them with the missing elements required for decision. This is important in therapy.

Combination with Other Techniques

The will not only can be combined, but inevitably is combined with the active performance of all the other techniques of psychosynthesis; and, inversely, the performance of any technique indirectly develops the will.

This raises the important practical question of when to introduce in the course of therapy the direct training of the will. With people with a very weak will it is best to introduce it at the beginning and thus avoid frustration, but this can be done without even mentioning the will itself, through training and encouraging them to use various active techniques, suited to their symptoms and to their needs. When, through the use of those techniques, they have unknowingly developed the will up to the needed point, then the therapist can introduce the direct training of the will as such. We thus have the paradoxical situation that the weaker the will, the later the directed training of it.

TECHNIQUE FOR THE TRAINING AND USE OF IMAGINATION

Purpose

Imagination is a function which in itself is to some extent synthetic, since imagination can operate at several levels concurrently: those of sensation, feeling, thinking and intuition. It includes all the various types of imagination, such as visualization—the evocation of visual images—auditory imagination, tactile, kinesthetic imagination and so on.

The imagination, in the precise sense of the function of evoking and creating images, is one of the most important and spontaneously active functions of the human psyche, both in its conscious and in its unconscious aspects or levels. Therefore it is one of the functions which has to be controlled when excessive or dispersed; to be trained when weak, and to be utilized owing to its great potency. This explains why in psychosynthetic therapy we are particularly interested in the regulation, development and utilization of imagination, since the practice of the technique of imagination is one of the best ways towards a synthesis of the different functions.

Rationale

In practice the real issue is between the will and the imagination. This recalls the paradoxical statement by Coué, that when will and imagination come into conflict, imagination wins. This is an empirical and paradoxical way of expressing a great and important law of the psychological life, which is described and explained in scientific terms by Charles Baudoin in his valuable *Suggestion and Auto-Suggestion* (London: Allen and Unwin, 1920).

The fundamental fact and law in this field has been formulated in the following way: *"Every image has in itself a motor-drive"* or *"images and mental pictures tend to produce the physical conditions and the external acts corresponding to them."* It is hardly necessary here to give instances of the immense power of images, for several psychologists have dealt with the subject; probably the first to do so in a systematic way was Théodore Ribot in his classic essays on imagination.

Not only psychologists, but also advertisers are keenly aware of the motor-power of imagination—or what they more vaguely call "suggestion"—and utilize it abundantly, or shall we say overabundantly, and very ably. It seems high time that this law should be utilized for higher and more constructive purposes; and the fullest use of it should be made for the purpose of psychosynthesis.

We will now take up separately the specific techniques for the evocation, training and utilization of imagination, i.e., the

Technique of Visualization, the Technique of Auditory Evocation, and the Techniques for the Imaginative Evocation of Other Sensations such as kinesthetic, tactile, gustatory and olfactory. The reader is also referred to the article, *Pictures and Colors: Their Psychological Effects;* see Appendix, p. 283.

TECHNIQUE OF VISUALIZATION

Purpose

The general purpose of evoking the imagination has already been discussed. The great importance and paramount value of visualization is that it constitutes the necessary preliminary training for, and furthers the purpose of, other important techniques. For instance, the clear visualization of the "ideal model" implies the ability to visualize. Therefore we will deal first with the technique of visualization; also in therapy we should at the outset explain to the patient the various uses of this technique; for example, that it is essential for the clear picture of the "ideal model" which is the goal of the psychosynthesis.

Visualization helps greatly in, and is one of the most suitable techniques for, the training of concentration in its first stages. Further, visualization helps, or rather implies and requires, the use of the will, and some of the exercises of evocative imagination which are described below, under Procedure, constitute a class of the so-called "useless exercises" which we have mentioned in dealing with the will.

Another purpose of visualization is to offer a starting point for or incentive to creative imagination; and finally it makes possible the effective use of symbolic visualization which will be dealt with when we take up specifically the technique of the use of symbols.

Rationale

In the Rationale on Imagination we mentioned the fundamental law that every image has a motor-tendency. Now we add something more: that every movement requires a previous image of the movement to be executed. This has been proved by certain forms of aphasia or rather one specific form of aphasia, the cause of which is the loss of the evocation of the image of the words to be pronounced. In short: visualization is a necessary stage for action.

In order to clarify our discussion, let us consider the differences between reproductive imagination and creative imagination, as they apply particularly to this specific technique. There is a fundamental distinction between conscious visualization of an image consciously chosen and the imaginative function which is spontaneous, creative and mostly operates in and on unconscious levels and then offers to consciousness the product or the result of its activity.

In the first case, we can consciously, deliberately evoke an image or set of images of what we have already seen; that is, strictly speaking, reproductive imagination. We can also consciously evoke an image of something we have never seen, i.e., build up an image which may include elements already seen but combined in a new way, which in this sense is a creation of a certain kind. But in these kinds of evocative imagination it is a *conscious* creation of a static image. Therefore, it is a creation of quite a different kind from the *spontaneous* creative function which we will take up later.

The real difference is that in evocative imagination it is a conscious process, deliberately carried through, while the other is the spontaneous function of creative imagination, although the starting point—as we will mention later—may be the conscious evocation of a symbol. It may be interesting to add at this point that—curiously, in a certain sense—it is much easier to evoke even a complex picture or image of something we have seen repeatedly (e.g., the front of a cathedral with its complicated details) than to create a new image, however simple.

Procedure

We shall describe a very simple exercise in the manner in which it could be given as an instruction to a patient or subject:

"First imagine the setting, which is a classroom with a blackboard, grey or dull black. Then imagine that in the middle of the blackboard appears a figure; let us say the number five, as if written with white chalk, fairly large and well defined. Then keep it vividly before your inner eye, so to speak; that is, keep the image of the five vivid and steady in the field of your conscious attention. Then on the right of the five visualize the figure two.

So, now you have two figures, a five and a two, making fifty-two. Dwell for a while on the visualization of this number, then after a little while, imagine the appearance of a four at the right side of the two.

Now you have three figures, written in white chalk, five, two, four—making the number five hundred and twenty-four. Dwell for a while on this number.

Continue adding other figures until you are unable to hold together the visualization of the number resulting from those figures."

The result of such an exercise is very interesting, and generally rather humiliating. As we first read the description it seems a very simple matter, but it has a deceiving easiness in its simplicity, for when we put it into practice, we see that it is not easy at all. The figures seem to have a wicked tendency to disappear or to change size or color, or to turn into fanciful forms, and even to dance in the field of our consciousness. We have to recreate them again and again. This humiliating experience is very instructive and profitable. It gives us an almost dramatic realization of how little we really control our psychological functions—in this case imagination and concentration—and reveals how weak and ineffective the will is in exercising such control.

This exercise also gives important clues to the various aspects of our psychological functioning, i.e., some succeed better with eyes closed, others with eyes open; some can very rapidly imagine and visualize the figures, but almost as rapidly these disappear or change; others instead have difficulty in creating and evoking the form of the figure, but after having done it the figure persists with little or no effort. Thus the fact of greater facility in visualizing with closed or with open eyes is an indication of the psychological type, i.e., in regard to extraversion or introversion. We have found that extraverted people can visualize more easily with closed eyes, because the open eyes tend to be instruments of their extravert interest in what they see before them. Thus, when they close their eyes they are forced—so to speak—to introvert, to direct their attention to the inner world. On the contrary, introverts have more difficulty with closed eyes, because their interest being already inwardly directed, all sorts of other pictures or other psychological processes crowd out the interest in the figures. However, keeping the eyes open checks in some measure the attention directed towards the inner world— while the outer world does not interest them sufficiently to create a difficulty in their visualization process.

As Jung pointed out, an individual may be both introverted and extraverted according to the different levels of his psychological functions; for instance, introverted in the feeling function while extraverted in the thinking function, etc. In this exercise we are mainly concerned with the sensation level, because it is one connected with vision. Therefore, extraverts on the sensation level will have much difficulty in visualizing with eyes open, and vice versa, an introvert on the sensation level would be flooded with organic sensations with his eyes closed.

As far as rapidity versus persistence of the visual image is concerned, we can also obtain certain diagnostic clues from them; specifically on what some psychologists call the respective prevalence of the primary and secondary functions. Those who visualize rapidly but whose mental pictures have no persistence have the primary function prevalent. But by primary function we do not mean that mentioned by Freud, who differentiates between the primary function of the Id and the secondary function of the Ego. We mean the distinction made by O. Gross and other psychologists between a primary and a secondary function. To explain the difference in simpler and clearer terms: it is the difference between the individual who reacts more promptly but also more superficially to stimuli, and the individual who reacts slowly or apparently not at all; but the stimulus starts a process of unconscious activities which sometimes later emerge again above the threshold of consciousness.

Another aspect to be considered in this exercise with figures is the extent of the area of attention. This is indicated by the number of figures which the subject can visualize at any one time. Finally the degree of vividness has also to be taken into account; this would correspond to the intensity of the light in the area of conscious attention.

The value of this exercise consists in the fact, among others, that it gives us a means of measuring any improvement resulting from the training in visualization by the subject. In this respect improvement is more important than initial ability, because the latter depends in great part on the subject being the visual or non-visual type. The degree of improvement is what is significant, not only as regards visualization per se but as regards the other functions involved in the exercise; i.e., concentration, attention, will.

Also there is the additional advantage of demonstrating to the patient or subject himself that he is making progress; which, of course, is vital as a reinforcement to his motivation to put forth further effort.

A *second exercise* brings in another factor, that of *color*. After the subject has gained some proficiency in the simpler exercise of the figures on the blackboard, we ask him to visualize *geometrical forms,* two dimensional and colored; e.g., a blue triangle, a yellow circle, or a green square. This has two purposes and advantages: first, to notice the difference in visualizing ability between form and color—and we do find a clear difference: some subjects can maintain the image of the form or shape, but have difficulty in visualizing the color and keeping it steady, or vice versa. Without going into the theoretical aspect of the matter which is outside the purpose of this Manual, this does suggest that the visualization of the form is more connected with the mental, thinking function, and color with the emotional function. Although this exercise is so simple, yet it brings out this significant difference—one which can also be found in art. For instance: the whole Tuscan School of painting put the emphasis on form, but the colors are not outstanding. On the contrary, the emphasis of the Venetian School is on very strong and intense colors.

The second usefulness of this exercise is that it is preparatory to the use of symbols in the Technique of Symbol Utilization. As we shall see later, when we describe those symbols, much use is made of forms, often complicated ones, and also colors.

A *third series of exercises* in visualization could be called *mental photography.* This is done in the following way:

The subject is asked to observe for a short time—generally for one minute—an image such as an illustrated postcard or a diagram or a mathematical or chemical formula. Then the patient is asked to close his eyes and to evoke the image he has just observed, and then give a detailed and full description of it. This technique also has several advantages. First, that it can give a numerical measure of the initial ability to visualize, and of its successive improvement, i.e., the number of details exactly recorded versus those inexactly described, or, as often happens, those invented. The second variable is the length of exposure, so to speak, necessary to gain a vivid mental picture of the image so that it can be correctly visualized later. Another variable which has more theoretical than therapeutic value is the length of the persistence of the image, found by asking, after a certain time, if the subject can still recall the image.

Apart from these variables, which we could call the measuring rod of improvement, this exercise has a special practical usefulness in its combination with two other techniques: those of observation and of memorization. It is needless to emphasize its value for mnemonic retention in making a clear visual picture of a thing to be memorized—particularly in the case of complicated algebraic or chemical formulas. When the image is rather complicated or when the power of observation—which implies concentration and visualization—is poor in the subject, it is good to let him repeat the observation a second time for half a minute, and sometimes even a third time—again for half a minute.

This is a valuable technique for many patients who may have very slight contact with the physical world, because it trains them to observe the physical universe, or parts of it, and relates them again to it. It is also valuable for individuals in whom the sensation function is not properly developed and who tend to live too much on the mental level. One particularly useful exercise of this nature is described by Rudyard Kipling in his book *Kim:* a variety of objects are placed on a tray; the subject is given say 30 seconds in which to look at them, after which the tray is removed or covered. He is then asked to describe what he saw. This is essentially one of the techniques of observation; as such it is well known but it can also be used as a technique of visualization, if the subject is asked to close his eyes and evoke in imagination the articles he has seen.

Indications and Applications

Some or most of the indications have already been mentioned in speaking of the usefulness of visualization. We can add that in these exercises, although in general they are passive, there is a varying degree of a constant flow of energies, and this must be taken into account, bearing in mind the general principle (which is one of the sound principles of psychoanalysis) not to suppress any activity or function. The indication is to teach patients to control their imaginative function without checking it by force or trying to suppress it. Therefore we teach them to utilize the imagination actively at will, and to switch it off at will, in order to permit it a certain expression, but only at the proper times and for specific purposes. Specific indications would be necessary in cases in which the sense of reality is deficient or tends to fluctuate. Other cases are those where the mnemonic function is, so to speak, uncontrolled: overimaginative individuals, in whom the flow of energies is much too strong.

Limitations and Contra-Indications

These are not outstanding. One is an exaggerated excessive interest in the technique itself without making use of it for the purpose of psychosynthesis. For example, certain obsessive compulsive individuals would sometimes use, or rather r suse, this technique and make of it a ritual which continues to utilize their chronic symptomatology. On the other hand, the visualization of certain geometrical forms (which theoretically should reinforce the ritualistic tendency of some excessive compulsives) has in some cases had the opposite effect, because it is a method of substitution. It replaces an egocentric emotion with an impersonal objective goal and is, so to speak, a case of therapeutic substitution . The only thing we have to watch as therapists is that the substitution does not become a symptom.

Combination with Other Techniques

As has already been mentioned, this technique naturally— one may say inevitably—is combined with other techniques and is helpful to them, e.g., Concentration, Will, Observation, Memorization. It also can be used as a preparation for the technique of the "Rêve éveillé" of Robert Desoille and also for the more complex exercises in symbolic visualization which we will describe later.

TECHNIQUE OF AUDITORY EVOCATION

Purpose

The general purpose of auditory evocation is, of course, the same as that of visual evocation; but it also has specific purposes as mentioned under Indications and Applications. Also it constitutes a useful and sometimes necessary preparation and training for the utilization of the power of sound and of music in the technique of musical therapy.

Rationale

Here again, this is generally the same as in visual evocation; we would only add that it has a specific quality and psychological influence which have not yet been studied sufficiently in a truly methodical way. This is a large field of research which could be very fruitful.

Procedure

There are two main groups of "auditory images," as we might call them, giving "image" a larger connotation than visual. The first group is that of *sounds and noises of Nature*. For instance, we can instruct a subject: "try to evoke the sound of the sea, the waves breaking against cliffs. Try to go through the whole process—the incoming waves, the crash or impact of the water on rocks, and then the quite different sounds as the water recedes."

Another example is that of evoking the sound of a waterfall. This sound is a continuous one, as compared to that of the waves. Yet another could be the whispering of the wind in the forest; and so on.

This brings up the question of subjects being auditory or visual types. Very often people with an auditory evocation also produce spontaneous visual images—they see the waves breaking on the rocks, they see the waterfall, and so on. This may call for a different procedure. In some cases we ask the subject to exclude as much as possible his visual images and to concentrate his attention on the purely auditory component of the evocation. In other cases we can be permissive, asking the subject to simply register both images and at the same time to try to judge which one is the more active, which is more facile than the other. Usually the visual is stronger than the auditory.

In deciding whether to ask for concentration on the auditory to the exclusion of the visual, or to allow both to occur concommitantly, in practice we generally use both methods in succession, because their rationale and aim are somewhat different. In the exclusion of visual images the accent is on concentration, control of psychological processes, emphasis, attention. In the other, instead, the objective is a more neutral observation of what is going on within oneself, and the ascertaining of spontaneous traits and processes in the psychological functions.

In both methods the exercise can be useful in bringing forth and developing the "I-consciousness," since in the first method it is the willing self which decides to include or exclude certain psychological processes from the area of consciousness; and it is also the willing self which observes the flow of images, both visual and auditory, as it occurs in the second method. However, in the exclusion there is an emphasis on the will, and in the admission there is an emphasis on the eye as a detached observer.

It is advisable to help the patient to recognize the value of the exercise (e.g., the desirability of gaining concentration, ability to evoke images, development of either the visual or the auditory images, I-consciousness, will) because this brings an increased motivation to the patient and also a growing ability to synthesize the various psychological functions, which after all is the goal of psychosynthesis and which we should always keep in mind.

The second large group of "auditory images" is that of *man-made sounds*, in particular what we call *music*. Here we have to distinguish between the direct influence of sound as such and the influence of the combination of sounds. The combination of sounds, which we call music, has therefore to be analyzed and differentiated into its various components. One is the rhythm, the second is the melody, the third the harmony (chords), and the fourth the quality (timbre) of the particular instrument expressing the music.

All this will be taken up at length in the chapter on musical therapy. But we have briefly mentioned it here because in the auditory evocation the emphasis can be put on each of the components separately. We can ask the subject to evoke a certain rhythm or to evoke a melody, or to evoke a chord, or the specific quality of sound of a violin or piano or cello. Each of these has a different aim, effect and indication. The ability of subjects to evoke such auditory images varies a great deal, and here the type is really outstandingly important. There are some who have an amazing facility of evocation of sounds and others for whom it is very difficult. We would say that the individual differences are greater than those indicated by visual images.

This technique is particularly indicated for all those who follow a musical career, for musicians, singers, and especially composers; for whom the facility of auditory evocation could be of help in preventing them losing some inspiring motive. Similarly, this technique is indicated for public speakers.

At this point we cannot digress to explore the psychical and psychosomatic effects—conscious or subconscious—of the use of this technique, nor its use in hypnosis or post-hypnosis. We simply stress the importance of simple auditory evocations as a means of gaining facility in this technique for its later use in combination with other techniques.

Another exercise—of great usefulness, in modern life especially—is the opposite of the foregoing. It is that of *excluding* from our consciousness sounds and particularly noises. This is not easy but can be achieved by training in a gradual systematic way. For instance, place near the subject a clock which ticks loudly and instruct the subject to listen to it for, say, ten or twenty seconds; and then, on a given sign, to dismiss this sensation and replace it in the field of consciousness with other contents. It is easier to achieve this substitution by contents of a different nature, but also a vivid evocation of a melody, of music, can submerge the impact of the outer uninteresting sensation (the tick of the clock). The same can be done with noises coming through a window from the street, or the whining of a child in an adjoining room, and so on.

In parenthesis, in regard to this question of the ever-increasing noise of traffic, one wonders what effects this has on the unconscious level. With many people it certainly creates tensions and may have an unfortunate effect and yet there are thousands who not only do not mind noise, but encourage and actively create it in preference to silence. This is particularly true of the young, especially teenagers who seem to enjoy noise and feel the need for a background of loud playing radios, and seem undisturbed by it even when studying. This is a paradox; it is contrary to what we think should happen and therefore it is an interesting psychological problem, to which we draw the attention of psychologists and therapists, but it is outside the scope of our present discussion.

Another type of auditory evocation is that of the bells of a country church, and this is particularly helpful for individuals living in a city. It seems to have a nostalgic tranquilizing and harmonizing effect.

It may also be valuable to ask the patient to attempt to evoke the different quality of a female versus a male singer; and further, within each, the different quality between, say, a soprano and contralto, or between a tenor and a baritone. These differences are not only of auditory qualities, but also have symbolic values, presenting different psychological characteristics. One could, in fact, include them in the category of visualization of symbols.

There is another technique, which is parallel to the one we described earlier as "mental-photography," and which can be called *auditory registration*. In this we ask the subject to listen to a short musical composition and then immediately afterwards to try to hear it again in imagination. The purpose, the procedure and the effects are parallel to those of mental photography. It is possible in this way to re-integrate and re-evoke some of the attendant emotions which one experienced while actually listening to the musical composition.

Another instance can be when we are sitting in a garden, relaxed and listening to the sound of birds. Then, after they have gone, we close our eyes and try to again hear their song. As we remarked about the auditory evocation of church bells, to people living in the midst of the city this auditory recall is particularly helpful, bringing back the sense of, and the contact with, living nature.

Indications and Applications

In general, these are the same as for visualization, but as the auditory evocation has a stronger, more intense resonance on the emotional states, there is a wider application of the technique, as we shall see, for either controlling or arousing emotional states and feeling of a positive nature.

Paradoxically, this technique of auditory evocation is particularly indicated in two extreme types: those with deficient auditory ability and those with excessive ability. For those of a deficient auditory ability the technique helps them to develop the function in order to utilize it either for therapy or in life in general. In contrast, for those with an excessive auditory sensitivity it serves to control it without suppressing it. As we said in regard to visual images, the function cannot be suppressed, but it can be controlled and regulated by the active systematic evocation of the will—the chosen auditory evocations substituting the involuntary and sometimes non-constructive or harmful auditory influences.

In certain patients, particularly neurotics, there is a high degree of sensitivity to sound, and especially to noises. In dealing with this kind of patient we first use a negative exercise; that of training them, as a regular exercise, to divert their attention from the noise instead of reacting with anger to it—which only increases their attention to the noise. Then follows the method of substitution: that is, to try to evoke vividly in imagination a pleasant sound of music, music that can replace the objective noise coming from outside. Exercises of relaxation are also helpful in this respect, for even without instruction, the patient during relaxation notices the noises less. This is a paradox, because in the quiet of relaxation he seemingly should notice them more; but this is explained by the fact that his interest in and emotional reaction to the noise is lessened as his interest shifts to the positive results of his relaxation.

We would emphasize that the foregoing facts regarding neurotics in no way substitute for or remove the necessity for dealing with the underlying causes, with the neurotic motivation of problems of which heightened auditory sensitivity is only a symptom. At this point we are discussing merely the symptomatic level and at this level the techniques are useful but secondary. There still remains the necessity for causal therapeutic action, and one must be on guard and not permit oneself to become fascinated by the theoretical interest and the possible lines of research which they open up.

Limitations and Contra-Indications

There is one important and serious contra-indication. This technique has to be avoided in every case in which the patient is apt to hear inner voices; that is, in which split parts of his personality or unconscious sub-personalities become so autonomous as to "speak" to the patient who generally erroneously considers it to be some external influence. In such cases the patient's attention should be deflected from all kinds of inner listening or auditory evocation; and even from outer listening. His attention should be directed to the outer world through the other senses, particularly sight, in addition to touch, taste and smell.

One of the inherent limitations, of course, is the rather widespread deficiency among human beings in auditory evocation, which makes it difficult for them to do the exercises; yet for whom they are particularly indicated. However, there is the limitation of time and of the range of possible experiences; and although the ideal purpose of psychosynthesis is the full development of every function, this, in many cases, would be unrealistic and should not be the main aim. A man or woman can "be," can feel and live creatively from a personal viewpoint, despite some functions being deficient, e.g., the auditory function.

Combination with Other Techniques

This technique can be combined, as can visualization, with the training of the will, attention, concentration, observation and so on. In particular it can be a very effective element in symbol utilization, and also in the "ideal model" of the personality, of an integrated, psychosynthesized personality, which we will discuss later.

TECHNIQUES OF IMAGINATIVE EVOCATION
OF OTHER SENSATIONS

There are four classes of such sensations which can be imaginatively evoked: the kinesthetic, the tactile, the gustatory and the olfactory. For the sake of simplicity and brevity, we will deal with the four classes simultaneously because our general observations will refer to all of them, with particular comments specific for each.

Purpose

The general purpose is the same as that of visualization, with the specific indication that kinesthetic evocation is a useful preparation for all the physical exercises connected with *bio*-psychosynthesis. In particular, muscular sensation, the sensation of tension or relaxation of the muscles, is important for the successful execution of the exercises of relaxation and for acquiring muscular skill. Olfactory evocations (e.g., the evocation of perfume) are also useful preparation for some of the later exercises in connection with symbol utilization. In contrast, gustatory and tactile evocations have no other purpose than the mere technical training of attention, observation and so on, which fall within the general aims of visualization.

Rationale

On the whole the rationale is the same as that for visualization. One may add that the fact of combining the evocation of the image with sensations derived from the different senses strengthens the association and the effect which one desires to produce. So, practice in the technique of evoking individually each of the sensory images is only preparatory to later combining them in exercises which will be described in the appropriate place.

The attempt at reinstatement or evocation of kinesthetic, tactile, gustatory, and olfactory sensations tends to give added vividness to the evocation of visual or auditory scenes or images. Also, the degree to which sensations occur spontaneously during the visualization of the scene or picture indicates the reality of the experience; and this becomes of particular importance in some of the exercises of symbolic visualization. It enables us to assess the degree to which the patient is actually experiencing the scenes that he is visualizing, or if he is simply going through an exercise lightly and on a superficial level.

Procedure

Here again the procedure is similar to that used for visualization and auditory images; but as tactile, gustatory, olfactory and kinesthetic images are generally weaker, their evocation can be made easier by having the patient actually experience the sensation and then immediately afterwards try to evoke it in imagination—just as was done in "mental photography." For instance:

For *tactile* sensations, ask the patient to pass his hand over the surface of a cold glass, or a fur, or, say, caress the back of a cat, and immediately afterwards try to do it in imagination over and over again until the ability to evoke tactile sensation is developed.

As regards *gustatory* sensation, some people who are very food and drink conscious have no difficulty in evoking the corresponding sensory images. For those who are not, we give them a cold drink with a marked flavor, or alternatively a hot drink of tea or coffee. Here, as we see in the tactile experiment, there is an association between the gustatory and the thermic sensations.

Similarly for *olfactory* sensation, we ask the patients to sniff a perfume, or better still a natural scent such as that of a rose or other flower with a strong perfume, and then we remove the stimulant and ask them to repeat the process in imagination—recalling as vividly as they can the special quality of the perfume.

Kinesthetic sensations which can have constructive application are those of an active kind; that is the awareness of right muscular tension—not too much and not too little, so to speak. There is a right and harmonious tension of the muscles necessary for any given action, one which gives a general subjective sensation of fitness and readiness to perform that action. This is probably achieved unconsciously by all athletes and sportsmen, but if it is done consciously it can be more effective. There can be a kind of "muscular anticipation," or the evocation of the kinesthetic sensations which will accompany the specific action.

We would mention here that a so-called "negative" kinesthetic sensation can also be useful, if limited to the exercise of relaxation, where one can usefully evoke the sensation of letting go muscular and nervous tension.

Indications and Applications

The general indication, and in a sense the most useful application, is for subjects or patients who have a deficient awareness of the body; i.e., for those who are so centered in their emotional life or, as in the case of some intellectuals, in their mental activity that they lose the sense of the relative value or even the reality of the physical body.

In contrast it is also indicated for those who take an antagonistic and a condemning attitude towards their bodies which, of course, is a familiar symptom in certain neuroses.

The value of this reintegration in consciousness of the body by means of these techniques of imaginative evocation lies in the fact that it is done "from above," so to speak, by the personal self who deliberately and actively assumes control of the physical body of expression. It is not being the prisoner of the body, having one's attention held by the body against one's will; it is, on the contrary, the personal will which first takes notice of and then control of one's necessary instrument of expression in the material world.

Another *exercise in tactile sensations* which we have found useful is the sensation of pressure. We ask the patient to become aware of the pressure of the band of his wrist-watch, and to attempt in imagination to follow the sensation all the way around the wrist. In many cases it will be found that this is a very difficult exercise, in that one may feel a certain amount of pressure in one part of the wrist but very little in another—particularly when the patient finally tries to become aware not only of the parts of the wrist which are pressured slightly by the wrist-band, but also of the total sensation. In general, awareness of muscular tension is useful in guarding against the tensions which often develop during one's work or other activities. As has been shown in many researches, a certain degree of tension in mental work is valuable, but too much uses up energy unnecessarily and may lead to headaches or even muscular spasms.

For this reason it is very useful for mental workers to practice a short relaxation every hour; short, so that the needed and right mental tension is not lost, and yet the body is freed from excessive tension. Such short relaxations depend on one's physical condition: if very tired, relax on a couch wherever possible; if not, stand up and move about. In both methods include deep breathing, but such relaxation should not be for more than five minutes. It provides a useful break, helps towards sustained work—a "second wind", so to speak; and those who are tense relax and those who are slack are helped to become active.

To produce an awareness of muscular tension is particularly

useful for individuals or patients who are chronically tense and yet do not realize the fact. So to help a patient to first recognize those parts of his body which are over-tense is an excellent preliminary and incentive to the practice of the exercise of relaxation. Many neurotics are quite unaware of how tense they are, and will often deny that they are tense at all. For this reason the therapist should observe the patient very carefully during the session and if he notices certain tensions it may often be valuable to pause and ask the patient if he feels tense; if he denies it, then ask him to carefully direct his attention to the parts of his body that you observe to be tense, so that he can become aware of what is going on at the muscular level.

Another way of making the patient aware of his tension is to tell him to lie down on a couch; but instruct him casually, without emphasizing the adoption of a restful attitude. When he has been lying down for a few minutes and thinks he is resting, you gently take him by the wrist and lift his arm for a little way and then without forewarning let it drop. What usually happens is that the arm does not drop freely, as if it were a dead weight, but more or less slowly. Then you can point out to him: "You see, you are not relaxed. If you had been, the arm would have fallen freely of its own weight, but in fact there was a muscular tension which prevented its doing so." This then serves as a prelude or introduction to the exercise of relaxation. At the end of the exercise you repeat the lifting of his arm—by which time it generally falls like a dead weight. If it does not, it is a sign that the patient did not succeed, or only partially, in the relaxation exercise.

The evocation of tactile sensation by means of caressing a piece of fur, of which we made mention earlier, is particularly useful, because the tactile sensation of fur is closely connected—at least on an unconscious level—with the basic feeling of warmth and closeness of contact that we received or should have received in our earliest infancy. As Dr. Klopfer has shown, and more recently Professor Harlow in his presidential address to the American Psychological Association, it is this feeling of warmth and closeness from which we derive our basic security. Klopfer has very imaginatively derived some of the interpretations of the Rorschach plates from this basic concept, and considers the reaction to shading as indicative of the way the individual reacts to the closeness of contact and the extent to which, and the way by which, his affectional anxiety has been resolved or left unresolved, repressed or denied. Therefore it is very interesting and revealing to ask a patient to give his subjective reactions while stroking a piece of fur; to use free associations, etc. Also to see whether this closeness of contact is something that the patient can do freely, whether he surrenders to it or reacts against it, attempts to avoid or denies it, or is disturbed by it. This may have very revealing diagnostic value and at the same time, as the patient repeatedly strokes the piece of fur (or imagines stroking it), there may be certain therapeutic values involved over and above the basic purpose of the technique.

Limitations and Contra-Indications

There is a definite contra-indication which should be taken into serious consideration. It concerns all those who already have a tendency to pay excessive attention to their physical sensations and consider them interesting or important, and who consequently would respond in the same way to their imaginary evocation. The more pronounced type, or rather class, of these people are the hypochondriacs—but cannot we say that all of us are to a small degree hypochondriacs, that we tend to give too much attention to physical sensations? There is the same contra-indication to the "autogene training" of Schultz in the case of hypochondriacs and also micro-hypochondriacs—because the "autogene training" tends to emphasize physical sensations too much, and in that sense may even become harmful.

Therefore, one should, in using these techniques, keep clearly in view their limited application; and that it is within the power of the self to evoke or dismiss at will images of every type of sensation. Then their use is constructive; but they should be limited as to the time spent on them, for they are after all secondary techniques, subservient to and useful for psychosynthetic exercises, but in themselves alone they have no real value.

We would like to re-emphasize the value of the negative aspect of these techniques, i.e., the ability to dismiss at will sensations and their images. Therefore, a refinement of the technique can be this: evoke a kinesthetic or other sensation for five seconds, then dismiss it from the field of consciousness for five seconds then again evoke it for five seconds, and then again exclude it, and repeat the process three or four times. By experiment one can see what length of time is right for each individual. One may have to use a slower rhythm, say ten instead of five seconds. The value of this is the development of the ability to evoke or to dismiss at will any content of the consciousness.

May we suggest that therapists experiment with these techniques themselves—it will give them useful experience in handling their patients, because we cannot be therapists in the full sense of the word unless we ourselves have experienced and struggled with every single one of the exercises of psychosynthesis. The ideal would be to undergo a didactic psychosynthesis; but when, for practical reasons, this is not possible, a therapist should really make a serious effort at a *self*-psychosynthesis. And a step towards that would be to do, either beforehand or at the same time as the patient, the particular technique or exercise we are asking him to undertake. This procedure has several advantages. The fact that the therapist himself does the exercise is a stimulus to the patient, who may feel that he is directly helped by this, either in a suggestive way or by osmosis or, one could say, "telepathically"; but even if there is no real "rapport influence" the suggestion—of the therapist doing the exercise—can be very strong and helpful.

Combination with Other Techniques

The most natural and useful combination is that with the technique of bio-psychosynthesis which includes all the active physical techniques. But another helpful combination is that with symbol utilization, where the combination of evoking various images coming from the various senses at once enhances the dynamic effect of the symbol utilized. More general associations have already been mentioned: with concentration, with awareness of the self as the directing and willing agent; and of course the strict relationship of this evocative technique with the "autogene training" of Schultz.

PLAN OF THE PSYCHOSYNTHESIS

After the assessment of the conscious aspects of the personality and the exploration of the unconscious — and generally after the use of some techniques for the preparation of the patient, such as the training of the will and the exercises in self-identification and visualization — comes the right moment for a definite planning of the level of the psychosynthesis to be achieved. First, the therapist has to consider and organize this plan. Then he has to decide how much or how little he will convey to the patient at this stage. This will vary greatly according to the cultural level, the condition of the patient and the troubles from which he is suffering. Therefore, no fixed rule can be given, except that generally the *goal* can be clearly indicated to the patient. It is good that he has a clear picture or vision of this as soon as possible. This is the image of himself as he can and eventually will be, when the psychosynthesis is achieved; in other words, that which we call the "ideal model" to which he will gradually conform.

An important and in some respects a critical moment of the therapy is that when its specific plan, as applied to a particular patient, has to be consciously defined. Various factors have to be considered: the first, already mentioned, is the plan of the psychosynthesis as thought through and outlined by the therapist to himself, for his own guidance in the work with the patient. The second is the plan as presented by the therapist to the patient.

Let us take up first *the plan of the therapist for himself*. It is the adaptation of the general pattern of psychosynthetic treatment not only to the diagnosis of the patient, to his cultural, intellectual level, etc., but also to those other factors which have nothing to do with the purely medical, psychological and scientific aspects of the treatment, such as the amount of time which can be given to the therapy, to the frequency of the sessions, and to the patient's family conditions. Although these are outside the scientific structure of psychosynthesis, in real life they intrude, sometimes in a disturbing way, and have to be taken into account in the planning of the psychosynthesis. To be more specific: a complete psychosynthesis, i.e., one as complete as possible from the scientific and ideal therapeutic standpoint, is very seldom possible of achievement, due to the personal limitations mentioned above. Therefore, the plan should be adapted to the existing conditions, and one of the tasks of the therapist is to see what is essential for adequate treatment of the patient, and therefore, which techniques are really necessary and which can be omitted without detriment.

One of the practical aspects in arriving at a plan and deciding on realistic goals to be reached by the patient during the therapy, is the capacity of the patient himself to benefit from psychotherapy. In this respect, patients vary very greatly in their intellectual and emotional reactions and these will have to be taken into consideration.

In view of the practical limitations it is valuable to consider what techniques could be taught to the patient, so that when the practical possibility of sessions with the therapist is exhausted, for financial or other reasons, the patient can at least—even in a limited way—continue on his own. For this purpose, the technique so chosen must be safe for use by the patient alone, and the patient himself must have progressed to a level which will enable him to use such techniques without harm to himself or others.

We would emphasize that the teaching of techniques to the patient and inducing, encouraging him to use them independently as soon as, and as much as, possible is a fundamental principle of psychosynthesis, independent of the aforesaid limitations. We consider a psychosynthetic treatment as going beyond its immediate medical usefulness and as presenting and introducing to the patient a dynamic conception of the psychological life, with its unlimited possibilities of development and self-realization. Therefore, at the end of the treatment, the instruction to the patient is: "You have seen the usefulness of psychosynthesis. Then go on and practice it throughout your whole life for the prevention of any recurrence of your troubles, and for a fuller, richer life and progressive self-realization."

After the therapist has been able to make first a tentative plan of the treatment then comes the second part, the problem of *how soon and how much of it to present to the patient*. The advantage of presenting a plan to the patient as soon as possible is that it gives him a clear picture of the next stages of the therapy and prepares the setting for the use of the Technique of the Ideal Model. Caution is needed not to present too wide a program to the patient, for this may be a source of discouragement to him. Here no general rule can be given, and the therapist must gauge how much the patient can receive and still retain a positive attitude to the plan.

Another problem in the planning is that of the respective amounts of definiteness and of plasticity in the plan, for one might err in both directions. We would advise, therefore, that it be made as definite as possible, because of the dynamic and the suggestive or creative effect of a clear picture; but be just as ready to modify it at any time, and even repeatedly, if some good and sufficient reason arises. Also the plan itself should be dynamic or, to put it another way, the therapist should have a definite picture of the goal, but also the partial plans of the various intermediary steps from the starting point to the achieving of the goal; and these can be plastic and modified according to new elements of judgment arising out of the dynamics of the treatment itself.

TECHNIQUE OF IDEAL MODELS

Purpose

The purpose is clear: that of utilizing the plastic, creative, dynamic power of images, particularly of visual images, which we examined in dealing with visualization. Here we emphasize the creative aspect of imagination in the sense that imagination creates mentally and emotionally, and then that which has been imagined and visualized is expressed outwardly through the use of natural means.

In therapy it is a process of substituting a realistic, attainable model for those already existing in the subject which do not have such qualities. We must become aware that each of us has within himself various self-models or models of the ego, or—more exactly, using our terminology—of the personality. Such models are not only diverse in nature, origin and vividness but they are in constant conflict between themselves, and this constitutes not only one of the major difficulties but is also one of the most useful fields of application of a right psychoanalysis. This awareness of the self-models is one of the purposes of psychoanalysis which we will touch upon in 'Combination with Other Techniques.'

Before dealing with the ideal model—of that which one can become—which is the true goal of this technique, we could classify in the following way the multiplicity of models which prevent or obscure our self-recognition of what we actually are at present:

1. What we *believe* we are. These models can be divided into two classes: those in which we over-evaluate ourselves, and those in which we under-evaluate ourselves.
2. What we *should like* to be. Here come all the idealized, unattainable models very well described by Karen Horney.
3. What we *should like to appear* to be to others. There are different models for each of our important interpersonal relationships.

This would seem at first appearance to exhaust the categories of models, but there are three other classes which are important and sometimes overpowering:

4. The models or the images that *others project on us;* that is, the models of what others believe us to be.
5. Images or models that others make of what they *would like us to be.*
6. Images which others *evoke and produce in us;* i.e., images of ourselves evoked by others.

We will clarify the last point because it is more obscure. The fourth and fifth classes are those of models which are projected on us but which we recognize as of "foreign" origin, so to speak, and which we do not accept and sometimes bitterly resent. Instead, those of the sixth class are the models which others succeed in making us accept, and therefore can be the most harmful.

7. There is finally the model of that which *we can become.* This constitutes the goal of the technique.

Before working with the patient on an ideal model, what we need to do first is to make the patient aware of all these models, which may be conflicting and some of which are largely unconscious. This brings in one of the deeper aspects of analysis; not so much to look for small traumas or small incidents of the past, but for the *dramatic, analytic situation of the present.* It is the present, existential situation of the patient, who—having these conflicting sub-personalities, models and ideals in himself—is at a loss how to deal with them. Some psychologists have called these models "self-images" or "self-concepts," but we suggest that a consideration of the various existing and conflicting models can be a rich and extremely valuable part of analytical work.

Rationale

The main point behind the rationale was mentioned in our discussion of the Technique for the Training and the Use of the Imagination, i.e., the utilization or taking advantage of the psychological law that every image has a motor-element which tends to be translated into action—which is a rather dry, objective way of indicating the creative power of imagination. This law was formulated by a pioneer of modern psychology, Théodule Ribot, in the first years of this century. The model must first be static and then "manifesting in motion." The stages are: first the *idea*, which if seen as desirable becomes an *ideal*, and when ardently sought after emerges or expresses itself in form and function. This definition, fully understood, removes the semantic confusion which has arisen in regard to the words "ideal" and "idealized." The frequent wrong connotation, of impracticality or unreality, should not deter the use of the designation "ideal" in speaking of the ideal model.

These stages of idea-ideal-form-function can be correlated with or are analogous to scientific or industrial blueprints preceding the manufacture of functioning models; or in some degree to gestalt field theories.

Procedure

There is no one "ideal model" but several, with diverse indications, as will be seen by their description. There is one which is being used unconsciously by most people all the time, that of an *external or indirect model*. This is the unconscious or conscious imitation of a human model, one who represents what is considered as desirable or who arouses admiration or represents an ideal. This falls within what is usually called "hero worship," because worship or admiration spontaneously and naturally evokes the urge to imitation. On the value and effectiveness of this technique Thomas Carlyle eloquently expressed himself in his well-known book *On Heroes and Hero-Worship*. Also we have Plutarch's *Lives*, which is a collection of hero-images, and *Representative Men* by Ralph Waldo Emerson. Hero worship which was much practiced in the past has, most unfortunately, been substituted in modern times by "idol-worship"—and by "idols" we designate those inferior models represented by some movie stars, sports and TV prize winners, successful businessmen irrespective of their character or moral stature, etc. Sometimes the external model chosen is a less ambitious and unrealistic person, some particular one whom we admire and who therefore creates a pattern to which we tend to conform. Perhaps such cases were more frequent in the past than the present: a person of one's own family—father, mother, or some other closely related adult; not infrequently one's teacher. In therapy the influence of the therapist, as a dynamic ideal model, can be used both constructively and destructively in the therapeutic relationship.

In utilizing this technique the first requirement is to discard unrealistic and unworthy models. But even when a model held by a patient is a good and helpful one, there are two pitfalls to be avoided in order that its influence may be really constructive. There should not be a passive or too close an imitation, because no one should become wholly like another. Some of the outstanding qualities of the model can be introjected, but not the whole of the personality characteristics.

The second danger to be avoided is a personal attachment to the human representative of the model. The model should be a model and not the living person. It should be an idea, an image, introjected, and not a personal attachment to the inspirer of the model. Often, at first, the two are connected, and rightly so. But gradually the process of introjection or subjectivation should take place, in order to dissolve the affective bond with the model-inspirer and to have the model become a dynamic, inner creative pattern.

How from a practical angle do we help the patient to discard an unrealistic or unworthy model?

The first step—which one could call the aggressive approach—is that of debunking the unworthy model: to show the reality behind the attractive mask, e.g., of a glamorous movie star, by showing all the human frailties of such a model-inspirer, drawing on biographical data to reveal the unhappiness and frustration of such a person. The same can be done for what has been called the "ideal of the animal man," i.e., the man wholly identified with his physical body, and only with that.

The therapist must not be afraid of a direct intervention and debunking of such idols, especially in this analytical or destructive stage of the treatment which is not directed to influencing the patient *towards* something, but to freeing him from hindrances to becoming his better self, his true self—this is an important point. We must be very cautious not to influence a patient according to our own ideal, of ourselves or of him; but every active, even aggressive, help in freeing him from limitation and the many kinds of images which keep him in bondage is of value.

The debunking of the "Hollywood-star-ideal" for instance—showing the hard facts behind the facade, through objective biographical details—is in no way a counselling. It is an active intervention by the therapist, not a counselling in the strict sense of the word, because it does not indicate in what direction the patient should now go, but shows him what are impossible or dangerous by-paths into which he could be induced to go.

We now come to the wholly conscious and direct use of the technique of the ideal model, that is, of the patient *visualizing himself* as possessing the qualities which it is good or necessary to develop and to build into himself. This is a very well defined model. It is not a general model of perfection, of complete psychosynthesis, but the model which represents the next and most urgent step or stage—that of developing an undeveloped psychological function, focussing on a single specified quality or small group of qualities, or abilities which the patient most needs in order to achieve, and even to proceed with, his psychosynthesis. He is asked to visualize himself in possession of that particular quality or actively using that particular psychological function. The visualization should be as vivid and "alive" as possible. The patient is taught and trained to see himself in a definite situation in which he wills to express and to put into action the needed quality.

With the help of the therapist, a form of dramatization can be developed, in which the subject sees himself in action and playing several roles. For example: each role implies personal relationships; therefore we can suggest to the patient that he visualize a scene fitting for each of the roles, functions or sub-personalities; e.g., a scene in which the subject plays successfully and satisfactorily the role of son or husband, of father or a professional or social role, etc. In playing a particular role the subject, by just imagining that he is playing it successfully, brings into action qualities which up till then had not been sufficiently developed. This, in effect, becomes a psychodrama-play-technique *in imagination,* and if well performed it has many, if not all, the advantages of actual psychodrama without its practical difficulties of execution.

Since, for many practical and therapeutic reasons, there is a choice of functions or qualities that we may select for development in each phase of the therapy, *how do we help the patient choose a particular function or quality upon which to concentrate?* This is a practical question. It is related to the stage of planning which we discussed previously. In the planning, both therapist and patient agree which part of the program to take up first, and this includes the choice of the functions or qualities to be developed through this technique of model-building and acting.

How is the technique presented to the patient? As simply as possible, for almost all are able to understand if it is presented in clear simple terms. We first tell him of the goal and the rationale of the technique. We assure him that it is very effective if practiced well, and then with him we build up the blueprint, the model. Frequently it is a collaboration, in which the therapist tentatively presents the outline of the model and asks if it is acceptable; or he suggests to the patient that he can modify it, and especially that he complete it more "concretely." The therapist then gives his approval and the patient starts in the same session to build a model with the active help of the therapist, who assures the patient that he too is building the same model with and for him. As we previously said, this active cooperation is encouraging, suggestive if not actually influencing.

As a practical procedure, it is generally preferable to carry out this technique with the eyes closed. We also favor that the patient be sitting, not lying down, since this is not an analytic technique to bring forth unconscious elements, but rather a conscious technique of building that which one has decided is advisable to build—with the "I" or self in control. In general, we limit the couch to analytical procedures and to relaxation exercises; and all the rest of the treatment is made with the patient sitting more or less in front of, or sideways to the therapist, which gives a more normal situation for interpersonal relationships and favors a quick interchange between patient and therapist—also, it has the advantage of eliminating all passive half-dreaming attitudes and reminds the patient that what is required of him is the action of his conscious self using his will.

Regarding the time to be given to this exercise in a session, it depends on the patient's ability for persistent concentration. In general we put the emphasis on the vividness and intensity of the visual evocation and not on its prolongation—because a very vivid image can have an instantaneous effect; just as a photograph taken in bright sunlight immediately impresses the film, so a very vivid image immediately imprints the plastic aspect of the unconscious. It is a vivid, short, repeated evocation; and it is useful to repeat it over and over again. By "repeat" we mean that we ask the patient to do this himself at least once every day, and also a few times in each session. As to how long this process needs to be continued—realizing, of course, that much depends on individual cases—we could say that the evocation of some form of ideal model should go on during the whole of one's life, changing the model periodically in order to develop successively various needed functions.

How is the desired model worked through into action? In other words, how do we help the patient translate images into concrete reality, or how can we help the patient to translate the desired good into actual altered behavior?

The first step requires the active will of the patient, encouraged by the therapist. The therapist can say: "Now you see that in imagination you can perform the role, be the model, quite easily, without those disturbing emotional and psychosomatic reactions. That shows that the ground is free. Now go ahead—live and relive it in imagination and then seek to play it in reality; you can go ahead with a good prospect of success." Sometimes we add "What can further help you is not to care so much about the results. Just try, make the experiment in a detached attitude. If you do not succeed this time, you will succeed the next." This experimenting can also be modified; for instance, if the patient is a performer, a musician, we can say "Just try to give your performance before a small group of friends and see what happens; and then, if you find out that it is possible to do this, then repeat the performance before a larger public." In short, the translation process is this: an active will, an experimental detached attitude and, if possible, a playful attitude, so that the subject can always focus his greatest interest on the experiment itself and not on the practical results. This latter point can be a great help.

At a somewhat advanced stage of the treatment we suggest a further use of the technique, i.e., that of a *general model*, a model of the whole new psychosynthesized personality. That, of course, requires much previous training and, being more complex, demands a little longer time for each visualization. The patient is asked to visualize himself as the new, whole-functioning, self-actualized being with the aim and the reward of completed (always in a relative sense) psychosynthesis. This includes the subject feeling himself integrated, freed from both his symptoms and his outstanding deficiencies, harmonized with the various functions, the various roles he has to play, not conflicting but cooperating in a many-sided, rich life.

This is a general model, the general pattern of a self-actualized individual. Each patient in cooperation with the therapist can make it more definite within, of course, the limits of his empirical possibilities.

Indications and Applications

These are very extensive. In all walks of life one sees the importance, even the need, of clear planning, preparing exact blueprints and even scale models of what one wants to create or build. There is exactly the same need in psychological and psychosynthetic purposes, and the same general procedure can and should be extensively used. Here, too, clear planning and a definite pattern are among the chief elements of success. Therefore all the required time, attention and concentration should be dedicated to this essential and often neglected phase of therapy and psychosynthesis, of education and self-realization.

In other words, this technique is indicated practically for every psychosynthesis and for all patients, because it is a necessary stage in all psychotherapeutic procedures.

Limitations and Contra-Indications

In apparent contrast to the "universal" indications just mentioned there is one important contra-indication of this technique. It is not really a contra-indication, in the sense of not using it at all, but in the sense of using it only after or at the final stage of another technique. These specific cases—quite frequent—are those in which there are present in the subject, more or less consciously, drives or attitudes which are in direct contrast to the model or pattern to be visualized and then realized. When there is this counter-current, so to speak, it would be a mistake to try to force upon a patient, to superimpose as it were, the ideal model or pattern. The result would be either a repression in the unconscious, with the well-known harmful effects, or the arousing of an active opposition which would forfeit or make difficult the success of the technique we are considering.

To give specific examples: when the subject has an intense fear or even a phobia of performing a certain action, or he takes a certain set attitude under certain circumstances. For instance, a student before an examination, an actor or a singer before a public performance, an employee before an interview with his boss. In all these cases where the emotion is intense it would not be possible to visualize over and over again perfect behavior in the given situation, repressing the fear or anxiety. The same can be said in visualizing an ideal of loving behavior towards some individual or group when there are in the subject strong hostile or aggressive drives against the same people. In these cases the technique would be preceded by the use of another one which has also great value in itself. This is the technique of imaginative training and desensitization described on pp. 226–28.

In other words, what one needs to do first, is to have the patient imagine, visualize himself, with some of his defects and undesirable traits, in the situation which is feared or avoided; this is needed to bring forth to consciousness those elements which should be worked through before the more desirable pattern is introduced and reinforced. To be more precise, the patient has to visualize himself in the given situation and then if, spontaneously, emotions of fear or anger come up, the patient tries not to fight them. This is the point: *not to fight them* but to be permissive, to accept and to experience them. And this has to be done over and over again for a sufficient number of times, for in doing this there is a spontaneous—not forced—freeing of what could be called "psychological allergy," and after a sufficient number of times the patient without any effort finds himself free from the negative emotions. Then he is in a position to perform effectively the technique of the ideal model.

This confirms one of the essential procedures of general psychosynthesis; that is, a right succession and combination of all that is best of psychoanalytical procedure and the best of the active techniques. Up to now, unfortunately, in most cases they have been adapted separately.

The above is an example of how an active Technique of Imagination and Visualization can be used for analytical purposes to bring forth into consciousness elements which heretofore were not fully accepted by the individual and therefore partly repressed.

The technique of visualization first serves as a discovery of these drives and tendencies, then as a catharsis or elimination, and thirdly as the active development of the opposite positive trends.

If we started with only the positive trend we would not really deal therapeutically with the situation. This explains the chief deficiency in emphasizing only the positive, forgetting and neglecting the negative aspects of human nature. This partially justifies the hostilities in certain circles against the more superficial optimistic advice given for peace of mind and so on.

The important point is that we need to deal in imagination with the negative aspects of the individual before we can fully impress the progressive desired good, although the desired good may be in mind before the negative aspects are brought up into consciousness. This brings to mind the difficulty that is often experienced with many patients when we ask them to visualize themselves having positive or so-called "constructive qualities." One part of them—the better part, so to speak—would like to acquire the good or at least express it more fully, but after doing this exercise of the ideal model once or twice they give it up. When this happens, it indicates that there are certain forces in the individual which run counter to the constructive tendencies, and these resistances need to be dealt with.

Combination with Other Techniques

A special combination is that with planning, because a concrete plan, not abstract general planning, implies a clear visual pattern of the end to be achieved. The other special combination, that just mentioned, is with the technique of active imaginative training.

In effect, there are two phases to the combination. In the first phase planning is done with the patient; in the second, visualization of desired qualities and situations. The visualization may bring up certain resistances; and even without resistances it may be useful to have the patient visualize himself in certain situations, such as being with his parents or children or his mate, and also at work; this may bring out certain negative reactions—which could be partly dealt with by the technique of imaginative training before going back again to the previous stage of the model of the desired goal. This means that you do not necessarily separate the techniques of the stages; e.g., "Now I am going to concentrate on planning, now I am going to concentrate on the visualization of situations which may bring forth negative—but also positive—reactions." It is a kind of fluid combination of all stages so that from the different points the patient progresses. He progresses in awareness and clarification of a realizable goal, and he also progresses in the awareness of those aspects in himself of which he was afraid, so that he can accept them and incorporate them better because the constructive aspect is also being reinforced.

In other words this is one of the specific procedures of psychosynthesis: what could be called a moving back and forth between the various stages and in the use of various techniques. It is a fractioned psychoanalysis or a partial use of a technique and then a passing to others; then a coming back again to a further stage in the use of that technique. This working in a fluid way might seem at first to be lacking order, but is in fact obedient to a higher order of organic development.

Another procedure in psychosynthesis is the use of not only verbal material but also imaginative visualized material, and any therapist who has really had experience in this process begins to realize that he is dealing with a very powerful technique, which because of its power represents both opportunities and dangers, and for which he must be fully prepared. Only those therapists who, if not at peace, are at least fairly comfortable with their own unconscious material (which sometimes is of a primitive kind) can be at home with similar processes in the patient, without imposing a rigid structure on what goes on.

This brings up again a point which cannot be emphasized enough: the thorough psychosynthetic preparation of the therapist himself. As to the points of danger, we recall those—well described by Jung—of the invasion of the consciousness by strong images from the unconscious, especially the deeper levels which he calls the "Collective Unconscious," and which contain the archetypal images.

TECHNIQUE OF SYMBOL UTILIZATION

Purpose

The purpose of this technique is to utilize the enormous and by far not yet realized potency of symbols in the dynamics of the psychological life. Symbols are constantly being used by everyone but generally in an unconscious way and often in unconstructive and even harmful ways. Therefore one of the urgent needs of therapy—and of education—is the realization of the nature and power of symbols, the study of the many classes and kinds of symbols, and their systematic utilization for therapeutic, educational, and self-realization purposes.

Apart from and in addition to this general, one could almost say universal, purpose of symbols in human life, there is a specific purpose for their use in psychosynthesis, because there are symbols which have a specific psychosynthetic integrating value and therefore directly serve the purpose of bringing about psychosynthesis, both in the individual and in groups.

Rationale

The rationale of the use of symbols is based on their nature and on their function, or rather functions. Let us first consider symbols from the psychodynamic standpoint.

Their primitive and basic dynamic function is that of being accumulators, in the electrical sense, as containers and preservers of a dynamic psychological charge or voltage. Their second function, a most important one, is that of transformers of psychological energies. A third function is that of conductors or channels of psychological energies. From the qualitative point of view symbols can be considered as images or signs of psychological realities of many kinds. (In C.G. Jung, *Psychological Types*, p. 601, Jung makes a distinction between signs and symbols.)

Symbols as accumulators, transformers, and conductors of psychological energies, and symbols as integrators, have most important and useful therapeutic and educational functions. And this can be considered also in reference to psychodynamics because integration is really a function of energy, specifically the function of what has been called syntropy as contrasted with entropy. Syntropy means a heightening of the tension of the voltage of psychological and also biological energy. The whole principle and theory of syntropy has been well expounded by the mathematician Fantappié.

In a sense it is a complete system of ingathering, storing, transforming, and finally of utilizing energies. The normal succession of the psychodynamic efficiency of the symbol is that of attracting psychological energies, storing them, subsequently transforming them, and then utilizing them for various purposes — particularly for the important one of integration.

Coming back to the qualitative nature and value of symbols it is well to make as clear as possible the relationship between the symbol and the reality which it represents. This relationship is based mainly, if not exclusively, on analogy. Analogy, we might say, is an important psychological link or connection between outer and inner realities. Analogy can be and has been much misused, or used in exaggerated and unreal ways. This was especially so during the Middle Ages, and this has produced a reaction, a devaluation, and even a rejection of it especially in science. But as it is a normal and really unavoidable psychological activity, the result has been — to use a colloquialism — "to throw out the baby with the bathwater," to renounce a precious avenue for knowledge.

One of the ways in which analogy can systematically be used is in attempting to find new and unusual relationships and to find hypotheses—or ways of looking at things—which one did not have before. It is a method which is full of rich possibilities for creativity, not only in an artistic sense and from a humanistic viewpoint, but also from a scientific standpoint. Of course, it needs to be followed by a systematic use of analytical thinking in order to check the value of the analogy. One can use analogy as a method for getting new and fresh slants on almost every subject. It can be systematically carried out and pays rich rewards, provided one is not carried away by the process. It is linked with that part of the creative process which one might call the "loosening stage," when one allows the unconscious to bring new and creative relationships; and then it has to be followed by a "tightening" process of checking and analytical thought. We cannot go further into this at this point since it finds its proper place as one of the techniques for creativity. But to put it in other words, every scientific hypothesis and every scientific model is in reality a symbol based on analogy, and the best modern scientists are well aware of this. Analogy is heuristic in function and nature, and gives a relative and not a "photographic" or exact picture of reality—which we never have anyway!

The possible and desirable integration of the various fields of knowledge by the method of analogy, and the methods of verification, systematization and incorporation of the body of knowledge, is quite parallel to that between intuition and intellect. In fact intuition is, among other things, an organ for the discovery of analogies.

The effect and unavoidability—if one can use such a word—of symbols is brought vividly to our consciousness by the direct recognition that *all words are symbols*. They are, so to speak, stenographic, condensed symbols. This is clearly shown by two words much used in psychology and in religion: "anima" and "spirit." "Anima" comes from the Greek "anemos" which means "wind." It is interesting to note that the word "spirit" has just the same symbolic meaning. "Spirit" comes from the Latin "spiritus," which originally meant "breath" or "wind."

Part of the rationale of symbol utilization is to revive symbols, to recognize the dynamic possibilities of words and images, which normally are taken at their face value instead of having the function of evoking the hidden realities behind them. The universal rationale of symbols was clearly condensed by Goethe in his famous verse at the end of "Faust":

> *Alles Vergängliche ist nur ein Gleichnis.*
> *(All which is temporary is only a symbol.)*

Another aspect of the rationale of symbol utilization is their effect upon the unconscious. Symbols can be visualized and this sets into motion unconscious psychological processes. This is an effective means for the transformation of the unconscious. To address the unconscious in logical terms is not particularly effective. In order to reach the unconscious, as in reaching any person — especially women and children, as Jung pointed out — we have to speak in its own terms. One should attempt to use the mode in which the unconscious normally operates, which is by way of symbols.

Besides the fact that symbols in themselves have integrating value — in other words, integrate within the unconscious itself — the technique of consciously utilizing symbols by visualizing them achieves a further integration between the conscious and the unconscious elements of the personality, and to a certain extent between the logical mind and the unconscious non-logical aspects of the person. Jung has said that symbols are transformers of psychic energy. This may be correct not just as a metaphor but in terms of actual psychological energies. Therefore, what we can do is to observe the results of the presentation of certain symbols to the unconscious of our patients, and then see if the setting in motion of certain unconscious forces produces a transformation of the outer personality.

Procedure

Procedures for the utilization of symbols are based on the knowledge and use of three ways of utilization of seven groups of symbols. The three ways are the following:

1. Presenting, offering, or suggesting the use of a definite symbol out of the first six classes or groups of symbols, which are enumerated below.

2. Fostering, or taking advantage of the appearance of, spontaneous symbols in the course of treatment, a procedure which was widely used by Jung.

3. An intermediate way, that used by Desoille, who in his method of the "rêve éveillé" first suggests a symbol, mainly that of ascending and of descending, and then lets the patient develop freely his own subsidiary symbols. This method, used ably as Desoille does, can give very good therapeutic results.

These three ways can be used alternatively and the skilled therapist will try all three with each patient and then put the emphasis on the one which reveals itself as being most fruitful. In the third method, of combination—suggesting symbols and allowing the patients to go on with their own subsidiary symbols—we may also include the techniques of Leuner and of Happich.

Symbols which may be presented to the patient can be divided into seven main categories. As this is a pragmatic classification, some symbols are included in more than one category. In general, only those symbols which have positive value for psychosynthesis are presented to the patient and are therefore listed here; for many negative symbols will have already emerged spontaneously during the analytical phase of the treatment.

1. Nature Symbols:

These include air, earth, fire, water; sky, stars, sun, moon. Among the chief nature symbols are the mountain (with its correlated technique of "ascent"), sea, stream, river, lake, pond, wind, cloud, rain, fogs; cave, tree, flames and fire, wheat, seed, flowers (rose, lotus, sunflower, etc.); jewel, diamond and various symbols related to light (including sunrise, sunset, rays of light, etc.) and darkness (including shadow), etc.

2. Animal Symbols:

Lion, tiger, snake, bear, wolf, bull, goat, deer, fish, worm-chrysalis-butterfly (as symbols of transformation); birds (eagle, dove, etc.); domestic animals (horse, elephant, dog, cat, etc.); and the egg.

3. Human Symbols:

a. *General human symbols:* Father, mother, grandfather, grandmother, son, daughter, sister, brother; child, wise old man, magician, king, queen, prince, princess, knight, teacher; the human heart, the human hand, the eye. Birth, growth, death, and resurrection.

b. *Modern human symbols:* These include the mountain-climber, the explorer (including the space explorer), the pioneer, the scientific investigator (physicist, chemist, etc.), the automobile-driver, the aviator, the radio or TV technician, the electronics engineer, etc.

4. Man-made Symbols:

Bridge, channel, reservoir, tunnel, flag, fountain, lighthouse, candle, road, path, wall, door, house, castle, stairway, ladder, mirror, box, sword, etc.

5. Religious and Mythological Symbols:

a. *Universal and Western Religious Symbols:* God, the Christ, the Holy Mother, angels, the devil, saints or holy men, priest, monk, nun, resurrection, hell, purgatory, heaven, the Grail, temple, church, chapel, the cross.
b. *Eastern Symbols:* Brahma, Vishnu, Shiva, the Buddha, etc.
c. *Mythological Symbols:* Pagan gods, goddesses and heroes: Apollo, the Muses (symbols of the arts and sciences), the three Graces (symbols of femininity in its refined sense), Venus, Diana (symbol of the woman who refuses her femininity), Orpheus, Dionysus, Hercules, Vulcan, Pluto, Saturn, Mars, Mercury, Jupiter. Wotan, Siegfried, Brunhilde, Valhalla, the Nibelungen, the Valkyries, etc.

6. Abstract Symbols:

a. *Numbers:* In the Pythagorean sense of psychological significance—for instance, one symbolizing unity; two—polarity; three—interplay, etc.
b. *Geometrical Symbols:*
Two-dimensional: Dot, circle, cross (various forms, such as the mathematical plus sign, the long-limbed Christian cross, the St. Andrews Cross or multiplication sign), the equilateral triangle, the square, the diamond, the star (five-pointed, six-pointed, etc.).
Three-dimensional: the sphere, cone, cube; the ascending spiral, etc.

7. Individual or Spontaneous Symbols:

These emerge during treatment or spontaneously in dreams, day-dreams, etc.

Of course, not all the numerous symbols can and should be used with every patient. That would require months, even years, and is not at all necessary for therapeutic purposes. Some classes of symbols are more suitable, more evocative, than others for different types of people, different conditions, different cultural backgrounds, different sets, different ages; and one of the tasks of the therapist is to choose those which—either obviously or after a few sample trials—prove to be the most useful and fruitful for therapeutic purposes. Also in various stages of the treatment different groups of symbols should be used.

How do we present these different symbols to the patient? There are three main ways: firstly, by simply naming the symbol or giving a short description of it; secondly, by observation, i.e., presenting to the patient a drawing or image of the symbol in question; and, thirdly, by visualization, i.e., asking the patient to visualize, evoke an inner image of the symbol. This latter procedure is needed for dynamic symbols, i.e., for symbols of action, which undergo transformation and pass through different stages.

The first procedure, of naming or description, is sufficient for very simple symbols; e.g., for geometrical symbols. Also it is the best for human symbols of a universal character such as father, mother, child, etc. These should remain general symbols, i.e., we point out their psychological meaning, and explain that they must not be defined in relation to a personal image—which might influence the patient adversely in various ways.

Observation, the second method, is used for more complicated symbols; e.g., symbols of natural scenery, or others which have numerous details and would take too long to describe or be difficult for some patients to actively visualize. For instance, we may present a picture of a meadow, including perhaps trees and a mountain, or a temple or other subjects which have a manifold structure.

In symbol presentation, requesting the patient to draw a particular symbol is a very good method and advantageous for all subjects who do not feel inhibited by being requested to draw. Many patients are, but they can be trained to overcome this resistance by assuring them that we pay no attention whatever to any artistic value nor give aesthetic consideration to their drawings, and that they are purely psychological documents.

In the sessions the time taken by the patient to draw may be more usefully spent doing something else, and in many cases we encourage patients to draw at home. The Technique of Free

Drawing is used also for other purposes—e.g., for the purposes of expression and catharsis; when the patient has trained himself in free expression by drawing, then in a further stage, that of the Technique of Symbol Utilization, we have the channel already prepared.

There is in theory a difference between static and dynamic symbols, but in practice, as often happens, the nice clear-cut theoretical classification does not obtain or have any relevant value. For instance, often when we present a static symbol, the symbol spontaneously becomes dynamic and changes under the inner eye of the subject, even against his will. In many such cases, one encourages the autonomous free development of the symbol.

In other cases we give instructions to the effect that the symbol should be dynamic, i.e., should develop and represent an action performed in the dimension of time. A very simple instance of this, but which has a particular therapeutic, and more exactly a psychoanalytic, meaning and utility, is that of undoing with patience a tangled knot. The meaning is obvious.

Another significant example is the building of a house or, even better, a temple. This symbol often exists in the collective unconscious and is meaningful and effective. A human, dynamic symbol that is full of meaning and which can be really transforming, is that of awakening: the passing from sleep to waking consciousness—and waking consciousness has various degrees of clarity, of perception, of insight. This has been widely used, but more specifically in the East, where the very name "Buddha" means "the awakened one." His personal name was Gautama, but his title was "the Buddha"—the awakened or enlightened, or the perfectly awakened one.

Some dynamic symbols, having various stages, constitute indeed a whole psychological exercise and therefore we will describe them separately in the section on psychological exercises (see p. 207).

Indications and Applications

Because of its importance and usefulness, this technique—with rare exceptions—can and should be used in every case; but the great problem in the use of symbols is the specific indication for each class of patients, for each patient, and for each stage of the treatment.

A general indication, of course, is that the choice of the symbol should be such that it is suited for the specific present problem or task of the patient. Here come in the experience, the skill, and even more, the intuition of the therapist.

Some symbols (i.e., *bridge* or *mountain*) clearly indicate a definite relationship with the patient's problem; and some human symbols indicate clearly that they are suited to certain interpersonal problems. A full discussion of the indications would require a book in itself, and cannot be undertaken here; but even a most detailed explanation can never take the place of the intuition and the psychological insight of the therapist. Here comes a clear indication for the therapist; that it is very useful for him, also, to have used the standard symbols, or at least one or two of each category, himself.

There is a class of symbols which have a special current indication, i.e., the series of *Modern Human Symbols,* which we listed earlier. From a certain point of view they have the disadvantage of being, or appearing to be, too prosaic and matter-of-fact, but in reality they are not so. It is interesting to observe how these matter-of-fact symbols excite the imagination of teen-agers and adolescents much more than what we have called "imaginative" symbols. Young people identify themselves easily, often spontaneously, with the modern "heroes," such as the aviator, the explorer of space. These arouse something very vital in them, a kind of model; they are symbols of daring, of adventure—sometimes of evasion of everyday life. Therefore they satisfy fundamental drives which have emerged with particular intensity in the present generation of teenagers and the young.

Some of these modern symbols have another great psychological advantage; they bring out clearly the right relationship between man and the machine—man as the builder, controller, master of the machine. The driver is the master of his automobile; he first chooses his destination, maps the successive stages of the route and then, seated comfortably in the driver's seat and with little physical effort, he makes the automobile his obedient, efficient tool or means for reaching his goal. This relationship can be easily introjected, i.e., the automobile can easily be considered and realized—we could almost say "lived"—as the symbol of the body and even of the whole personality, which the conscious self through his intelligent planning and his will can make an instrument for attaining his goal, plans, and intentions.

The use of modern technology for therapeutic purposes is a vast field of application which is still at its very beginning. In future methods of psychotherapy perhaps special short motion pictures will be made, to present certain symbolic scenes in action, which the patient can then respond to and identify with. This is already common practice in personnel training.

Animal symbols can be used both diagnostically to find out with which particular animal the individual identifies, and also as means of evoking certain needed psychological traits. The technique of Hanscarl Leuner, for instance, of asking the patient to visualize himself in a meadow, looking towards the edge of the woods, and waiting until some animal comes out of the woods, allows for the choice of the animal to come from the unconscious of the patient. And from this choice certain psychological characteristics can be surmised, characteristics represented by the traits usually associated with this animal.

Instead of the earlier mentioned symbol of the automobile, we can—for some people—use the horse. This is an even more evocative symbol, because there are the stages of first the wild horse, then its taming, followed by its utilization and the right affectionate relationship between the man and the horse; all of which symbolize the right way of treating the physical body, mastering it but not maltreating or condemning it. This was indicated with delightful humor by St. Francis when he spoke affectionately of his body as "brother ass."

The subject of the symbol of *Fire* or *Flame* is so alluring and vast that one can become seduced by it and enmeshed in the enchanted world of symbolism. There is a tremendous amount of research work to be done in the utilization of symbols, so here we will only give enough to indicate certain specific applications.

Fire is one of the most ancient and most effective symbols. Incidentally, this suggests that we might add to the list of mythological symbols that of Prometheus, who stole fire from heaven. On the purely human level it is a symbol of heat, of protection from cold, and defense from wild animals for primitive man. Also it is a symbol of transformation processes—of cooking, of the changing and purification of raw materials and minerals; therefore it is an important chemical symbol connected with transmutation and sublimation. Further, it is a symbol of destruction, of danger; and finally it is one of the purest—if not the purest of all—symbols of the spirit, both the spirit in man ascending toward the universal spirit, and of "fire coming down from heaven."

One of the very important symbols is the *human heart*, which has been mentioned by Blackwell. A fruitful way to use this symbol is to ask the patient to visualize a huge heart, bigger than himself, and in this heart a door. Then ask the patient to open the door and to enter into the heart. What he finds there varies with each patient. But the actual use of this symbol, as a technique, reveals the importance of the ability of the therapist in handling it. It is a technique which, to be really or most effective, cannot be done in a mechanical routine way; for, step by step, the therapist has to decide intuitively which is his part in leading the imaginative scene. Here, for the therapist, is the razor-edged path—so to speak—between being too passive on the one hand and being overly suggestive in indicating images, on the other. He should indicate only the minimum amount of imagery which helps the patient's unconscious to bring forth further imagery.

Another technique of symbol utilization which is full of possibilities uses the symbol of the *door*. The door, of course, may represent an entrance into a new life or life-cycle; and one of the ways in which it can be used is to ask the patient to visualize a door, sometimes a door in a high wall or in a house, depending upon the situation, and on the door to visualize a word. Sometimes the choice of the word may be left to the patient, especially for analytical purposes, and has therefore a symbolic significance at that stage of therapy. At other times the word may be suggested by the therapist: e.g., "fear," "worry," "anxiety," or "doubt," etc., and at other stages of the therapy, positive words such as "hope," "peace," or "love." The possibilities are endless, of course. The patient is then asked to open the door, and what is found on the other side of the door has sometimes very profound significance. A very good description of the use of such symbols is given in the valuable article by Robert Gerard on *Symbolic Visualization* (which may be obtained from the Psychosynthesis Research Foundation, New York).

Another class of symbols is the group of *childhood symbols*. These are very interesting and, used with skill, can be very helpful from the following angle: they refer to the pre-psychotic stage or state of the patient, and so link him up with the normal part of him which at present is hidden or submerged by the psychotic inrush. Therefore, it must be a symbol through which the therapist may come into contact with, and emphasize and encourage, the normal part of the personality.

Mauz discussed the use of symbols in psychotherapy to evoke positive feelings, in an article "The Psychotic Man in Psychotherapy", published in 1948 in the *Archiv für Psychiatrie*. He used early childhood images which would evoke positive feelings, images such as "Christmas Eve" and "Christmas," a carousel and flying balloons, a parade at a festival, a river at sunrise; he also mentions a song from a children's songbook, and so on. He stresses that the therapist should relate these themes to the patient as much as possible, using the patient's own words and images taken from the patient's own history. In this respect the technique would then become not only one of using symbols but complete symbolic scenes, and is in effect an extension of symbol utilization.

Here we would add a general remark about the *functioning and results of symbols*. In addition to the kind of symbols just mentioned, which have an "opening up" effect, so to speak, or a clearing out and positively stimulating effect, there are many symbols which act as a bridge between the personal and spiritual psychosynthesis. Of course, in practice, there is no sharp distinction; and in using the symbols just mentioned certain aspects of the procedure have themselves a bridging effect. To be more exact, there are two main ways of arriving at spiritual psychosynthesis: One could be called the abrupt, dramatic way, as seen in cases of religious conversion and in the forms of sudden illumination or awakening—and the latter is the technique used in an extreme way by Zen-Buddhism. But in many cases, and perhaps at present in the majority of cases, there is instead a gradual development from the integrated personality towards the inclusion of superconscious elements, a gradual approach of the personal self-consciousness towards the spiritual Self, from self-identity in the personal sense to spiritual realization. Therefore in therapy—and also in education—the preferred and more general way to be encouraged, and to which the patient has to be helped, is the gradual one, which presents several advantages which it is not necessary to enumerate. The use of symbols often spontaneously produces this development from a personal psychosynthesis to at least a beginning of spiritual psychosynthesis. It is well to keep this in mind. Later, when we deal with spiritual psychosynthesis, we will speak of symbols of the Self and other symbols which have only, or predominantly, a spiritual significance and effect.

Limitations and Contra-Indications

Taking up first the contra-indications one may say, paradoxically enough, that this technique is contra-indicated, or at least to be used with great care and within limits, with those subjects for whom symbolism is the line of least resistance, who have a spontaneous production or over-production of symbols. The reason is that in these cases symbols represent an escape from reality and a substitution for normal life, for functioning in ordinary life. This is outstanding in a certain class of psychotics who, as Jung has stated and as each of us may confirm, give most interesting cosmological and cosmic symbols of great theoretical meaning, but of little therapeutic use. This is also true in a lesser degree for a number of introverted psychoneurotics. Therefore, in those cases this technique has to be used with discretion, and with them a symbol should always be used as a bridge to outer reality and not as a way to keep the interest and the attention in the inner world of phantasy.

The limitation of this method concerns types opposite to those just mentioned. This method is difficult to apply and gives scanty results with subjects of the opposite psychological make-up— extremely extraverted or very intellectual—who have a very objective attitude in their conscious personality and little or no communication with their unconscious. These people dislike symbols, or at least symbols do not appeal to them; they can perform in a mechanical way the technique or exercise as suggested, and very easily too, but they do not find interest in it. The symbol does not give results because there is a separation between the conscious personality which looks outward and the unconscious which remains unexpressed. To speak colloquially: the conscious and the unconscious turn their backs to each other. In such cases this technique can be attempted only at a later stage of the treatment, when the excess of extraversion has been corrected and a certain degree of communication has been established between conscious and unconscious activities.

What we have mentioned in connection with extremely extraverted patients also applies to very rigidly compulsive individuals, who often have very little symbolic activity; yet it is for these individuals that the technique can be particularly useful in loosening up, so to speak, their rigidity. But here also it can only succeed after other bridges have been created; for instance, the development of the undeveloped or inferior functions of emotion, feeling and imagination in general—and then encouraging their use specifically in the domain of symbols. The same is true for the over-intellectuals, the over-sophisticated; those who are proud of their mental cleverness are blocked or create blocks in the use of this technique.

In *borderline psychotics* this technique has to be used with great caution. For example, even the most apparently innocuous symbols may suddenly assume a threatening aspect.

This brings us to a general observation about the problem facing the therapist of the choice of the technique to be used, among the many available. And here we would mention the Rorschach Test: we quite appreciate its usefulness for typology or differential psychology and for diagnostic purposes. Its drawbacks are only of a practical nature, i.e., it takes much time both to perform and to correctly analyze the results; and there is a danger of becoming over-technical, too much interested in all the details, the formulas and percentages of the results. Therefore it seems to us that it belongs more to the psychological laboratory than in psychotherapeutic sessions. And in many cases it appears that the use of simple symbols gives more quickly, and as fully, the same result as a more laborious and technical Rorschach. This is a consideration which therapists should keep in mind — not to become too much interested and side-tracked by the technique, by theoretical interest, by the ideal of perfection, but to remain close to the immediate practical and humanitarian purpose of the therapy, to make the patient whole.

Combination with Other Techniques

It does not seem necessary to describe the various combinations with other techniques because these will result spontaneously from the description of the exercises in which symbols are used and form a central part of the exercise.

CHAPTER V

Spiritual Psychosynthesis—
Techniques

INTRODUCTION

The preceding chapters have been concerned with the techniques of achieving a personal psychosynthesis. Such a personal psychosynthesis for many patients is a much desired and quite satisfactory achievement, making of them harmonious individuals, well adjusted both within themselves and with the community to which they belong and in which they play a useful part.

But there have always been a certain number of human beings who were not and could not be satisfied with such a normal achievement, however worthy it may have appeared to others. For such people there must be a different solution, another wider and higher type of psychosynthesis—Spiritual Psychosynthesis.

Related to this subject are the indications from many sides of an interest in and a general trend—or should we say a groping—towards the realization and acceptance of that field or range of consciousness which we call "spiritual."

The first problem is to clarify the meaning of the word "spiritual," which has been and is being used often in a loose and indefinite way, and much confusion and misunderstanding exist on the subject; therefore it is appropriate to clarify the meaning in which the word is used in these pages. This necessarily involves the all-important and not often clearly realized difference between "superconscious" experiences and psychological activities and the spiritual Self.

As the scientific method is to proceed from the known to the unknown, and particularly from *facts* and from direct *experience* to the formulation and interpretation of what has been observed and experienced, we will not attempt to define nor to discuss at the outset what "Spirit" in its essence may be, but will start with the fact of spiritual experience and spiritual consciousness. For instance, we do not need to know the ultimate nature of electricity in order to apply and use it in the countless modern appliances, just as we do not need to solve the theoretical problems of the ultimate nature of man and of many physiological and psychological processes and functions in order to deal with them for therapeutic or educational purposes.

We would therefore emphasize our neutrality towards those "ultimate" problems, for our concern is to focus on living psychological experience and psychological facts found through the exploration of the unconscious. This is an attitude of realism, and in its best and proper sense a pragmatic position. But this pragmatism should rightly include the experience of individuals who have had wider and deeper levels of realization than the average man—in other words, we should not exclude experience of what we are calling the "superconscious." What has been called by various people or thinkers "spiritual" corresponds in great part to what can empirically be called "superconscious" or "those functions generally not active in average man."

What distinguishes psychosynthesis from many other attempts at psychological understanding is the position that we take as to the existence of a spiritual Self and of a superconscious, which are as basic as the instinctive energies described so well by Freud. We consider that the spiritual is as basic as the material part of man. We are not attempting to force upon psychology a philosophical, theological or metaphysical position, but essentially we include within the study of psychological facts all those which may be related to the higher urges within man which tend to make him grow towards greater realizations of his spiritual essence. Our position affirms that all the superior manifestations of the human psyche, such as creative imagination, intuition, aspiration, genius, are facts which are as real and as important as are the conditioned reflexes, and therefore are susceptible to research and treatment just as scientifically as conditioned reflexes.

We accept the idea that spiritual drives or spiritual urges are as real, basic and fundamental as sexual and aggressive drives; they should not be reduced to sublimation or pathological distortion of the sexual and aggressive components of the personality—although in many neurotic cases such elements are, of course, also present.

What we hope to see developed over a period of years—and certainly do not claim has yet been achieved—is a science of the Self, of its energies, its manifestations, of how these energies can be released, how they can be contacted, how they can be utilized for constructive and therapeutic work. At this stage, since we do not have scientific instruments which enable us to measure these energies directly, we still have to rely on essentially a phenomenological position, in the sense of insisting on the experience itself, and hoping that sooner or later—maybe not in the lifetime of the author—science will attack this problem on a rigorous "energy" basis. However, we must also realize that even if science were able to measure the energies within the constitution of man—which would include emotional, mental, and spiritual energies—this would not make the work of the study of the experience itself less important. Just as in the study of physiology knowledge of neuro-physiology, of the electrical impulses, is very important but does not replace the psychological approach of studying feelings and emotions, so in the same way, the science of the Self should advance on two fronts: one purely in terms of energy, which may perhaps lead to the genius physicists, the Einsteins, of the future; and the other, the psychological, experiential approach.

At this point it seems advisable to explain in what sense psychosynthesis is "neutral" towards religion and philosophy.

First, it must be clearly stated that "neutral" does not mean "indifferent." Religion can be, and has been, considered at two different stages:

1. The "existential religious or spiritual experience"; that is, the direct experience of spiritual realities. This has been realized by the founders of religions, the mystics, some philosophers and, in varying degrees, by many people.

2. The theological or metaphysical *formulations* of such

experiences and the *institutions* which have been founded, in various historic periods and "cultural spaces," in order to communicate to the masses of men who did not have that direct experience, its fruits and outcomes. Further, the *methods, forms* and *rites* through which the masses of men may be helped to participate—indirectly—in the "revelation."

From another angle the French philosopher Henri Bergson in his book *Two Sources of Morality and Religion* (New York: Doubleday, 1954) emphasizes the difference between *static* and *dynamic* religion.

Psychosynthesis definitely affirms the *reality* of spiritual experience, the existence of the higher values and of the "noetic" or "noological" dimension[a] (as Frankl aptly calls it). Its neutrality refers *only* to the second phase: that of the formulations and the institutions. It appreciates, respects and even recognizes the necessity of such formulations and institutions; but its purpose is to help to attain the direct experience.

First, it offers its assistance to those who do not believe in religion nor have any clear philosophical conception. To those who refuse to accept the existing historic formulations, psychosynthesis offers methods and techniques towards spiritual realization. But those who have a living faith, those who belong to a Church or are followers of a philosophical school, have no reason to be afraid of psychosynthesis. It does not attempt to interfere with or to change their position; on the contrary, it can help them to make a better use of the methods and teachings of their own religion. Moreover, psychosynthesis can help them to understand that the same experiences may find expression through different enunciations and symbols; and in this way, it can help them to understand formulations dissimilar to their own and to be broadminded towards them. It can even go so far as to make them see the possibility of a "psychosynthesis of the religions"; which does not mean creating a unique religion and abolishing

---

[a]"This is another logotherapeutic term which denotes anything pertaining to the spiritual core of man's personality. It must be kept in mind, however, that within the frame of reference of logotherapeutic terminology 'spiritual' does not have a primarily religious connotation but refers to the specifically human dimension." Viktor E. Frankl in his paper read before the Annual Meeting of the American Ontoanalytic Association in Chicago, May 7, 1961.

the existing ones; it means that understanding and appreciation between the different religious confessions can be developed, and some fields of cooperation can be established.

This trend towards synthesis is already apparent and is spreading more and more; psychosynthesis is only bringing its own contribution to it.

One of the special positions of psychosynthesis is that all the so-called higher or spiritual states of consciousness and the parapsychological experiences are just facts, because they influence reality—inner reality and outer behavior. We endorse that expression of good pragmatism by Goethe: *Wirklichkeit ist was wirkt* ("Reality is that which is effective"), and in so far as these phenomena—whether termed spiritual, mystical, or parapsychological—change the inner reality and the outer behavior of an individual they are real and must be taken into consideration by any one who has a true scientific spirit and open-mindedness, and does not make the fatal confusion of science being restricted to the quantitative.

We emphasize that neither psychology nor other sciences rely solely on quantitative measurement; there are concepts, experiences, and qualitative realizations which are just as sure, well-demonstrated and therefore as scientific as quantitative procedures. This raises the basic question of what is scientific. The fundamental point in the scientific method is to reason well, i.e., to first objectively observe and describe the facts, the experiences, and then to think rightly about their meaning, nature, effects, consequences, and eventual utilization. Therefore the true scientific mind is the one which functions correctly as a mental mechanism, avoiding all the sophisms, all the rationalizations, all the possible causes of error in the functioning of the mental machinery (such as the personal equation, the limitation of a particular school of thought, and unwarranted generalizations, etc.). The latter are some of the "idols" which Francis Bacon mentioned and which surely deserve to be not only studied but kept constantly in mind while doing scientific work. It is not the subject matter that makes the study scientific, but the way in which any subject matter is dealt with.

Of real moment is the further factor in the scientific attitude which some of the foremost scientists have utilized—either spontaneously or deliberately. We refer to the recognition of the creative role of such psychological functions as imagination, intuition and creativity in scientific research, in the explanation and coordination of data and its interpretation. This has been well attested to by many scientists (e.g., mathematicians like Henri Poincaré) and was significantly stated in *Foundations of Modern Physical Science* (Reading, Mass, Addison-Wesley, 1958).

At this stage of our discussion, however, we will exclude as much as possible even the permissible use of the psychological functions of imagination, intuition, creative hypothesis and so on, and stick strictly to facts, i.e., to experiences and verifiable psychological experiments, and to verifiable results of the application of psychospiritual techniques. Let us recognize that we are as yet at the stage of field survey and tentative exploration, of description of results and reports on the use of active methods of verification and development. We are not yet at the stage of "theory-building." A great amount of research is required with no "theory-building" so that we can remain true to the original scientific purpose and function of psychosynthesis.

The Investigation of the Superconscious

The basic premise or hypothesis is that there exists—in addition to those parts of the unconscious which we have called the lower and middle unconscious, including the collective unconscious—another vast realm of our inner being which has been for the most part neglected by the science of psychology, although its nature and its human value are of a superior quality. The reason for such curious neglect would in itself constitute an interesting piece of psychoanalysis and would shed much light on the psychology of psychologists. This higher realm has been known throughout the ages and, in the last decades, some daring investigators have started to study it in a scientific way, thus laying the foundations for what Frankl aptly calls the "height psychology" (Frankl: *Der unbewusste Gott*, Amandus, Wien, 1949).

Before starting to deal with this subject, it is perhaps necessary to make a clear distinction, in order to avoid the confusion which has often been made, between the superconscious or "higher unconscious" and what has been called "supercon-sciousness," but which it would be more exact to call "a higher state of awareness or spiritual consciousness." This raises the all important and not often clearly realized difference between "su-perconscious" experiences and psychological activities and the spiritual Self.

The superconscious precedes consciousness of the Self, because — as we shall see — there are very many people who have had conscious experience of facts or of functions which are gen-erally superconscious; i.e., those that generally do not enter spontaneously into the field of consciousness, but which in some cases make a spontaneous, unexpected, sometimes unwanted irruption into the field of consciousness — parallel to, or in a sense inverse to, the irruption into the field of consciousness of instinc-tual or emotional drives and forces.

What is necessary is to differentiate this superconscious but previously unconscious material from the type of material that may come from the lower levels of the unconscious which have been extensively studied by Freud and his followers. It seems that in some of the extreme cases of irruption from superconscious levels the material that comes arrives — so to speak — almost ready made, and has very little connection with previous experiences. It is not something which arises in the usual way from the lower unconscious as the result of now released but previously re-pressed experiential contents; it is something new and, as said above, sometimes has little relationship to precedent personal experiences of the individual.

At this point it is necessary to remember that while there is a difference of quality, the superconscious shares some of the other characteristics of the whole unconscious. The superconscious is only a section of the general unconscious, but which has some added qualities that are specific. On the whole it partakes of the nature of the unconscious and the general possible relationships between the unconscious and the personal consciousness.

Viewed in terms of energy, we may consider the contents of the superconscious as energies having higher frequency than some of the contents of the lower unconscious. We could say, more definitely, that psychodynamics and its laws — and in part the methods derived from them—are the same for the three levels of the unconscious. The difference—and it is very real—consists in what is specific to the superconscious in terms of certain *values*, because—and here we come to the point now being increasingly recognized in psychology—*valuations are unavoidable.* It would be easy and perhaps amusing to show how many implied, unconscious, unrecognized valuations there are in many of the so-called purely objective and descriptive expositions of psychologists. It seems to the writer to be more truly scientific to admit that the function of valuation is a natural, necessary and useful activity of the normal human pysche.

In considering the definite values characterizing the superconscious, and which are different from those of the lower and even the middle unconscious, we start with the examination of the spontaneous phenomena, and then proceed to those which can be experimentally determined, produced or activated.

The spontaneous manifestations are demonstrated by that minority of human beings commonly designated as "geniuses." These are comparatively rare, but the rarity of phenomena is no reflection at all on their reality. The appearance of comets is very rare compared to the constant presence of stars and galaxies and yet comets are just as factual cosmic facts as an ever-present star. The study of genius can lead to a scientific understanding of the superconscious.

A first, interesting, important, and significant differentiation is that between two classes of geniuses. There are, of course, intermediate stages but for the purposes of clarification we will first describe the two main clearly distinguishable classes:

1. The first class is that of the great universal geniuses who have an all-round expansive self-realization, those who have manifold superior abilities, who have given successful demonstrations of their greatness through their creative action in various fields. Pythagoras, Plato, Dante, Leonardo da Vinci, Einstein are outstanding examples. This class of geniuses—who have achieved a more or less permanent Self-realization with many ways of expression, who are adjusted and have achieved an inner and outer equilibrium—can be represented in the following diagrammatic way:

Diagram I

1. Lower Unconscious
2. Middle Unconscious
3. Higher Unconscious or Superconscious
4. Field of Consciousness
5. Conscious self or "I"
6. Higher Self
7. Collective Unconscious.

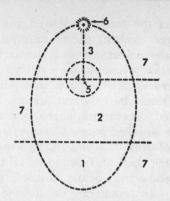

The diagrams as shown here are specially stratified for practical visual purposes. The lower part, number 1, represents the lower part of the unconscious, the middle part (no. 2) the middle unconscious, and the upper part (no. 3) the superconscious In reality, however, it is quite possible, although at this time we do not have scientific proof, that the different unconscious levels are in reality different fields of energy which interpenetrate, but which would be almost impossible to present in a two-dimensional diagram.

The position of Nos. 4 and 5 in the diagram indicates that there is a certain degree of elevation of the conscious personal center, which has reached the nominal borderline between conscious and superconscious, and the field of consciousness has penetrated to some extent into the superconscious level. This condition is not absolutely constant, but it is fairly stable to the same degree to which the consciousness of the normal, adjusted man can be called stable.

2. The second class of genius is that of those who have some extraordinary gift specialized in one direction. Through that gift they produce works (generally of art, literature, or music) having an exceptionally high quality, but their personalities are not above that of the average level; and in some cases even below the average in the sense of being maladjusted and remaining in many respects immature at a personality stage which corresponds to that of adolescence. Here the examples are many; an outstanding one is that of Mozart, who composed—or rather, to be more scientifically exact, through whose nervous system

floods of excellent music were transmitted—when he was only a few years of age, and who continued to transmit high quality music throughout his short life while candidly admitting that he did not know where this music came from or how it was composed, that he heard or felt it within himself and that he only had to write it down.

This process can be described as descent, entrance and pervasion or occupation of the field of consciousness by the product of psychological functions active at a level outside and above that of the normal conscious personality.

This second class of genius productivity can also be presented easily by the use of the diagram:

Diagram II

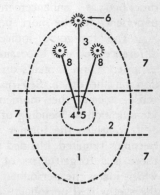

1. Lower Unconscious
2. Middle Unconscious
3. Higher Unconscious or Superconscious
4. Field of Consciousness
5. Conscious self or "I"
6. Higher Self
7. Collective Unconscious
8. Contents of the Superconscious

The stars or clusters—numbered 8—in level 3, the area of the superconscious, indicate activities (e.g., creative literary or musical activities) which project their outcome into the field of the normal consciousness of the personality, a field which remains at the same level. The projection is into the personal "I" or self which remains practically unchanged and merely receives— sometimes surprised and intrigued—the new and unexpected contents or the results of something working within him.

There are people who—either spontaneously or through some strenuous inner exercise of prayer or meditation—can temporarily project their consciousness upwards along a specific line corresponding to their type and way of functioning towards the levels of the superconscious, getting at times very near to the spiritual Self. But this is a passing condition, it does not last, and they relapse back to their normal level after such intense inner experiences.

This also occurs during the intense focussing of abstract thought that advanced mathematicians, physicists, etc., experience, and at these moments they often get real intuitive flashes of understanding which they then translate into understandable mathematical terms. Included in the same general area of experience are two other types: those aesthetic experiences which at their highest pitch give a kind of ecstasy and superconscious realization; and those other experiences in moments of danger, as in war or in certain phases of mountain climbing, which instead of paralyzing with fear stir a man to heroic action. This has been described as "enhancement of being," a real superconscious experience for the short spell in which the situation lasts.

The foregoing indirectly explains and emphasizes the difference between becoming aware of superconscious levels of experience and contents on the one hand, and pure Self-realization on the other. Self-realization, in this specific well-defined sense, means the momentary or more or less temporary identification or blending of the I-consciousness with the spiritual Self, in which the former, which is the reflection of the latter, becomes reunited, blended with the spiritual Self. In these cases there is a forgetfulness of all contents of consciousness, of all which forms the personality both on normal levels and those of the synthesized personality which include superconscious or spiritual levels of life and experience; there is only the pure intense experience of the Self. This has already been described in dealing with the Exercise in Dis-identification.

As we are here concerned mainly with the techniques of psychosynthesis we cannot go into all the possible ramifications of the theoretical aspects of this subject, but we will take them up whenever in the course of the procedure of the description of the techniques a need for theoretical explication should arise.

Symbols for Spiritual Psychosynthesis

We now come to the specific application of the technique of symbol utilization with its objective of realization of the spiritual Self. This process is necessarily an indirect one because every symbol constitutes an intermediary, and as such, symbols are particularly useful and for certain individuals necessary because of the great difficulty of a direct realization of a state of awareness which to the ordinary consciousness appears—although mistakenly—as abstract and as lacking in definite qualities. This is a paradox, for the spiritual Self is the greatest reality, the real essence of our being. Therefore, owing to this difficulty, the help of symbols is particularly indicated.

There are two main groups of symbols which can be used to indicate or to evoke the spiritual Self.

1. The first group is composed of *abstract or geometrical and nature symbols*. The first and foremost is that of the sun; and similar to it is the star, and another, a sphere of fire. Among the nature symbols is that of the rose, used for example, by the Persian mystics, by the troubadours of the Middle Ages, by Dante in his *Divine Comedy*. In the Far East, especially in India, instead of the rose the lotus is commonly used as a spiritual symbol— sometimes the lotus with a jewel at the center.

Abstract geometrical symbols are often combined with the symbol of the sun or a star; e.g., the visualization of an equilateral triangle which symbolizes the three aspects of the personality— physical, emotional and mental—and above the apex of the triangle a sun or star, with radiating rays, symbolizing the Self. This is a very apt symbol to illustrate the process towards and the achievement of spiritual psychosynthesis through the action of, the pervasion by, the spiritual Self of the reconstructed or renewed personality.

2. The second group of symbols of or for the attainment of the spiritual Self is of a more or less personified type. In this group we find the Angel, the Inner Christ—in the mystical sense, the Inner Warrior, the Old Sage, and the Inner Master or Teacher. The last symbol, of the Inner Teacher, is particularly useful because it introduces and is an instrument of a technique which is very important and fruitful in establishing a relationship between the personal self and the spiritual Self. This is the Technique of Inner Dialogue.

The choice of symbols is, of course, governed by the philosophical and religious—or non-religious—background of the patient. Religious symbols such as the Inner Christ would obviously be meaningless to an atheist or agnostic, and in such cases a symbol such as the Inner Teacher or certain nature or geometrical symbols would be indicated.

The Technique of Dialogue

In presenting this technique to the patient he is asked to imaginatively dramatize the following situation: he imagines himself as being in a quandary, having a specific personal or interpersonal problem which he does not feel he can solve by the ordinary rational means of the conscious personality. We then point out to him that if there were a very wise man, a teacher who had the spiritual and psychological competence to take up the problem with him and give him the right answer, he would certainly take considerable pains to obtain an interview with the teacher and seek his wise counsel. To this the patient generally signifies his agreement, and we then explain to him that there is a wise teacher within him—his spiritual Self who already knows his problem, his crisis, his perplexity. Although he need not make an outer journey to reach the teacher, it is necessary to make an inner journey, more exactly an ascent to the various levels of the conscious and superconscious psyche, to approach this inner teacher and then in imagination to simply state the problem, talking to the imagined teacher realistically as if he were a living person and, as in everyday conversation, courteously awaiting a response.

On occasion the answer is immediate and spontaneous; it is received clearly and comes with authority and an absence of all doubt. But this occurs in only the more fortunate cases, for sometimes there appears to be no answer at all. This should not be a reason for discouragement. Sometimes the answer is delayed and comes in an unexpected moment, when the personality is not looking for it and is perhaps occupied with other concerns — a condition that seems to facilitate the reception of the message, because eager expectation and tenseness can constitute an obstacle to receptivity.

There are more indirect and intriguing ways of receiving or finding the answer to the problem. The process or mechanism of this transmission is difficult to understand and often its existence is more than many people realize or are ready to admit. It apparently involves the whole gestalt of a person's life and the subtle unconscious psychological interplay between the patient and his environment. However, it is not necessary to know the mechanism of transmission—the fact is that sometimes the answer comes seemingly spontaneously through a third person or through a book or other reading matter, or through the development of circumstances themselves. In a certain sense this should not surprise us too much, and it might indicate the fact that enlightening impressions or psychological communications are reaching us all the time, even when not consciously sought. It is we who do not recognize the many and varied "signals." But the fact of formulating a question and being in a state of general expectation helps us to register and recognize what would otherwise remain hidden.

In this technique of the inner dialogue we should put the emphasis on the dialogue itself, more than on the "teacher," and experience indicates that what really interests the patients IS the answer, IS the dialogue and NOT the way and means to reach it.

Here we would mention Martin Buber, who has eloquently written on the importance of the dialogue, both the vertical dialogue with God and the dialogue between human beings. He rightly emphasizes the difference between the human—and in a sense spiritual—relationship and the relationship which is established between the "I" and the "It," meaning by "it" everything that is objective, natural, technical and mental; and he says that a great sin of modern man is to treat a fellow-being as "it" and not as "thou." In this Buber is entirely right and has called attention to a very important deficiency in modern relationships. But we must say that—as so often happens and is a trait of human nature—Buber sometimes overstates and exaggerates the dialogue situation, going so far as stating that this relationship is the true and only reality, that there is no reality either in the individual alone or in God alone, that it is the relationship which is the primary fact, and that one cannot dissociate either oneself or God from the living relationship. He makes the relationship the reality and the two subjects of the dialogue relative and secondary, and in this we think that he goes too far.

The truth in this overstatement is that in actual life a relationship is always present, recognized or unrecognized, conscious or unconscious. The individual is never absolutely alone and God (or the spiritual reality) is never purely transcendent, but always in living relationship with the manifestation. This is not the same thing as saying that the relationship IS the reality.

Of the personified symbols of the spiritual Self, that of the Inner Christ is one that we use in cases of individuals who are fairly open to Christian symbolism, in line with the general rule of using as much as possible the subject's own terminology in relation to the whole setting of his beliefs and preferences. As we mentioned earlier, in the case of atheists it is possible to use abstract, geometrical, or nature symbols or that of the inner teacher without going into a laborious discussion as to the existence or non-existence of a deity. In modern life, with the great majority of cases, it is better to stick to the empirical approach of techniques and the actual results of the techniques, eliminating every philosophical or religious question.

With devout Christians who have a certain mystical bent the symbol of the Inner Christ is readily accepted, for often it is not new to them because many Christian writers or mystics have used it, and one is merely calling the attention of the subject to the specific use of the symbol in connection with his own spiritual psychosynthesis. This with many people is the taking up and renewing of an earlier experience.

One may add that the concept of the Inner Christ is not always well defined in the minds of many Christians. There is a certain confusion in their minds between the Inner Christ in its precise restricted sense as a personification of the Self, and the Biblical Christ as the world Figure and Son of God, speaking to their soul inwardly. With this type of person, for practical purposes it is not always necessary or even advisable to make the distinction sharp. If the symbol works—that is the important thing.

In connection with this we draw attention to the famous book *The Imitation of Christ* attributed to Thomas à Kempis. Without attempting to give any religious or theological opinion or judgment on it, from the purely psychological point of view the first three books of *The Imitation of Christ* appear clearly to be a dialogue between the aspiring personality and the Self as the Inner Christ.

One thing that is important to remember is that in spiritual psychosynthesis the mystic experience per se is not the goal; and that the goal of spiritual psychosynthesis has the very practical purpose of increased creativity, of increased ability to give of oneself to some chosen field, and that for certain types of individuals this may be achieved without any mystical experience whatsoever.

It may be useful to make here some semantic observations on the word "mystical" which is very loosely used, both in its positive and negative connotation. Without dealing as amply with the subject as it well deserves, we would say that "mystical" in the good and precise religious sense means: union of love with God, a state of spiritual ecstasy accompanied by bliss, self-forgetfulness, and a forgetting of all outer reality and environment. This is the mystic experience as such, but it is limited and whatever value it may have, it is yet only one stage or episode not only in spiritual psychosynthesis but also in the development of the true perfect Christian. Several Christian teachers have rightly pointed out that the mystical experience is not an end in itself, but from it the subject has to draw the fire, enthusiasm and incentive to come back into the world and serve God and his fellow men. So the mystical experience while having positive value is not an end in itself and is a partial experience of the spiritual life.

There are many ways in which one may have a living contact with the Self, which have no mystical quality at all, taking mystical in the precise sense just mentioned. The dialogue between the spiritual Self and the personality can be unaccompanied by any emotional exaltation; it can be on a clear mental level, in a sense impersonal, objective, and therefore unemotional. This is a fact that it is well to realize, particularly in treating patients who have no strong orthodox religious beliefs or affiliations.

Exercises for Spiritual Psychosynthesis

We outline here three exercises—each of which combines various techniques—that have been found in practice to be particularly effective, both in therapy and in self-realization. These are:

1. Exercise on the Legend of the Grail
2. Exercise based on Dante's *Divine Comedy*
3. Exercise of the Blossoming of the Rose.

Exercise on the Legend of the Grail

This exercise can be done by an individual alone, but it is particularly effective as a group exercise for intra-group psychosynthesis. We will therefore outline its use by a group.

At each meeting— usually held weekly—the leader of the group or therapist describes the series of symbols, and their significance, to be found in the text of Wagner's operas "Lohengrin," "Parsifal," and the various books on the Grail Legend and the Grail Knights. Each time a symbol is described and its significance explained, passages of music by Wagner appropriate to the theme are played; following this the group is requested to think about and reflect upon the symbol in order to realize its significance.

Each member is asked to introject the symbol, so to speak, to identify himself with it. For instance, at the first group meeting, the identification is with Titurel; and then subsequently with each of the characters in the succeeding symbolic scenes of the opera. The group members are also encouraged to make practical experiments with the symbol in their daily life, to keep it present in their thoughts, and to see how much use they can make of it in their everyday life. They are also asked to write down any ideas that may come to them, as well as experiences they may have in connection with the symbol, and to bring them into the group discussion at the next meeting. This is a relatively new experiment in the use of symbols which tends to create or stimulate a lively interest in the entire project.

It is suggested that the following series of symbols be presented during this group exercise:

1st week: Titurel as the symbol of a man who is dissatisfied under the worries of existence, and who therefore decides to leave the world with which he has been identified. He sets out to climb to the top of the mountain and persists with courage until he reaches the summit.

This is an application of the Technique of Ascent. It can be interpreted—and applied in practice—as the ascent of the center of consciousness during the exercise from the ordinary level of awareness to ever higher levels, seeking to reach superconscious levels, and to approach the spiritual Self. In a wider connotation it is the whole process of ascent during the course of therapy or the period given to self-realization.

2nd week: The watch in the night. Titurel spends the night in prayer on top of the mountain asking for inspiration. His kneeling under the sky is a symbol of invocation.

Here we have the use of the techniques of concentration, contemplation, invocation, and silence—the higher active introversion.

3rd week: The response to Titurel's invocation. A point of light appears in the sky, then a host of angels appears. During the presentation of this symbol to the group the prelude to "Lohengrin" may be played. An Angel brings the Cup (the Grail of the legend, the symbol of Love) and the Spear (the symbol of Power or Will).

In a more general sense the cup is a well-known symbol of the feminine aspect and the spear of the masculine, and it is significant that in the opera the Angel brings both to Titurel, indicating that he—and later the other Knights—will have to make use of both of them, thus symbolizing that they must make the synthesis within themselves of love and will.

4th week: The founding of the Order of the Knights; Titurel finds and chooses his co-workers and creates the group.

This is a symbol of interindividual psychosynthesis. In cooperation the Knights build the Castle and the Temple; and here again the Castle represents the Power aspect, and is a symbol of might, while the Temple is the symbol of the religious aspect of Love, the place of communion with the Spirit. In the legend the Castle is built to defend from hostile attack the whole territory chosen as the dwelling place of the Knights; while the Temple is where they perform their ceremonies, where the cup and the spear are kept. The Castle represents the human aspect and the relationship with the outer world, and the Temple represents the inner life and the source of inspiration for the outer activities.

5th week: The life of the group of Knights in the community which they have created; the successful functioning of the Order, symbolizing group psychosynthesis, brotherhood, friendship, group cooperation.

That group harmony and cooperation is a most difficult undertaking—not only because of the different individualities and the possible clash of psychological types and temperaments, but also because of disrupting influences coming from outside—is very dramatically and effectively brought out by Wagner in "Parsifal." In the opera, the magician Klingsor who had been expelled from the Order because of his moral unworthiness had built another castle at no great distance from the Grail Temple; and being furious at his rejection he tries to destroy the work of the Grail Knights, using Kundry as his tool. He instructs her to tempt the Grail Knights, in particular Titurel who at that stage of the legend is the Head of the Grail Order. Titurel yields to Kundry's temptation, and Klingsor inflicts on him a wound that will not heal. Titurel is thus prevented from performing his duty, as Head of the Order, to fulfill the ritual.

6th week: The mission of the Grail Order in the world. The appeal by the men of the plains for help; the descent of the Knights from the mountain into the plains for the selfless purpose of service to humanity.

This appeal from the plains is the main subject of Wagner's "Lohengrin." Elsa, who has been unjustly deprived of the Kingdom of Brabant, prays to God and appeals for help. The appeal reaches the Grail Castle and Lohengrin descends to the plains to help her, and eventually succeeds in reinstating her into her kingdom. The descent into the plains illustrates a very important principle of spiritual psychosynthesis; viz. that the realization of the spiritual Self is not for the purpose of withdrawal but for the purpose of being able to perform more effective service in the world of men.

This is an important point which has to be emphasized over and over again. There is no division, no separation between inner and outer, between spiritual and worldly life. In psychosynthesis there should be a dynamic balancing of the two, a wise alternation.

7th week: The Knights, having performed their missions of service in the world, return to the Castle and meet in their ritualistic ceremony. At the ceremony a white dove appears from above and the spear is seen hovering over the cup.

This is symbolic of the recharging with spiritual energy, periodically needed for more efficient service. The Grail Knights commune as a group, and having been "charged" for the future year of service they depart, leaving a nucleus who always remain in the Castle and perform the duties of the community life there.

Exercise on Dante's Divine Comedy

Dante's *Divine Comedy* is a unique performance of human genius, comparable in certain respects only to Goethe's *Faust*. One of the unique features is that Dante used symbolism with full awareness, for in his theoretical treatise "Il Convivio" (The Banquet) he clearly states that there are four different meanings to the *Divine Comedy*. The first is the literal meaning. The second is allegorical, i.e., symbolical, but a symbolism, he says, of a human and poetical nature, of which he gives an example taken from mythology. The third meaning is the moral one, which is on a higher level than the allegorical. But there is a fourth and still higher meaning, which he calls anagogic, i.e., leading upwards.

The central symbolical meaning of the *Divine Comedy* is a wonderful picture of a complete psychosynthesis. The first part—the Pilgrimage through Hell—indicates the analytical exploration of the lower unconscious. The second part—the Ascent of the Mountain of Purgatory— indicates the process of moral purification and gradual raising of the level of consciousness through the use of active techniques. The third part—the visit to Paradise or Heaven—depicts in an unsurpassed way the various stages of superconscious realization, up to the final vision of the Universal Spirit, of God Himself, in which Love and Will are fused.

This is the essential meaning, but there is also a wealth of further symbolism. As an instance: at the beginning of the *Comedy*, Dante finds himself in a dark forest, and is in despair. Then he sees a hill illumined by the sun, and meets the Latin poet, Virgil, who symbolizes in the poem human reason. Dante sets out to climb the hill, but three wild beasts, representing the unredeemed unconscious, bar the way. Virgil then explains to him that he cannot climb the hill directly, but has first to make the pilgrimage through hell, i.e., experience a deep psychoanalysis, and he leads Dante on this pilgrimage, helping him, encouraging him, explaining to him the various phases of the process.

Virgil accompanies Dante through the whole ascent of the Mount of Purgatory. But when Dante has reached the summit Virgil disappears; i.e., human reason has accomplished its function and cannot go further. Then the guide becomes Beatrice, who represents Divine Wisdom, and only she is competent to lead Dante into the regions of the superconscious.

The main theme or leitmotiv of Dante's *Comedy* is that of first a descent and then a double ascent—the ascent of the mount of purgatory and then through the various heavens of paradise. This bears an interesting similarity to a modern method of psychotherapy based on the same themes of descent and ascent, i.e., the Rêve Eveillé of Desoille *(Le Rêve Eveillé en Psychothérapie,* Paris: Presses Universitaires de France, 1945). In this method the patient is asked to visualize himself climbing up to the top of a mountain—and in some cases of going further on up into the sky, using any imaginary means such as a ray of light or a cloud. He is also asked to visualize a descent into the depths of the sea, or into a cave going deep into the earth. Desoille has found empirically that during the descent the images which are evoked in imagination are related to the unacceptable or threatening power of the unconscious and also to certain complexes and to images related to parental figures with which negative emotions are connected. In contrast, in the ascent of the mountain there is the evocation of positive and constructive feelings; also newly experienced feelings of love and wisdom are often evoked by this technique.

It is also considered to be a method of sublimation, since it is possible for the patient to take some of the images encountered in the depths of the earth or ocean and bring them up, symbolically, to the surface, observe them, and then continue with the ascent of the mountain. An example is the case history, reported by Dr. Robert Gerard of Los Angeles, in which his patient encountered an octopus in the depths of the ocean which threatened to engulf him. However the subject was asked to visualize himself going up towards the surface, taking the octopus with him. On reaching the surface, to the surprise of the subject, the octopus changed itself into the face of his mother. The patient was thus able to experience directly the extent to which the mother was engulfing and possessive, and so threatened him with loss of identity. Then—although this is not possible in all cases— the patient was asked to climb the mountain in company with his mother. As he climbed higher and higher with her, he began to see her in a different light, as a human being in her own right, a person with both qualities and limitations, who had struggled under difficult circumstances. She was no longer threatening to him. Upon reaching the summit, he experienced for the first time deep feelings of compassion for his mother. This experience contributed toward a marked improvement in his affective life.

Returning to Dante's *Divine Comedy* and the exercise based on it, we would stress that it should only be used with competent subjects, i.e., patients with a sufficient cultural background and spiritual outlook. With such patients we ask them to read the poem carefully in the light of its four meanings and its symbolism; and to seek to identify themselves with Dante. We ask them to report periodically and discuss the results, encouraging them to ask for further explanations of the deeper meanings. For those who cannot do this difficult task themselves it may be necessary to divide the poem into the various stages of the descent and ascent, which can then be taken in turn.

This exercise can also be used as a group exercise, and this method will probably grow in importance as the general principles and elementary exercises in psychosynthesis become better known and more generally adopted.

Exercise of the Blossoming of the Rose

The flower has been regarded and used as a symbol of the Soul, of the spiritual Self, of Divinity in both the East and West. China adopted the image of the "Golden Flower," while India and Tibet adopted the lotus (in appearance similar to the water-lily), which has its roots in the earth, its stem in the water, and its petals in the air, where they open under the rays of the sun. In Persia and Europe the rose has been extensively used. Examples are to be found in the *Roman de la Rose* of the Troubadours, the mystical rose exquisitely described by Dante in *Paradise* (Canto XXIII) and the rose at the center of the cross that forms the symbol of some religious orders. Usually it has been the already open flower that has served as a symbol of the Spirit, and, although this is a static representation, its visualization can be very stimulating and evocative. But even more effective in stimulating psychospiritual processes is the *dynamic* visualization of a flower, that is, of its transition and development from the closed bud to the fully open bloom.

Such a dynamic symbol, conveying the idea of development, corresponds to a profound reality, to a fundamental law of life that governs the functions of the human mind as well as the processes of nature. Our spiritual being, the Self, which is the essential and most real part of us, is concealed, confined and "enveloped" first by the physical body with its sense impressions; then by the multiplicity of the emotions and the different drives (fears, desires, attractions and repulsions); and finally by the restless activity of the mind. The liberation of the consciousness from the entanglements is an indispensable prelude to the revelation of the spiritual Center. The agency for achieving it—and this applies in nature as much as in the realm of the mind—is the wonderful and mysterious action of the intrinsic vitality or "livingness," both biological and psychological, that works with irresistible pressure *from within*. This is why the principle of *growth*, of *development*, of *evolution* has been receiving much attention in psychology and education and will be increasingly applied in the future. It is the foundation of one of the most effective methods of psychosynthesis and forms the basis of the exercise now to be described.

1. Procedure

We describe the exercise as it is presented to a patient or to a group:

Let us imagine we are looking at a rosebush. Let us visualize one stem with leaves and rosebud. The bud appears green because the sepals are closed, but at the very top a rose-colored point can be seen. Let us visualize this vividly, holding the image in the center of our consciousness.

"Now begins a slow movement: the sepals start to separate little by little, turning their points outward and revealing the rose-hued petals, which are still closed. The sepals continue to open until we can see the whole of the tender bud.

"The petals follow suit and slowly separate, until a perfect fully-opened rose is seen.

"At this stage let us try to smell the perfume of this rose, inhaling its characteristic and unmistakable scent; so delicate, sweet and delicious. Let us smell it with delight. (It may be recalled that religious language has frequently employed perfume as a symbol, e.g., 'the odor of sanctity'; and incense is also used in many religious ceremonies.)

"Let us now expand our visualization to include the whole rosebush, and imagine the life force that arises from the roots to the flower and originates the process of opening.

"Finally let us identify ourselves with the rose itself or, more precisely, let us 'introject' it into ourselves. Symbolically we *are* this flower, this rose. The same life that animates the universe and has created the miracle of the rose is producing in us a like, even greater miracle—the awakening and development of our spiritual being and that which radiates from it."

Through this exercise we can effectively foster the inner "flowering."

2. Comments

The results with patients have varied greatly in different cases; but sometimes they have been apparently out of all proportion to the simplicity of the exercise. There has resulted with some patients a true Self-realization, and awakening of hitherto latent inner qualities that certainly speeded up the healing process.

The efficacy of the exercise depends on the ability to introject the rose, to experience the sense of the living symbol, so that the symbol works in us creatively. There is deep similarity between the process of unfoldment in a plant and what happens inwardly in ourselves. Here one could speak at great length—and with some patients one can wisely do so—about the secret of self-realization, of actualization, of the ordinary personality considered as a "seed" of what one can become. There are also many psychoanalytic elements—of resistance, of doubt, of oscillation, and so forth; so the patient is, of course, encouraged to speak freely of his spontaneous reactions, and then these are analyzed again and again until they are dissipated, and the blossoming or unfolding takes place freely and unimpeded.

There are other exercises, analogous to the three described above, which involve a succession of images and combine various techniques; for instance, the exercise of visualization and introjection of the *Cycle of Wheat:* from the tiny seed all the way through the many processes which end in a loaf of bread; i.e., the tilling and fertilizing of the soil; the sowing of the seed; the action of sun and rain; the seed growing into a plant, maturing, flowering and the forming of the grain; the ripening, the harvesting, the storing and grinding of the grain; finally the making of bread which, eaten as food, is transformed into living organic substance for maintaining the human body.

Similarly, the exercise of the *Cycle of Coffee:* the planting and growing of the coffee plants, the harvesting and grinding of the beans; the making of coffee by the action of fire and water; the aromatic factor; finally its stimulating and psycho-physiological effects on man.

A further exercise is that based on the growth from seed of a tree; its growth and process of maturity also belongs to this series of symbolic exercises.

The symbolism in these exercises is apparent, and they can be used with all the significance that they contain for the process of psychosynthesis. They are suited for the more objective and practical type of patient; they also help patients discover the symbolism in nature and in natural processes.

We would insert here a general word of caution about the individual meaning that symbols may have for different subjects. Symbols cannot and should not have a uniform interpretation — the same symbols can mean very different and even opposite things to different individuals and this particularly applies to patients with serious psychological disturbances. We would therefore repeat this important note of warning about unwarranted generalizations and interpretations based on preconceived significances of certain symbols in the therapist's mind.

TECHNIQUE FOR THE USE OF INTUITION

In this discussion we assume that intuition exists as an independent and specific psychological function. It was called by Jung an irrational function; to use his own words: "this term does not denote something contrary to *reason*, but something outside the province of reason" (Jung, C.G.: *Psychological Types*, New York, Harcourt, 1933, p. 569).

We will consider intuition mainly in its cognitive function, i.e., as a psychic organ or means to apprehend reality. It is a synthetic function in the sense that it apprehends the totality of a given situation or psychological reality. It does not work from the part to the whole—as the analytical mind does—but apprehends a totality directly in its living existence. As it is a normal function of the human psyche, its activation is produced chiefly by eliminating the various obstacles preventing its activity.

Intuition is one of the least recognized and least appreciated, and therefore one of the repressed or undeveloped functions. It is repressed by a mechanism similar to that of the repression of unconscious drives, but generally the motivation is different. Repression of the intuition is produced by non-recognition, devaluation, neglect and lack of its connection with the other psychological functions. Regarding this last point, a true cognitive process implies not only the function of intuition as such, but also its intelligent apprehension, interpretation, and inclusion in the existing body of knowledge.

It is necessary to make a definite distinction between so-called day-by-day intuition and real spiritual intuition. For instance, the intuition as described by Bergson is predominantly on the personal levels, while intuition according to Plotinus is purely spiritual. Intuition according to Jung is on both of these two levels; and for our present practical and therefore limited purposes we will take the Jungian attitude and speak of intuition fundamentally as a function which can be active on different levels, and can therefore assume different aspects but remain fundamentally the same.

Purpose

The purpose of activating the intuition is that of putting at the disposal of the individual a precious function which generally remains latent and unused, thereby leaving the individual incomplete in his or her development. Another purpose is that of offering to the individual an instrument of cognition and of approach to reality, and a means of interpersonal relationships through the intuitive understanding of other human beings. A further purpose is to help him to discriminate between genuine intuitions and false or supposed intuitions which are really either sentimental generalizations or imaginative notions with no foundation in reality.

Rationale

As with every other function, intuition is a psychological experience. Any one who feels has emotions; he experiences as an immediate content of his consciousness the emotion or feeling, and looks not for any demonstration of its existence or reality. The same is true for the function of thinking; there are people of low psychological development who really never think in the proper sense of the word, and it would be hopeless to try to demonstrate to them the existence of thought and the working of the thinking function; and yet, thinking does exist. The same reasoning is true for intuition. Anyone who is intuitive, who spontaneously and naturally uses the intuition, experiences what it is without any need of explanation or demonstration.

The essential distinction between cognition by way of intuition and cognition by way of the thinking or feeling functions is that intuition has the following characteristics: it is immediate and direct, not mediate and progressive as is thinking; it is synthetic or holistic, i.e., it is an immediate apprehension of a whole, one could say of a Gestalt, and not of different parts later put together to form a whole. Intuition in its purest manifestation is devoid of feeling in the ordinary and right meaning of the nature of emotion, of a warm reaction of the personality—generally either positive or negative toward the object apprehended. Intuition, as well as the other psychological functions, can be activated, following the general law that attention and interest foster their manifestation. It has been said that attention has feeding power; it has also a focusing power. One could even say that it has an evocative power, and attention really implies appreciation and therefore valuation.

Procedure

The first step is of a negative character—the temporary checking or elimination from the field of consciousness of other functions which generally have a spontaneous and uninterrupted activity. Constantly sensations from the outer world or from the body intrude into the field of consciousness; emotional reactions do the same, and often the mind is over-active and undisciplined. All this obstructs, fills the field of consciousness, and makes either the entrance or the recognition of intuitions impossible or difficult. Therefore, it is necessary to carry out what we might call a psychological cleansing of the field of consciousness; metaphorically, to ensure that the projection screen is clear and white. This permits in the subject a sympathetic opening of the consciousness towards, or a reaching actively for, that truth or section of reality with which he seeks to come into contact for the solution of a human or an impersonal cognitive problem.

The second stage is then possible, in which he quietly waits for the result of the approach, this nearing, which in successful cases becomes a contact with and even an identification of the subject with the looked-for experience of reality or truth.

In this process we emphasize the necessary cooperation of the will (in every technique there is the god behind the machine—"deus ex machina"—which is the will). Just as in the first part of the procedure, of the stilling or cleansing of consciousness, there is a conscious and active action of the will, so also in the second part, that of relaxation and quiet waiting, the will continues to function, although in a subtler way and, as it were, remaining in the background. This is so because in order to maintain an attitude of relaxation and quietness—and one which is not purely passive—the will is still required, to act, metaphorically, as the watchman at the door of consciousness to exclude intruders.

To further clarify the difference between the action of the will in the first and second stages, we could say that in the former the will actively ejects the occupants of the "room of consciousness" and in the second stage the will merely watches at the door so that no unwanted intruder can enter.

A characteristic of intuitions is that they are fleeting and, curiously, very easily forgotten, in spite of the fact that at the time they enter the field of consciousness they are very vivid and the subject does not think he can or will forget them easily. Such intuitions can be likened to a stray bird entering a room, circling swiftly around it, and then after a few seconds flying out of the window. The practical deduction from this "fleeting" characteristic is to write down immediately any intuitions we may have— more particularly when we recall the distorting effect of time on all our recollections. Also, of course, it is correct scientific procedure to write down immediately and with precision the supposed intuition for its necessary checking later.

Preparatory to utilizing the technique with patients the first requirement is the assessment, in which we ask the patient if he has ever had intuitions and, if so, if he found them reliable or not; or what his reaction is to his intuitions, i.e., does he overvalue them or feel superior because of his supposed intuitive ability? According to the patient's reactions the approach is correspondingly changed. In the first case—where the fact or possibility of intuition is questioned—the value of intuition has to be emphasized and examples given; and in the second case—of over-valuation—the difference between intuition and "hunches" or imaginative flights has to be explained and emphasized.

If the patient at an early stage of the therapy recounts intuitive experiences, then that clearly indicates the opportunity to take up the subject with him there and then. If, on the contrary, the patient does not show evidence of intuitive activity it is better to postpone dealing with this rather subtle and difficult subject until the treatment requires it—generally at a rather late stage.

Indications and Applications

The general application is for cases where the patient is seeking the attainment of understanding in its fullest psychological sense. Only intuition gives true psychological understanding both of oneself and of others. Whenever one wants to reach a true understanding of the essence of the specific quality of a human being, of a group, or of human relationships, the use of intuition is indicated and even necessary.

A general field of application is in *valuation,* for sound valuation is often the outcome of an intuitive perception of the essence or purpose of a person, an activity or of a situation. Then, as with every other intuition, this valuation has to be checked and examined through other functions such as that of critical analysis; but one can say that the intuition is the specific organ of psychological function for achieving understanding and true valuation.

Another large field of application is that of the sciences. There also it can be used to reach the truth in a synthetic way, a truth which has a universal or general value—such as a principle, a law, or as a general method of procedure, even if applied to a specific problem.

Concerning specific indications there is first the psychotherapist himself. We cannot conceive a true and successful therapist who has not developed and uses the intuition. For this reason, this technique should be given special attention in every didactic psychosynthesis. And of course this applies also to educators certainly no less than to therapists. Regarding education, children and adolescents often have a very active intuition, because it is not checked and interfered with by over-activity of other functions. Therefore, in education, intuition should be dealt with at an early stage.

The greatest need for intuition is in intellectual or over-intellectualized people; i.e., for those who have an active or over-active mind but specifically for those who identify themselves with their mind and are proud of their intelligence. Such intellectuals often have a very lopsided development and are in great need of psychosynthesis in general, and of the activation of the other functions which, as we mentioned earlier, very often remain undeveloped. Even the sensation function can be warped by intellectualism, and the feeling nature is sometimes shamefully suppressed, with the will practically nonexistent—but they share this last deficiency with the majority of human beings.

In contrast, we have cases—especially among women—where the intuition is active but in a "rough" undiscriminating way; in a technical sense "impure." In such cases the indication would be to refine, to purify it, to separate it from heterogeneous elements.

Limitations and Contra-Indications

The limitation—which also applies to all other techniques and the use of all other functions, but which has to be reiterated—is that the separative use of any function can give only limited, one-sided results. It is in the cooperation and synthetic use of all human functions that success—either in cognition or in action—can be achieved. Therefore, however valuable intuition may be, it should be used concomitantly with the other psychological functions.

The contra-indications arise in the case of certain types who are too prone to be affected and impressed by hunches, by imaginative ways of pretended knowledge, and who have not enough mental capacity to exercise the necessary discrimination and to develop the fine ability to distinguish between true and false intuitions. In such cases, the development of intuition should be postponed to the stage in which the other complementary and supplementary functions have been cultivated. Here, of course, comes in the need to be able to check the validity of an intuition and to know how this can be done.

Combination with Other Techniques

The most important combination is that with a controlled mental activity and mental discrimination. To use an analogy, it is a necessary and difficult marriage. Often it is a stormy marriage which sometimes ends in divorce. First there is a good number of those who do not even contemplate such a marriage. They are content to either use only the intuition or only the intellect. Even when this attempt at matrimony is begun, there are various difficulties: in some cases one of the partners is too imperative and devaluates and keeps in subjection the other—and it can be either one that makes this mistake, with all the drawbacks of repression, of overt or covert rebellion. In other cases there is an oscillation, a fight between the two in which temporarily the one or the other predominates.

Many intellectuals are to a certain extent afraid when an intuition intrudes into their thought processes; they are diffident and treat it very gingerly; consciously or unconsciously, in most cases they repress it.

To speak more directly, and without metaphor, of the true relationship between intuition and intellect, intuition is the creative advance towards reality. Intellect has, first, the valuable and necessary function of interpreting, i.e., of translating, verbalizing in acceptable mental terms, the results of the intuition. Second, to check its validity; and third, to coordinate and to include it into the body of already accepted knowledge. These functions are the rightful activity of the intellect, without its trying to assume functions which are not its province. A really fine and harmonious interplay between the two can work perfectly in a successive rhythm: intuitional insight, interpretation, further insight and its interpretation, and so on.

One of the techniques involved here is the use of the will to maintain the emotions in a quiet tranquil state. One of the favorable conditions toward the reception of intuition is when one is in a state of emotional quiet and not overly emotionally involved; and in achieving this the Exercise in Dis-identification that we dealt with earlier can be helpful. Also, the Exercise for Evoking Serenity given below is particularly applicable here.

EXERCISE FOR EVOKING SERENITY

1. Assume a physical attitude of serenity; relax all muscular and nervous tension; breathe slowly and rhythmically; express serenity on your face with a smile. (You can help yourself in this either by looking at yourself in a mirror or by visualizing yourself with that expression.)

2. *Think* about serenity; realize its value, its use, especially in our agitated modern life. *Praise* serenity in your mind; *desire* it.

3. *Evoke* serenity directly; try to *feel* it; with the help either of the repetition of the word or by reading some appropriate sentence, or by repeating many times a suggestive phrase or motto. For example: "Both action and inaction may find room in thee; thy body agitated, thy mind tranquil, thy soul limpid as a mountain lake."

4. Imagine yourself in circumstances which would tend to agitate or irritate you; for instance, being in the midst of an excited

crowd—or in the presence of a hostile person—or confronted by a difficult problem—or obliged to do many things rapidly—or in danger—and *see* and *feel* yourself calm and serene.

5. Pledge yourself to remain serene throughout the day whatever happens; to be a living example of serenity; to radiate serenity.

*   *   *   *

Note: This same pattern can be used for the purpose of evoking and developing any other psychological quality such as Courage, Decision, Patience, etc.

CHAPTER VI

Technique of Imaginative Evocation of Interpersonal Relationships

Purpose

The purpose of this technique is to enable the patient to achieve the right inner attitude towards other people and to successfully perform intended actions involving others. This is achieved in two stages: the first is to eliminate the hindrances, unconscious or conscious, blocking the free attainment of that right inner attitude. This includes not only the development of desirable attitudes towards other people but also the development of desirable attitudes towards oneself. The second stage is a gradual training in developing facility in outer interpersonal relations.

Rationale

The rationale of the first stage, of the elimination of obstacles, is the same as that on which the technique of catharsis is based, i.e., the elimination through the outward expression of emotional charges which exist either in the unconscious and/or in the conscious. This may involve something more than simple catharsis, namely an understanding of the negative emotions, and so on.

The rationale of the second stage is that of the creative effects of imaginative visualization and the evocation of positive images. These create the "model," and arouse the impulse to successful action.

Procedure

The procedure is best explained by an actual description of the technique in action, applied to one of the simpler types of cases, i.e., of preparing for and making possible the performance of an action which appears difficult and arouses fear and anxiety.

The first step is to ask the patient to give a verbal description—as accurate and detailed as possible—of the action to be performed. Let us take the instance of a scholastic oral examination; the student is asked to describe the building and room where the examination will take place, and to give as many details as possible about the examining professor, the subject of examination, the possible questions which may be asked, etc.

After the patient has given that description, he is asked to lie down in a comfortable position on the couch. Then with the help of the therapist an exercise of relaxation is given (such as that on p. 223). When a degree of relaxation has been achieved the therapist repeats the description of the examination fully and realistically, coupled with the instruction to the patient to vividly imagine the scene as if he were actually participating in it. The patient is further told to permit his reactions to emerge freely without any inhibition, i.e., all the reactions evoked by the imaginative living through the examination, such as the subjective emotional states and their accompanying psychosomatic reactions, such as trembling, perspiring, etc. This acts as a catharsis.

The procedure then has to be repeated in further sessions. Often in the second session the reactions are just as intense as in the first, but with successive repetitions they become less and less intense until they spontaneously disappear or become very weak. This completes the first stage of the technique which may be called that of "imaginative desensitization" and the time has come when the patient can be encouraged to prepare to actually face the previously feared ordeal.

This second stage could be called "the visualization of the desired attitude and successful performance." However, this often happens by itself, for in the final repetitions of the first stage the patient may spontaneously feel that he has already gained the right attitude, i.e., in imagination he can now take the examination calmly, confidently, and without any emotional reaction. When this comes spontaneously, it is proof that the negative emotions have really been eliminated.

This procedure, with its two stages, can be modified or adapted to other situations, such as interpersonal relationships with parents or with superiors, which may arouse if not fear, at least anger and aggressiveness.

It is particularly useful to have the patient visualize himself in all sorts of interpersonal relationships with parents, persons of the opposite sex, etc. In these cases it is advisable to have the patient lie on the couch in order to allow the free emergence of all kinds of feeling reactions. And only after this has been repeatedly experienced in a succession of sessions do we ask the patient to adopt a sitting position, and to begin more specifically to visualize the desired attitude and relationships.

For instance: we have in mind a woman patient who had difficulty in her relationships with her parents. We prompted her to recall and re-live past scenes with them, and for the first time in her adult life she fully experienced the rage and hatred that she had felt at the time of those long past incidents. Only after these had been repeatedly experienced in imagination did we move to the next stage of visualizing the possible "love" attitude of this woman towards her parents.

There are many individuals, seemingly normal and psychologically healthy, who yet are uneasy in interpersonal relationships, and because of this put distance between themselves and other people. Again, before they can be asked to visualize themselves in close intimate relationships of warmth and affection with other human beings it is necessary to have them re-experience the fears and other hostile feelings—often unconscious—which are the basis of the difficulties in their personal relationships.

Indications and Applications

These are clear from what has been mentioned in the preceding paragraphs. They are very wide; but to summarize, they cover three main classes of situations:

1. The performing of difficult or feared actions.
2. The realization of harmonious interpersonal relationships, and other more complex kinds of social behavior.
3. The development of awareness of one's attitudes towards oneself and their modification into more constructive and realistic ones.

The effects of this technique have been very gratifying. The subjects often acquire a new and joyous sense of freedom, of independence, of mastery over situations, tasks, and relationships.

Limitations and Contra-Indications

There are really no definite and serious contra-indications, provided the therapist takes care, in the stage of the free emergence of reactions from the unconscious, that the conscious personality of the patient is not submerged by an uncontrolled inrush of other unconscious repressed contents released through the opening made. Such unconscious contents have their origin in the deeper layers of the unconscious, and even in the so-called "collective" unconscious. As Jung has pointed out, this can be a real danger and many of us have had occasion to confirm this in our therapeutic experience.

The best protection against this danger, in certain cases of borderline psychosis, lies in using this technique only after a certain measure of consolidation of the conscious personality has been achieved, and only after the patient has gained an awareness of the laws and mechanisms of the psychological life.

It is also possible—as has been described by Desoille in his technique of the "Rêve Eveillé"—for the therapist to suggest certain protective images; and also to present less threatening images at the point where he feels that the patient may become overwhelmed by unconscious material.

Combination with Other Techniques

This technique can be usefully combined or alternated with all the psychoanalytical procedures; for instance, with catharsis. It is also closely allied with, and in a sense preparatory to, the imaginative evocation of the ideal model.

COMMENTS ON
THE TECHNIQUE OF HENRI BARUK
FOR THE RELATIONSHIP BETWEEN
THERAPIST AND PATIENT

In his *Traité de Psychiatrie* (Paris: Masson, 1959, Vol. II) Professor Henri Baruk describes his main technique in the treatment of psychiatric and psychoneurotic patients. He emphasizes a group of techniques which concern the attitude of the therapist, his preparation and his relationship with his patients.

The first and more general task is that the therapist must realize the global influence that his personality—or rather that he as a human being—exercises on the patient. This happens spontaneously, naturally and inevitably, but he then proceeds from this spontaneous and unconscious influence to an increasingly conscious and direct one. Further, he eliminates those aspects of the influence which might be harmful or create an obstacle in the treatment, emphasizing—or even developing, if absent—certain possible influences which are directly constructive and helpful in the treatment.

This point has also been dealt with by other therapists, for instance: Alfonse Maeder in *La Personne du Médecin-un agent psychotherapeutique* (Neuchatel, Delachaux & Niestlé, 1953), and the German psychotherapist, Tochtermann in *Der Arzt als Arznei* (Dusti Verlag, Remscheidt, 1955).

Baruk's specific technique is based on his fundamental conception that in every patient, including serious psychiatric cases, behind the pathological facade of symptoms and disorders there is an aspect which remains unaffected, and the characteristic of which is moral conscience. This has been dealt with in several of his books and he has given satisfactory proof of the reality of his conception. (Henri Baruk: *Psychiatrie Morale Expérimentale, Individuelle et Sociale,* Paris, Presses Universitaires, Second Edition, 1950). Baruk, accordingly, in his therapy directs himself to the healthy aspects of the patient, particularly to his moral conscience. He identifies his procedure with a word he himself created: "CHITAMNIE," which means in his interpretation "the method of trust"; i.e., trusting the patient.

This was and is of special interest to us because for very many years we have used a similar technique, arrived at independently of Baruk. However, our emphasis is not so much on moral conscience, but consists in the attitude of addressing oneself to the better part of the patient, together with the same spirit of confidence, of trust in and appreciation of the patient, mentioned by Baruk. Our experience in putting and demonstrating trust in the patient has yielded very gratifying results. This has been done specifically in serious situations, such as with patients who have attempted suicide. In such cases the ordinary procedure would be to keep on the safe side and have the patient committed to an institution; but in contrast, in those cases we have addressed the patient in terms such as the following:

> "You know the serious nature of what you have committed. Professional procedure, and in a sense even my duty, indicate that you should be placed in an institution for your own protection. But there is an alternative which I offer to you: if you will give me your word of honor not to make any other attempt at suicide for a determined period of time (generally we specify one month; in more serious cases, one week) I am willing to begin with you an intense psychotherapeutic treatment. You realize the serious consequence to yourself and indirectly to me if you were to make another attempt at suicide during this period. So, if you feel that you have enough control over yourself to sincerely give me your word of honor not to make any further suicide attempt for this short period of time, then I am willing to take the risk. And, at the end of this period, you will know enough about psychotherapy and the general possibilities of this treatment to judge for yourself if you are ready and willing to go on renewing your pledge—or if you should not feel able to renew your pledge, then you will willingly go to an institution. There my treatment can be continued, but you will have external protection from your self-destructive impulses."

In every case in which we have adopted this method the result has been positive. During those periods, of course, the treatment has been very intensive, sessions being held either daily or every two days.

This subject of the psychotherapeutic relationship is fundamental in psychotherapy, and we have but touched on a subject which warrants a deep study and the development of a series of appropriate techniques which would help the therapist in the development of the right inner action. We realize, of course, that in this respect the personality of the therapist is one of the most important factors.

In America, Rogers has strongly emphasized the importance of trust in the ability of the patient to marshal certain positive, constructive forces, and to these Rogers addresses himself. However, we do not go along completely with him in a purely nondirective approach, for we feel that active techniques are necessary in cases where the therapist is faced with much more than a simple counseling situation. Further, we think that the role of the active counselor is a normal constructive role in interpersonal relationships. It should be a function equivalent to that of "the wise guiding father" who, through example and the answering of spontaneous questions of his children, has won their confidence and respect. The role of the father is to give such guidance as can avoid many trials and errors and even serious mistakes, and thus shorten and make easier the way to the desired self-direction, self-realization of youth. In some respects the mother can also play this role, especially with daughters in helping them to understand their right feminine roles; but this requires that the mother herself has fully realized this role and is adequate to the task.

Referring again to the methods of Henri Baruk, may we observe that the moral sense or conscience is one of the direct characteristics of the spiritual Self, although it is not the only one. We think, therefore, that the therapist in addressing himself to the better and higher nature of the patient, while yet giving full consideration to the moral aspect, should not limit himself to that moral sense alone, but realize the advisability of appealing to the other aspects and activities of a spiritual and superconscious nature—such as are described in the corresponding sections of our exposition.

There is a limitation in this technique as it concerns psychotic cases and psychiatric patients. This is evidenced in Baruk's writings and his description of certain cases in which he describes the effects of his technique. It demands a great deal not only of patience and attention and interest on the part of the therapist, but also of time. Therefore, it is necessary that not only the therapist assume this attitude of trust, but also all the people who have to deal with the patient during the course of treatment. They too should be instructed to assume the same attitude, so as not to undo what the therapist is endeavoring to accomplish; and further, they should be asked to actively cooperate with him, to help create an atmosphere of confidence in the patient. Therefore, all the time devoted by the therapist to this end, in training members of the family and nurses or other assistants, would be well spent. This training of nurses and assistants is valid not only for one or two patients, but for all those with whom, later on, both the therapist or the nurses will have to deal. This is being increasingly recognized, particularly in America, under the term of "therapeutic community."

There is one point which perhaps needs clarification, that there are different levels of moral conscience, and that it is very important to distinguish between them. On the one hand there is the moral conscience that Freud discussed at length under the title of "super-ego," which is to a great extent introjected from parental prohibitions and parental commands. This type of conscience is on the level of the personality, so to speak, and to a great extent is tied in with very strong affective charges of fear of consequences, of doing things wrong, etc. This has a rigidity to it, and a type of an almost childish "black-and-white" sort of morality.

In contrast, the moral conscience that issues from the spiritual Self is quite different. It is a wise, loving type of moral conscience; it is not harsh, and follows to some extent the principle so well expressed in the words of the Christ: "Love thy neighbor as thyself." This means "love thyself" with a real wisdom and understanding of the problems of the personality; therefore, this type of conscience does not have rigidity and, going beyond specific codes of conduct, has a certain quality of universality of values attached to it.

This distinction is very important and has to be kept well in mind to avoid the repressive moralism against which psychoanalysis and in general the modern world have reacted, sometimes in a violent and extreme way. But there is to be found in the personality the elementary manifestation of the higher, true, genuine, spiritual morality which has been emphasized — and rightly so — by Baruk. It is the sense of justice. Baruk says that even in the most seriously affected patients this sense of justice persists. Many violent patients are infuriated by real or supposed injustices done to them, even of a very small kind, because they are symbolic of injustices rendered to them in the past; and Baruk, in dealing with such patients, examines particularly and deeply this point of justice and injustice, with — it seems — very good results. He has gone deep into the subject and has developed a test for the sense of justice which he calls — using a Hebrew word — the Tsadek-Test. This was expounded by him in his book *Le Test Tsadek, le jugement moral et la delinquence* (Paris, Presses Universitaires de France, 1950).

SOME GENERAL COMMENTS ON THE TECHNIQUES

We would repeat what was said at the outset, these are only introductory notes on the techniques of psychosynthesis. They are first approximations which should be practiced and put to the test. We will be glad to receive from fellow clinicians any comments, reports, elaborations, additions, and experiences with specific cases; and we will heartily welcome any cooperation of this kind.

We have been asked if we can provide statistics covering the results of the application of the techniques. We are of the opinion that statistics of this nature would be difficult to compile and of doubtful value for the following reasons:

1. The treatment of each patient calls for a combination and alternation of techniques that differ according to the specific features and needs of each.

2. Each patient is considered, investigated, and treated more from the standpoint of his specific individual constitution and situation than as a member of a class.

In other words, we aim more at making an *assessment* (as indicated in this Manual) than a standard diagnosis. In fact, we often find in the same patient symptoms that are generally attributed to or classified under different psychiatric labels; such as combinations in different proportions of psychosomatic disorders, neurotic manifestations, sexual abnormalities, etc.

Concerning results, we can state that the best ones have been achieved in the cure of psychosomatic disorders, phobias, and homosexual tendencies.

Another fact we have ascertained is that the success of a treatment is positively correlated much more with the degree of active cooperation on the part of the patient than with the nature and intensity of his symptoms. This explains the paradoxical finding that in some cases more serious troubles respond to treatment more readily than less serious ones. The former may arouse in the patient a stronger incentive to accept and meet the demands made by the treatment.

For these reasons, we feel that research can be more profitably directed towards the intensive study and treatment of a comparatively small number of cases—resulting in detailed and thoroughly discussed case histories—than towards a more general treatment of the large number of cases needed for statistical purposes.

May we again suggest that fellow therapists will find it interesting and rewarding to experiment themselves with the techniques before or parallel to their utilization in therapy—or, modified and adapted, in education.

There are many techniques that we have not been able to discuss in these pages, but it is hoped that it will be possible during the coming years to present some of the remaining techniques. Further, there is still the big task of illustrating by means of actual cases how the various techniques are applied in specific therapeutic situations. However, it is felt that at this stage it is more important to present the essence of some of the fundamental techniques rather than go into too much detail. This also has the advantage that future presentations will incorporate combined experience of a much wider and larger group of therapists in both Europe and. America.

Part Three

SPECIAL
APPLICATIONS

MUSIC AS A CAUSE OF DISEASE AND AS A
HEALING AGENT | TRANSMUTATION AND
SUBLIMATION OF SEXUAL ENERGIES

CHAPTER VII

Music as a Cause of Disease
and as a Healing Agent

The healing properties of music were well known to the peoples of the past and they made considerable use of it. Among primitive peoples songs and musical instruments such as the drum and the rattle were used not only in order to increase the effect of herbs or drugs, but also as independent means of healing. Such practices have persisted until the present day among American Indians. Paul Radin (22), in his essay "Music and Medicine Among Primitive Peoples," reports that "among the Ojibwa, for example, the so-called *jessakid* practitioners are supposed to function simply by sitting near the patient and singing songs to the accompaniment of their gourd rattles. Similarly, among the Winnebago, those who have obtained their powers from the bear spirits can heal wounds by merely singing their songs." (p. 17)

It was known by the ancient civilizations that music has healing properties, and they deliberately used it for such purpose. In Finland's epic poem, the *Kalevala* (15), we read of a sage who succeeded, by means of his music, not only in appeasing the fury of a mob, but actually in hypnotizing the people, sending them to sleep. In the Bible (5), it is reported that King Saul, being tormented by an evil spirit, called upon David, the skillful player on the harp; and "whenever the evil spirit. . .was upon Saul. . .David took a harp and played with his hand; so Saul was refreshed, and was well, and the evil spirit departed from him." (I Sam. 16:23) According to the Arabs, music has a beneficent effect on animals. They say that the singing and playing of the shepherds make the flocks thrive. Among the Greeks music had a special place as a curative agent. Homer (12) narrates that the flow of blood from the wound of Ulysses was staunched by the melodious song of Autolycus.

We have more precise information on the use which Pythagoras made of music. "Pythagoras," writes Porphyry (21), "based musical education in the first place on certain melodies and rhythms which exercised a healing, purifying influence on human actions and passions, restoring the pristine harmony of the soul's faculties. He applied the same means to the curing of diseases of both body and mind. . .In the evening, when his disciples were about to retire, he would set them free from all disturbances and agitations of the day, steadying their somewhat wavering minds and inducing peaceful sleep which brought with it propitious and even prophetic dreams. And when they arose in the morning he. freed them from lingering sleepiness by means of special songs and melodies." Porphyry also relates that on one occasion, after Pythagoras had striven in vain to calm and restrain a drunken man who was attempting, as an act of revenge, to set fire to a house, he succeeded in pacifying him by means of music.

Plato (18) accorded just as much importance to music as a powerful means of psychotherapy and education, as is shown by the following statement (among many others) to be found in his *Republic*: "Rhythm and harmony sink deep into the recesses of the soul and take the strongest hold there, bringing that grace of body and mind which is only to be found in one who is brought up in the right way." (p. 88)

Aristotle (4) mentions among the various functions of music that of emotional catharsis, which shows an interesting similarity with the aim pursued by modern psychoanalysis.

We cannot deal here with the many other instances of the appreciation and use of music for healing purposes by the Greeks and the Romans and, later, from the Renaissance on through the eighteenth century. Those interested in the history of musical therapy can find ample information in two essays, one by Bruno Meinecke, and the other by Armen Carapetyan, contained in the book *Music and Medicine* (22).

In the nineteenth century, owing to the prevailing material-istic trend, this method of psychotherapy was comparatively neglected. One may even say that the tonic effect of music came to be more appreciated by the military than by the medical profession—every regiment with its own band and constant use made of martial music, of spirited marches to raise and keep up the morale of the soldiers. A few medical doctors, however, did make use of musical therapy. Among them was Hector Chomet. In his book, *The Influence of Music on Health and Life* (7), various cases of healing by means of music are mentioned. He reports the case of a woman subject to epileptic fits who one day hap-pened to be listening to music when the symptoms of an ap-proaching attack set in; the fit, however, did not occur. From that time on, at the first appearance of the symptoms, she arranged for music to be played, and in this way succeeded in entirely overcoming the attacks.

In the present century, and particularly in the last decades, there has been a renewed interest in musical therapy which has shown itself chiefly along three lines: as a means of soothing pain; through collective application in hospitals, especially in psychiatric clinics, with the general aim of producing calming or tonic effects on the patients; and as a means of occupational therapy.

A truly scientific musical therapy, and particularly its indi-vidual applications—namely those which aim at curing specific troubles in particular cases—should be based on a precise knowledge of the various elements of which music is composed and of the effect which each one of them has, both on physiolog-ical functions and on psychological conditions.

The principal musical elements are: *rhythm, tone, melody, harmony, timbre.*

1. Rhythm

This is the primordial and fundamental element of music. The music of primitive peoples consists solely of rhythm. It is, indeed, what the poet d'Annunzio has called it, "the heart of music." Rhythm is the element which has the most intense and immediate influence on man, and it affects directly both the body and the emotions.

Organic life is based on various rhythms: the rhythm of

respiration; the rhythm of the heart-beat; the rhythm of the various muscular movements; the rhythm of activity and rest; the rhythms of the various bodily functions, not to speak of the more subtle vibratory rhythms of every cell, every molecule and every atom. It is therefore not surprising that the rhythms of music exercise a powerful influence on those organic rhythms, either stimulating or calming them, harmonizing or creating discord and disruption.

The psychological life of the individual as well as that of his body has its various and complex rhythms: the rhythms of elation and depression; alternations of sorrow and joy, of fervour and lassitude, of strength and weakness, of extraversion and introversion. All these conditions are extremely sensitive to the influence of the rhythm of music. There are also certain activities wherein the rhythms of the body, the emotions and music interpenetrate and become fused in one integral rhythm. This happens in dancing, which one may truly call living music, expressed with one's whole being.

In rhythm itself we must distinguish various elements: chiefly *tempo* or speed (andante, moderato, allegro, etc.) and *meter* or grouping of beats. Each of them has its own specific influence; for instance, the more rapid the tempo, the greater is the emotional tension produced. A valuable analysis of the psychological effects of the various metric patterns or designs can be found in the chapter by Howard Hanson (11) on "Emotional Expression in Music," of the book already cited, *Music and Medicine* (23).

2. Tone

Every note, while physically produced by a specific rate of vibration, has at the same time both definite physical and psychological effects. As is well known, sound has great power over inorganic matter; by means of sound it is possible to cause geometric figures to form on sand and also to cause objects to be shattered. How much more powerful then must be the impact of this force on the vibrating, living substances of our sensitive bodies!

Each musical note has a specific *quality*, which cannot be expressed in words. This quality produces psychological effects, but one cannot ascribe a specific emotional quality to each note, and the various interesting attempts to relate each note to a corresponding color have not given any sure results, as the asserted correlations varied from individual to individual. More efficacious than isolated sounds are successions of tones in which the effect of each single note is increased by its combination with others of a different pitch.

3. Melody

The combination of rhythms, tones and accents produces those musical "units" or "wholes" which are called melodies. These are the results of the creative activity of the composer—an activity which is often spontaneous or inspired. Speaking in psychological terms, such musical creations as well as other kinds of creative artistic production are elaborated in the various levels of the unconscious, often in the superconscious. Melodies, being a synthesis of various musical factors, are a very apt means for the expression of emotions. They produce on the listener intense and manifold effects. They arouse not only emotions but also sensations, images and urges, and greatly influence the nervous system, respiration and circulation, in fact, all vital functions.

4. Harmony

While melody is produced by a succession of sounds, harmony is produced by the simultaneous sounding of several tones which blend with each other, forming chords. According to the respective rates of vibration of these sounds, the result will be either an harmonious blending or a jarring discord, both of which have definite physiological or psychological effects. Thus we may say that the prevalence of dissonances in modern music, being the expression of the discord, conflicts and crises that afflict modern man, tend with their suggestive influence to accentuate and exaggerate the evil.

5. Timbre

The difference in the nature and structure of the various musical instruments, the human voice included, gives to sound a special quality which can hardly be defined in words, but which is easily recognizable, because it evokes special emotional responses. Everybody who has some musical sensitivity feels the specifically different *quality* of the impressions made by a violin or a flute, by a trumpet or by a harp, by a soprano or by a bass voice.

A composer, through the skillful combination of various instruments of an orchestra, can produce most powerful psychological effects.

Negative Effects of Music

Before considering the healing effects of music and their utilization, we must frankly recognize and examine its possible harmful influence. This should not surprise or shock us. Everything which is *effective* can be so either for good or ill. It is well to make the point clear that the medical effect of music does by no means have to coincide with its aesthetic value. There is "bad" music (from the standpoint of art) which is harmless, and on the other hand there is music by some of the best composers which can be definitely harmful. It is not a paradox to state in regard to music of a harmful character, that the more expressive it is aesthetically the more noxious it can be.

The harmful effects of music on body and mind are due to various factors. The most important of these is the kind or quality of the music. But there are others of a secondary character which can be influential and at times even decisive. These are: the amount of the music heard; the combination and succession of different kinds of music; the psycho-physiological constitution of each listener; the particular emotional state in which he or she is at the time. Thus, a piece that is disturbing and upsetting to one person may have no or little injurious effect on another; for instance, a listener who is sensitive to music and whose passions are strong and not under control, will be influenced in a very different way from a listener of the intellectual type who is emotionally cold and unresponsive. If a person is in love, he will be much more disturbed and excited by erotic music than when his passion is dormant or when it has burned itself out, leaving only the cold ashes of disappointment. In some extreme cases, when listeners are abnormally sensitive, music can be the cause of serious troubles. Evidence of this has been given by MacDonald Hastings, who in his study on "Musicogenic Epilepsy" mentions twenty cases, eleven of them his own patients, in which epileptic fits were brought on by music. (Quoted by F. Howes in his book, *Man, Mind and Music*, p. 158) (13)

Then there is the manner of the arrangement of the concert program, when different and often opposite impressions, experienced in immediate succession, arouse confusing and conflicting emotions. Frequently in concerts the soothing effect of a piece will be destroyed by the exciting nature of the one that follows; the cheerful stimulation of a third piece is neutralized by the depressing influence of a fourth, and so on. Such contrasts can be variously appraised from the aesthetic point of view, but they certainly cannot be approved from the medical standpoint. Also the excessive amount of music at long concerts, showered upon the listeners, can cause nervous fatigue and psychological indigestion.

The kinds of music apt to produce injurious effects are manifold. First, there is the music that arouses the instincts and appeals to the lower passions, that excites by its sensual enchantment. To the musical pieces of this kind, among those having artistic value, belong the Venusberg scene in Wagner's *Tannhauser* and certain parts of *Salome* by Richard Strauss. Concerning the latter, Frank Howes (13), President of the Royal Musical Association, expresses the following severe judgment: "Some small quantity of art can best be described as *fleurs du mal*. Out of the festering corruption grows an exotic, gaudy, sinister, fascinating beauty. Fascination is an ambivalent emotion in which the attraction is enhanced by the concomitant repulsion. Strauss's *Salome*, from the Dance of the Seven Veils to the end, is an instance of such fascination; it dazzles, seduces, repels and conveys just that hothouse beauty of evil, the lurid, livid fungus growing on the dunghill." (p. 71)

A second group of musical pieces of a harmful kind consists of those that are very melancholy and depressing, as they express languor and weariness, grief and distress, agony and despair. This kind of music may have great artistic merit and may have afforded relief to the composer himself and been a means of artistic catharsis, but it is likely to act like a psychological poison on the listener who allows its depressing influence to permeate him. Of this kind are certain pieces by Chopin, notably his nocturnes, in which that unhappy soul has given vent to his poignant melancholy and to his weakness and homesickness. They have contributed to the cultivation of that languid and morbid sentimentality which afflicted the young women of the romantic period of the last century.

Another type of music apt to be injurious consists of those musical compositions which, while representing interesting experiments in new forms of musical expression, reflect, with their frequent dissonances, their lack of form, their irregular and frenzied rhythms, the modern mind in its condition of stress and strain. Many modern dances, particularly jazz, combine overstimulation with the disintegrating influence of their syncopated rhythms. Howard Hanson, in his very good essay, already cited (11), exposes in a drastic way the widespread injurious influence of jazz. He says this: "I hesitate to think. . .of what the effect of music upon the next generation will be if the present school of 'hot jazz' continues to develop unabated. Much of it is crass, raucous and commonplace and could be dismissed without comment if it were not for the radio whereby, hour after hour, night after night, American homes are flooded with vast quantities of this material, to which accompaniment our youngsters dance, play and even study. Perhaps they have developed an immunity to its effect—but if they have not, and if the mass production of this aural drug is not curtailed, we may find ourselves a nation of neurotics which even the skill of the psychiatrist may be hard pressed to cure. It seems, therefore, only poetic justice that musical therapeutics should develop at least to the point where music may serve as an antidote for itself." (p. 265)

Music, even when it is not directly stimulating the passions nor inducing depression and discordance, can be harmful owing solely to the fact that it arouses and nourishes an excessive state of emotion which, when it is not transmuted into constructive activity, weakens the character. This wallowing in sentimentality was sternly denounced by William James in his *Principles of Psychology* (14) in these words:

"There is no more contemptible type of human character than that of the nerveless sentimentalist and dreamer, who spends his life in a weltering sea of sensibility and emotion, but who never does a manly concrete deed. Rousseau, inflaming all the mothers of France, by his eloquence, to follow Nature and nurse their babies themselves, while he sends his own children to the foundling hospital, is the classical example of what I mean. . .Even the habit of excessive indulgence in music, for those who are neither performers themselves nor musically gifted enough to take it in a purely intellectual way, has probably a relaxing effect upon the character. One becomes filled with emotions which habitually pass without prompting to any deed, and so the inertly sentimental condition is kept up. The remedy would be, never to suffer one's self to have an emotion at a concert, without expressing it afterward in *some* active way." (p. 125-126, Vol. I)

Finally, music can, and often does, have injurious effects on the performers themselves, who are subjected to a combination of harmful elements: muscular and nervous fatigue as a consequence of intense technical study and the excessive quantity of music, both heard and performed; the anxiety caused by public performances; the particular contrast of psychological attitudes required by the performance itself, which demands on the one hand perfection of technique, concentrated attention, and self-control; and on the other an emotional identification with the mood expressed by the music, needed to produce that warmth of expression, that powerful suggestion which fascinates the audience.

For these reasons performing musicians need, more than anybody else, to train their will, to control their emotions and to help themselves, or be helped, by a judicious use of relaxation and of all available means of psychotherapy.

Special attention should be paid to film-music. Superficially considered it would seem that such music is of no importance since in a cinematographic performance it is the picture which is of primary importance. However, such is not the case. From the very beginning—that is to say, at a time when the later invention of the sound-film could not yet be foreseen—cinematograph performances were accompanied by music, which proves that the important effect of music on the spectators was well recognized. It is a psychological law that the impressions which come to us through our senses are much more effective if related emotions, through the aid of other sense organs, are awakened within us.

There is also another psychological reason why accompanying music has a special effect upon the spectator. The *conscious* attention of the latter being completely concentrated upon the pictorial performance produces, instead of lessening the influence of the accompanying music, a tremendous increase in the effect which the picture has. Research pertaining to the mechanism of suggestion and to the part the unconscious plays in the life of the psyche has demonstrated that impressions received during the exclusion of waking consciousness and of critical judgment penetrate much more deeply into the individual; they affect man not only psychologically but also in his body and are even able to call forth functional disturbances.

Since music definitely increases the individual's receptivity to the impressions conveyed by film episodes, it seems highly desirable—from the medical as well as the educational standpoint—to thoroughly examine film music and, where the effect is found to be harmful, to take steps to correct it. Often such accompanying music is sensual in character or overtly emotional and its effect upon the listener-spectator is enervating. Indeed, often through such music feelings of oppression and terror, created by film scenes, are reinforced so that their exciting effect is thereby greatly increased.

Positive Effects of Music

After having dealt with the dark aspects of the picture, let us now consider the bright ones.

Music can indeed be a powerful healing agent. There are many and diverse ways in which it can and does exercise a beneficent influence on both body and mind. First of all, its effect can be wonderfully restful and refreshing, and we need not emphasize how valuable this is in our times of physical exhaustion, nervous tension and emotional and mental excitement. The general and obvious prescription for the elimination of these conditions is a rest cure. But so many men and women of our day do not know how to rest, or even what real rest means. They are accustomed to constant movement and noise so that they are unable to keep still and endure silence. Here music comes to their rescue. As Father Gratry (10) pithily says: "There is no agent so powerful in giving us real rest as true music. . .It does for the heart and mind, and also for the body, what sleep does for the body alone." *(Les Sources)* Indeed, many peaceful and solemn adagios, many soothing lullabies and barcarolles induce with their soft charm a beneficial relaxation in a more natural and healthy way than any chemical sedative.

More specific applications along these lines, with the purpose of inducing calm and soothing pain, have been made with patients undergoing dental treatment or surgical operations.

The following characteristic examples, which the New York Times reported a few years ago, will illustrate the kind and the results of such attempts: "The University of Chicago clinics experimentally introduced music to alleviate tensions of patients undergoing surgery. . .So successful was the experiment that the University of Chicago medical research center will introduce music with anaesthesia in its six major operating rooms and its six preparation rooms, when it opens Chicago's first cancer research institution, the Nathan Goldblatt Memorial Hospital. . .Music with anaesthesia is especially applicable to abdominal surgery, but it has been used in almost all types of operations. It has been found especially helpful to the peptic ulcer patients who are already so tense and nervous that the routine medical sedatives are not very effective. It is very important in cases where the patient is too old or ill to receive sedatives."

We have indicated how intensely music can work upon the feelings, and have pointed out the danger of this fact, but in many cases an emotional stimulus may be very opportune and helpful. For instance, there are a great many persons belonging to the practical or to the mental type who have an undeveloped or repressed emotional nature, and this is apt to make them arid, dissatisfied, shut-up within themselves. To them music may give the magic touch which reawakens and warms the heart and restores communion with nature, humanity, and God.

Then there is a kind of music, both instrumental and vocal, of a strong and virile nature, which arouses the will and incites to action. Such music has stimulated innumerable individuals to noble deeds, to heroic self-sacrifice for an ideal. Against all negative and depressive emotions, such as despondency, pessimism, bitterness, and even hate, music of a gay, vivacious and sparkling character, and also music that expresses true humor, acts as a true counterpoison. It cheers and gladdens, smoothing the wrinkled foreheads and softening into smiles the hard lines of tightly closed lips. Such effects are produced by many compositions of Haydn, Mozart, and Rossini.

What more efficacious, genial and acceptable means than music could a doctor devise for giving joy; that joy which the intuition of the ancients and the investigations of modern science alike declare to be a powerful tonic for both mind and body?

The particular stimulating action which music exercises on the unconscious can have many good effects; for example, it can stimulate memory, a function that depends largely on the unconscious. In this connection the following statement by the accomplished musicologist, Mario Pilo (17), is of interest:

"For myself, music performs a special action in arousing my memory, which is capricious and undisciplined, subject to lapses and slips that are often very annoying. More than once music has enabled me to retrieve from its hiding place, quite suddenly, some reluctant and elusive memory: Several years ago, a Neapolitan melody of no special merit, which was being played on a mandolin by a neighbour, enabled me in a few minutes to remember the subject of a manuscript I had lost years ago, also the ideas contained in it which I had tried in vain, at intervals, to put together again."

Music can and does also quicken and facilitate intellectual activity and favour artistic and creative inspiration. There is, among others, the case of the Italian author Alfieri who relates that he conceived nearly all his tragedies either at the moment of listening to music or immediately afterwards.

Through its influence upon the unconscious, music can have a still more definite and specific healing effect of a psychoanalytic character. If of an appropriate kind, it can help in eliminating repressions and resistances and bring into the field of waking consciousness many drives, emotions and complexes which were creating difficulties in the unconscious.

Music can help also, through its charm and uplifting influence, to transmute and sublimate those impulses and emotional energies so as to render them not only harmless, but make them contribute to the deepening of experience and the broadening and enriching of the personality. We have the works of a great composer who, having lived through periods of intense stress and strain, was finally able to rise to some extent above his personal pain and to draw inspiration from it, expressing strength, joy and faith, and praising the goodness of life. I am referring to Beethoven. In some of his sonatas, particularly in the later ones, the releasing and sublimating process is easily discernible. The storms and alternations in the first parts of these sonatas are followed by a peaceful and triumphant conclusion.

And there is the poet Francesco Chiesa who intuitively perceived, and expressed with admirable art, this psychoanalytic and sublimating action of music, this high lesson of strength and optimism. In his poem *L'Uccello del Paradiso* (The Bird of Paradise), he describes the emotional and mental states induced by a violin recital. (See page 264)

The previously discussed process of integration into the conscious personality of unconscious contents, and their subsequent transmutation and harmonization, can in a certain respect be regarded as a process of synthesis. But there is a more specific process of psychosynthesis which is of three kinds, or rather, consists of three stages, each wider and more inclusive than the preceding one. They can be called respectively: spiritual psychosynthesis; inter-individual psychosynthesis; cosmic psychosynthesis.

The first — spiritual psychosynthesis — recognizes the inclusion and integration into the conscious personality of higher psychospiritual elements of which it is not consciously aware, because they reside in the highest sphere of the unconscious, the superconscious.

Truly religious music is very effective in producing or favouring such a synthesis. It awakens and stimulates the spiritual "germs" which exist in every one of us, waiting to come to life. It lifts us above the level of everyday consciousness, up into those higher realms where light, love and joy ever reign. There are many musical compositions which produce such effects. We can mention only a few of the most significant examples, omitting the consideration of less accessible ancient and Oriental music: the Gregorian Chant which still evokes the highest religious emotions; then there is Palestrina, of whom it was said by Scott (25), in his chapter on "Beethoven — Sympathy and Psychoanalysis," that he "was the first European composer to restore music to its original function — that of constituting a definite link between man and God."

Next we must mention J.S.Bach whose music not only arouses the deepest religious feelings, but has a still greater synthesizing influence which we shall discuss later; nor should we fail to mention Handel and his impressive oratorios.

Among the later composers we find three who are markedly different from each other, but whose music, in diverse ways and with dissimilar techniques, produces powerfully spiritual effects: César Franck, that pure and noble soul who succeeded in giving adequate musical expression to the *Evangelical Beatitudes;* Richard Wagner, who in *Lohengrin* and *Parsifal* evokes with the magic of sound the flight of an angelic host from heaven to earth, the feeling of spiritual love and compassion, and the sacred rites of the Grail Brotherhood; Aleksandr Scriabin who, through the use of daring combinations of sounds, endeavors to lift the consciousness to the heights of rapturous bliss and ecstasy.

The second kind or stage of psychosynthesis — inter-individual psychosynthesis — is one which is established between an individual and his fellowmen within a group of which he forms a part — from the smallest combination consisting of a man and a woman, to the family group which includes the children, on to the various social groups, the national groups and ever greater units, until his consciousness embraces in an harmonious relationship the whole of humanity.

Such inter-individual psychosynthesis is promoted by all music which expresses collective emotions and aspirations. It includes national anthems, marches and folk songs belonging to particular occupations or group activities; harvest songs, grape-gathering songs, etc., and many choruses from the operas of Verdi and others. The highest and most effective musical expression of the psychosynthesis of humanity is Beethoven's Ninth Symphony, which reaches its climax with the intonation of Schiller's words *Seid umschlungen, Millionen.* (Be embraced, ye millions of men.)

The third stage — cosmic psychosynthesis — consists of an ever increasing recognition and acceptance by the individual of the laws, the relationships and the rhythms governing life itself, in its widest sense. It could be called the discovery of, and the tuning in with, "the harmony of the spheres," the conscious participation in the great life of the universe. This subject has been ably treated by Aleks Pontvik who expounded his views and has related some of the results of his musical experiments in a stimulating little book entitled *Grundgedanken zur Psychischen Heilwirkung der Musik* (20). (Fundamental Thoughts on the Psychic Healing Effect of

Music.) In this book the author adopts the Pythagorean conception of the universe as an ordered whole. The cosmos is built according to harmonious—and that means musical—laws and proportions. And he quotes in this connection Brantzeg's summary of Kepler's development of this principle (16): "Before all things were created there was geometry. This, since eternity, is a reflection of God; it gave Him the original *pattern* for the artistic structure of this world in order that it may become similar to its Creator. The fundamental elements of geometry are the divisions of the circle. They produce harmonies, they create earthly forms through the harmonious consonance of music and they give to the constellations of the zodiac their cosmic pattern. In music, harmony is the result of the composer's intuition, but among the stars it is produced by the geometrical necessity of the heavenly mechanics. God has given to the human soul harmonious proportions."

According to Pontvik, the following conception gives the key to psychotherapy in general, and to musical therapy in particular: healing can be attained only by starting from the whole. "It means the establishing, or re-establishing, of an harmonious equilibrium through the reconciliation of opposing elements within the whole. Thus the healing process of psychoneuroses can be indicated in musical terms as a progressive development which brings about, or restores, the fundamental harmonious chord." (p. 30) (20)

The technique of this healing action consists, according to Pontvik, in the evocation or musical expression of primordial symbols corresponding to what Jung calls archetypes. The music which can especially produce this kind of healing influence is that of J.S.Bach. Pontvik found in his experience that Bach's music evokes religious symbols, particularly that of a temple, the harmonious proportions of which are in their structure analogous to those of the universe. He supports his contention by two interesting quotations; one from Albert Schweitzer, who not only has to his credit great humanitarian achievements but is, besides, one of the most prominent authorities on Bach. Schweitzer (24) calls a composition by Bach "an expression of the Primal Power which manifests itself in the infinite rotating worlds." The other quotation is from the writings of a Chinese sage: "Perfect music has its cause. It arises from balance. Balance arises from that which is right. That which is right arises from the world's significance. Therefore one can talk about music only with one who has become aware of the world's significance."

One of my students expressed in the following way the effect of Bach's music upon her: "When, last evening, in the light of the moon, I listened to the Second Suite, I became aware of all the grandeur of Bach's poise. His music is really a marvellous harmony of the three divine aspects; a song of love, unfolding itself in the light of intelligence, and impelled by will. That is why it enriches so much."

Musical therapy, in order to prove effective, should be applied according to certain rules which are based on psycho-physiological, rather than on aesthetic or artistic principles. Here are some of the more important ones:

1. Prior to the performance, the patient or group of patients should receive *adequate information* about the piece to be executed. Its nature, structure and particularly the effect to be expected, should be explained. In this way the listeners can contribute intelligently to the influence of the music upon their unconscious, and consciously assimilate it. For the same reason it is useful for the listeners to know beforehand the text of pieces which are to be sung, or to have the text right under their eyes. Often, also, in regular performances the strain to catch the words (which are not usually clearly pronounced, or which are submerged by the sound of the orchestra) interferes with the effect aimed at.

2. It is advisable for the patients to *relax* as much as possible before and also during the musical performance. This, too, helps them to "open the doors of the unconscious," so to speak, and to receive the full benefit of the musical influence. Such relaxation can be induced by a comfortable physical position, by subdued illumination, by verbal suggestions made by the doctor, and also by a short introductory musical piece of a soothing nature, even if, subsequently, one wants to produce stimulation or joyousness through appropriate pieces.

3. The *right dosage* is of importance. In general, a musical treatment should be of *short duration*, in order to avoid fatigue and, therefore, possible defence reactions.

4. *Repetition* can be, and has been found to be, helpful. G.W. Ainlay, who combines the qualities of medical doctor, violinist, pianist and composer, states in his valuable paper on "The Place of Music in Military Hospitals" (2) the following: "It is quite astounding to see the good effects and relaxation that may be produced in certain types of neuropsychiatric patients by repeating soothing measures or phrases. The repetition seems to act like a gentle massage if properly done." (p. 328) However, we should remember that repetition of motifs and small sections is often adequately expressed in the compositions themselves, and that, if repetitions are too insistent, they can become annoying and even obsessing. Such an effect, for instance, is produced on some people by Ravel's *Bolero*.

5. The *volume* or *loudness* of the music should be *carefully regulated*. Generally, one should adopt a low volume of sound, not only in the case of soothing music, but also when music is brilliant and stimulating. The desired effect is produced by the rhythm and other qualities of the music previously mentioned (tone, melody, harmony, timbre), and not by the amount of sound which, when great, is apt to tire or jar the nervous system.

6. For the same reason as indicated in point two of these rules, it is advisable for the patient to rest for a while also *after* hearing the healing music. This favors its full and undisturbed action in and on the unconscious.

7. Due to the fact that the unconscious is not only active spontaneously during sleep, but also receptive to outer influences, musical therapy can be applied during the patient's sleep as well. The fact that music does affect the unconscious during sleep was proved many years ago by a series of experiments made by one of my co-workers, Dr. G. Stepanow, using the following technique. After having performed a piece of music during the subject's sleep, he awakened her and asked her to tell him what she had been dreaming. He found in every case that these dreams had been definitely affected by the nature of the music performed.

The therapeutic use of music during sleep is particularly indicated for children, for psychiatric cases, and in general for people who are restless and agitated when awake.

8. The *choice* of the musical pieces to be used requires careful thought and is more difficult than may appear on first

consideration. It is sometimes necessary that the guiding principles, which would seem obvious and of general application, be
qualified and even disregarded. Here are two such instances:

It would seem to be a matter of common sense to adapt the
music to be performed to the social and cultural level of the
listener. Indeed, in the majority of cases, simple uncultured people ask for, and enjoy, popular music and appear to be unresponsive to, and bored by, classical music. Yet there have been
many instances in which such people were deeply affected by
music of high quality by the great composers. Pontvik mentions
several such cases, and one that is particularly convincing is
quoted on page 259 under *Collective Applications*. This may be due
to the fact that the main effect of music is on the unconscious and
that, to some extent, the unconscious is independent of the conscious level and accomplishments of the personality. In the case of
uncultured people, therefore, it is advisable to attempt to use the
simpler but most impressive works of the great composers.

Another obvious rule would seem to be that of using music
of a specific character (soothing, stimulating, cheerful) in order to
arouse the corresponding emotions and conditions which appear
to be lacking in, and are needed by, the patient. However, in
actual practice the matter is not so simple. Cheerful music may jar
on a person weighed down by grief. A patient in a state of excitement and agitation may not be impressed by solemn adagios
and become still more restless. On the other hand, when an
individual who is dejected hears sad music, it can have an uplifting effect. In this connection I can quote a statement by one of my
patients: "When I hear sad music composed by a man who suf-
fered, as did Chopin, Beethoven and Tchaikovsky, I feel that I
am 'seconded,' and in feeling the beauty of that music I forget
that I am not well. . ."

But there is another and more general reason which com-
plicates the choice of the music to be used. It is a fact that the
appraisal of the very character of a given composition, and consequently its subjective effect, can vary according to the listener. As
C.M. Diserens pointed out in "The Development of an Experimental Psychology of Music," (8) a positive correlation between
many musical works and the moods aroused by them in the
listener does indeed exist, and this has been proved by the ex-

periments made by Bingham, Hevner, Campbell, and others. But the percentage of such correlation varies considerably from piece to piece, and there is in every case a larger or smaller minority of listeners whose reactions differ from or even oppose those of the majority. For instance, according to the data gathered by Capurso (6) from his experiments with 1075 subjects, 50% of these considered Wagner's *Ride of the Valkyries* as joyous, stimulating and triumphant, whereas 32% ascribed to it an agitating and irritating influence. In the case of Paganini's *Perpetual Movement* the respective proportions were 82% and 14%. Moreover, even the same listener can receive a different impression of the same work according to the varying psychological or physical conditions in which he or she is at the time.

Owing to these individual differences in the reactions to music, it is advisable to ask each subject or patient to furnish a report—as accurate as possible, and preferably in writing—on the effects of music on him, both in the past and after each application of musical therapy. Such reports have a threefold purpose and usefulness. First, they offer data on which to base the further choice of music to be used in that particular case. Second, they represent for the patient a training in self-observation and in exactitude of expression which has psychotherapeutic value. Third, they contribute to the accumulation of relevant material for the progress of musical therapy. For this purpose I have prepared a *Questionnaire* which will be found at the end of this chapter. (See p. 261)

However, we should not base our judgment regarding the effects of a musical composition only on such reports, which depict the immediate and conscious reaction of the hearer. There are other effects which operate on unconscious psychological levels, and emerge only later, or even remain unrecognized, while they may influence the general condition of the patient.

The accumulation of such data and a careful observation of the therapeutic effects will in the future facilitate the selection, in an increasingly reliable way, of the musical pieces best suited to each patient and his particular trouble. Until such progress has been achieved, the specific "prescriptions" of musical pieces for various morbid conditions, given by some writers on the subject, should be regarded with the utmost prudence and qualification.

Meanwhile, there is one type of music which can safely be applied with satisfactory results in all cases, regardless of the patient's difficulties and physical age; and that is kindergarten and folk music. This, according to Ainlay (2), seems to "re-supply, or re-activate, the mother-child complex and so offer temporary security and sanctuary." Another more general reason is that the unconscious, or more exactly a considerable part of it, is of a primitive and childlike character. Such music should be used preferably in the first therapeutic applications, or as a prelude to other specific pieces.

9. In the future, the development of musical therapy may make it possible for musicians, who are also psychologists or doctors, to compose special music aiming at definite therapeutic effects. This may not be as remote as would appear on first consideration. One of my students, who was an accomplished pianist, took up the study of medicine, and planned experiments in this direction. The technique she worked out for the treatment of obsessive ideas is reported in her own words on page 262.

10. *Combined use of musical therapy with other kinds of treatment.* Of course, no medical treatment should be confined to music; this can be only one of the various means used by a doctor. But here we refer to a specific use of music more or less simultaneously with other kinds of therapy. Up to now there have been mainly two kinds of such combined therapeutic applications:

(a) *Music and Anaesthesia.* In order to hasten or facilitate anaesthesia, music has been and is being applied, both by individual doctors (generally dentists) and in hospitals. On page 247 we have already mentioned the use of music for this purpose in the University of Chicago clinics. Recently (1955) similar applications have been introduced at the Vaugirard Hospital in Paris with marked success. We cannot enter here into the technical details of such applications, but interested doctors can find a description of them in the periodical, *Anaesthesia and Analgesia,* Vol. 29, 1950 (3), and in E. Podolsky's book, *Music Therapy* (19). In such cases the choice of suitable music is comparatively easy: it only needs to be soft, slow and soothing.

(b) *Music and Psychotherapy.* The two main objectives of psychoanalysis—namely, that of bringing into the light of consciousness psychological elements hitherto confined to the unconscious, and that of releasing and transmuting instinctual and emotional energies—can be greatly promoted by the use of appropriate music. The same can be said concerning the awakening and activation of the superconscious spiritual elements and the integration of the personality aimed at by psychosynthesis.

For these purposes music can be used, according to the specific effects desired, either before or after a psychotherapeutic treatment, or during an interval in the course of such treatment. Music can help also to solve inter-individual conflicts and bring about right human relations. A significant instance of such an effect deserves to be quoted in full. Here is what Aleks Pontvik (20) reports in *Contributions aux Recherches sur les Effets Psychiques de la Musique* (an unpublished, privately circulated article):

"We ourselves have had the experience that suitable music at the critical moment of a discussion between two human beings can play a determining role in the sense that somehow its influence can be 'disarming.' It takes the sting out of aggressiveness and renders it unfit for the battle by dissolving the effects before they have a chance to express themselves.

"We are able to report the case of a couple who had firmly decided on a divorce. They were sitting at a table, engaged in a violent discussion which left nothing to be desired as far as its acridness was concerned. Then someone came into the adjoining room and began to play the piano. The discussion had just reached the point where a definite decision regarding their separation was imminent.

"Suddenly, however, nothing came of it. Within half an hour an agreement was reached. Someone in the adjoining room had played Haydn for half an hour. Of course, one must not generalize this case. Subsequent examination of the matter, however, yielded interesting details on the interposition of the musical effect on the critical, problematical, intellectual situation of these two human beings. Above all, both felt pleasantly, calmingly paralyzed. They felt somehow that the conflict had 'split off' and become non-essential. It was a 'disarmament' in the best sense of the word."

11. *Musical performances by the patients themselves*. This is the most effective kind of musical therapy because it combines several

beneficial results. It furnishes a direct and easy outlet for pent-up emotions; it awakens the higher feelings and uplifts the consciousness; it offers all the advantages of occupational therapy. An eloquent testimony to these effects has been given by Georges Duhamel, the great French novelist, essayist, poet and surgeon, in his excellent book, *La Musique Consolatrice* (9). The experience which he reports occurred during World War I, while he was serving as a military surgeon at the front. He writes: "Whenever I happen to ponder upon music, upon the upliftments and clarifications I owe to it, upon the graces it has showered upon me, upon the secret relief for which I owe to it an everlasting gratitude, and upon the place it occupies in my thoughts and even in my decisions, I often evoke certain days of the year 1915." (p. 69)

"During my hours of rest, in the evening, I drank deeply of the humble song I played on the flute. I was still very unskilled, but I kept at it, closing my lips tightly and measuring my breath... By and by my most painful thoughts went to sleep. My body, which had been completely occupied with the effort of enlivening the magic tube, became lost to thought. My soul, purged of its miseries, relieved, freed from all anguish, rose, lightly, in luminous serenity." (p. 72)

"I began to grasp that music would permit me to live. It could certainly not diminish the horror of the massacre, the suffering, the agonies; yet it brought to me, at the very center of the carnage, a breath of divine remission, a principle of hope and salvation. For a man deprived of the consolations of faith, music was nevertheless a kind of faith, that is to say, something that upholds, reunites, revives, comforts. I was no longer forsaken. A voice had been given to me with which to call, to complain, to laud and to pray." (p. 75)

Still more effective, but possible only for the minority of those who have special musical talent, is *creating* music, either through free improvisation on an instrument or through actual composing.

12. *Collective Applications.* These, too, are of two kinds, receptive and active. Concerning the first, it has been ascertained that even an indiscriminate listening to music of various kinds, such as that offered by the radio, has a helpful effect. For instance—similar to very many other hospitals—at the Central

Hospital of Milan, a number of radio-earphones were placed at the disposal of the patients with good results. The invalids became calmer to the extent that care could be noticeably reduced. Concerning the second, the training of psychiatric patients to play together in small bands has yielded very gratifying consequences. It is remarkable how amenable even serious cases are to this kind of organized collective activity; and the patients like it. The chaplain and organist of the Asylum for Insane Criminals at Montelupo, Italy, stated that the worst punishment for the inmates was to be excluded from participation in the musical performances. Another very helpful means is that of teaching patients to sing together in choirs.

A wide use of music in hospitals, particularly in military and psychiatric wards, has been carried on in the United States since the second world war.

In a "convalescent reconditioning program" G.W. Ainlay (2) has outlined a detailed plan for many different applications of music.

There is considerable scope for the application of musical therapy in prisons. Criminals in many cases should really be considered as sick, neurotic, or psychopathic individuals and therefore, as human beings, to be treated by means of psychotherapy and re-education. Correspondingly, prisons would increasingly lose their character of places of punishment and acquire that of institutions in which offenders are kept in seclusion for reasons of social security, but are, at the same time, actively helped towards recuperation. Good beginnings have been made in this direction, but much more could and should be done as rapidly as possible.

Definite applications of music have been made upon the inmates of prisons in various countries. An impressive example of the potent therapeutic effect of music, and a confirmation of the statement previously made about using "great" music with uncultured people also, was contained in a press article a few years ago quoting the report issued by the "Prison Musical Group" of Paris:

"The bold idea of introducing high-class music into Paris prisons has been crowned with complete success. One audience consisted of about two hundred women whose average age was barely thirty. Musical pieces of a very high order were played to them for an hour. We believe that in order to touch human beings of low character we must offer them the highest. In our opinion, this music in the prisons is not an entertainment for the prisoners, but a *real means of cure* capable of arousing individuals, of moving them and of assisting them to take their proper place in life.

"From the first bars the majority of the women were in tears. Under the impression of music, one of the girls who had been arrested for vagrancy and for leading an immoral life, broke down and retracted her assertion, which she had made to the authorities, that she was alone in the world. She revealed her secret to the director and gave him the name and address of her grandmother. The girl, who would have been sent to a convict settlement, was returned to her relatives and undoubtedly owes her salvation to the effects of music."

The field of musical therapy is indeed large, and the fruits it can yield are significant and precious. Its cultivation calls for a widespread cooperation between physicians, psychologists and musicians.

We trust that the magic of sound, scientifically applied, will contribute in ever greater measure to the relief of human suffering, to a higher development and a richer integration of the human personality, to the harmonious synthesis of all human "notes," of all "group chords and melodies"—until there will be the great symphony of the One Humanity.

REFERENCES

1. Agrippa Von Nettersheim, H. C.: *De Occulta Philosophia* Lib. II, Cap. 14, Antwerp: 1531.
2. Ainlay, G.W.: The place of music in military hospitals. In Dorothy M. Schullian & M. Schoen (Eds) *Music and Medicine,* New York: Schuman, 1948.
3. *Anaesthesia and Analgesia Current Research* (Bi-monthly), Vol. 29, 1950, Cleveland, Ohio: International Anaesthesia Research Soc., Wade Park Manor, E 107th & Park Lane.
4. Aristotle: *Politics & Athenian Constitution,* Trans. Warrington, J., New York: Dutton, 1959.
5. Bible, The: I *Sam.* 16:23 — King James version.
6. Capurso, A. & Others: *Music and your Emotions,* New York: Liveright, 1952 (for Music Research Foundation, New York).

7. Chomet, H: *Effets et influence de la musique sur la santé et sur la maladie*, Paris: Germer-Baillière, 1874.
—— *The Influence of Music on Health and Life*, Trans. Flint, Laura A., New York: Putnam, 1875.
8. Diserens, C.M.: The development of an experimental psychology of music. In Dorothy M. Schullian & M. Schoen (Eds) *Music and Medicine*, New York: Schuman, 1948.
9. Duhamel, G.: *La Musique Consolatrice*, Monaco: Editions du Rocher, 1944.
10. Gratry, A.J.A.: *Les Sources*, Paris: Doumol, 1891.
11. Hanson, H.: Emotional Expression in Music. In Dorothy M. Schullian & M. Schoen (Eds) *Music and Medicine*, New York: Schuman, 1948.
12. Homer: *Odyssey* XIX,Trans. Andrew, S. O., New York: Dutton, 1953.
13. Howes, F.: *Man, Mind and Music*, London: Secker & Warburg, 1948.
14. James, W.: *Principles of Psychology,*Vol. I, New York: Dover, 1951.
15. Kalevala, The: Everyman's Series, Vol. I & II, New York: Dutton, 1958.
16. Kepler, J.: *De Harmonice Mundi*, Book V, Augsburg: 1619.
17. Pilo, M.: *Psicologia Musicale*, Milan: Hoepli, 1912.
18. Plato: *The Republic*, Book III, 401, Trans. Cornford, F. M., Oxford: University Press, 1942.
19. Podolsky, E.: *Music Therapy*, New York: Philosophical Library, 1954.
20. Pontvik, A.: a. *Grundgedanken zur Psychischen Heilwirkung der Musik* (Fundamental thoughts on the psychic healing effect of music), Zurich: Rascher Verlag, 1948.
—— b. *Contributions aux Recherches sur les Effets Psychiques de la Musique*, Unpublished. Privately circulated article.
21. Porphyry: *De Vita Pythagorae*, Edit. A. Nauck: Leipzig, 1885.
22. Radin, P.: Music and medicine among primitive peoples. In Dorothy M. Schullian & M. Schoen (Eds) *Music and Medicine*, New York: Schuman, 1948.
23. Schullian, Dorothy M. and Schoen, M.: *Music and Medicine*, New York: Schuman, 1948.
24. Schweitzer, A.: *Johann Sebastian Bach*, Leipzig: Breitkopf & Hartel, 1915.
25. Scott, C.: *The Influence of Music on History and Morals*, London: Theosophical Pub. House, 1928.

QUESTIONNAIRE ON MUSICAL THERAPY

1. What beneficial or harmful effects of instrumental and vocal music have you noticed?

   (a) Upon your physical health in general, and upon different bodily conditions (in particular, blood circulation; nervous system; physical pains; etc.).

   (b) Upon your emotional life (emotional release; joyous elevation or depression; excitement; excessive emotions).

(c) Upon your imagination.

(d) Upon your intellectual or artistic activities (memory; intellectual work; inspiration; creativity).

(e) Upon your will and your external activity.

(f) Upon your spiritual life.

2. Could you cite specific effects derived from given musical compositions? Have you noticed that the same piece of music has produced on you different effects, according to the different physical or psychological states in which you were on various occasions? Can you quote some specific instances of such different effects?

3. Which of all these effects have you been able to observe in others?

4. What physical or emotional effects do music and singing have upon you *as performer*?

5. What are the effects produced upon you by rhythmic movement (rhythmical gymnastics; dancing)?

MUSICAL THERAPY OF OBSESSIVE IDEAS

The case of a patient suffering from an obsessive idea — an idea which dominates him and renders his actions compulsive — offers an instance of the application of musical therapy by means of a special technique for creating unconscious associations.

Listening to a piece of music brings about an involuntary association between the music and the more or less latent emotions and thoughts of the patient. It is this association, which has been demonstrated by experiments, that forms the basis of a special music-therapeutic process whereby it has been found possible to disperse, or at least to modify, a morbid condition generated by an obsessive idea. It is, of course, necessary that the patient should never before have heard the music to be used, because any familiar piece would already have "impressed" other thoughts and emotions on the patient, likely to interfere in a negative way. The use of original pieces of music adapted by specialists to each particular case would be ideal.

This therapeutic technique can be briefly described as follows. The patient is invited to let go and to "live" his state of anguish with as much intensity as possible. At the same time he is made to listen to a piece of music selected for its ability to reflect his emotional state. The experience is then repeated until it is observed that an actual and intimate fusion between the music and the obsessive idea has taken place in the patient; until, in fact, the former is seen to evoke immediately the emotion associated with the latter. When this pattern of response has been firmly established, a short interlude precedes the second phase of the treatment.

This time the patient is invited to imagine that he is cured and freed from every trouble, that he is able to overcome, normally and naturally, the trials which he has regarded as fearful and difficult. He is made to listen, as before, to another piece of music, this time in harmony with a feeling of victory and inner peace. This phase is more difficult because, if the patient has succeeded easily in yielding to his anguish, he encounters serious obstacles in trying to identify himself with the picture of being cured; the principal reason being that, in the first phase, the situation is "lived," while in the second it is only imagined.

These two phases are a preparation for a third, which is the actual therapeutic stage after the two pieces—the one expressing anguish, the other the overcoming and the release—have been profoundly assimilated and identified by the patient with his own feelings. This time the patient is asked not to think of anything in particular, but only to allow the music he is about to hear to flow into him and affect him as it will. The composition should begin with the principal theme of the first piece with which the patient will, more or less consciously, associate his feelings of anguish. A bridging passage should follow, designed to link the first theme to a clear statement of the main theme of the second piece. The structure of this passage should express the inner conflict of the patient, his efforts to conquer his condition of anguish and to attain inner peace; the struggle between the two themes gradually culminating in the triumph of the second theme, which is then reinforced by variations of it.

Many such "auditions" may be required before a cure is arrived at, or substantial improvement obtained. The process is mainly an unconscious one wherein the patient, listening to the development of the musical conflict, will feel an upsurge of his real conflict—thanks to the technique of establishing the associations previously. He will pass through crises of anguish and experience moments of hope, to arrive at last at the stabilization of a state of tranquility and well-being.

Such is briefly the technique of this specific method of musical therapy. It is particularly applicable in the case of patients who lack a strong "will to get well."   M. V.

THE BIRD OF PARADISE

Naught could I see, closed in I was, low down
Behind a moving mass of hats, behind
A sombre wall of shoulders; then every whisper ceased
When he, the artist, forward came: all in an instant,
Like a sudden hush of waters
When winds get still. . .My eyes, unneeded now,
I closed, and motionless remained, and silent.

But yet there was no darkness 'neath my lids,
Only faint shadow, dewy and silver-glowing.
The morning dawned all red, the violin
Began for him to whisper its first notes,
Its primal tones of wonder and delight.

Uplifting then my gaze I seemed to see
From out the flaming sun a Bird of Gold
Winging a rapid flight. From earth uprose
A mighty tree whereon the wanderer,
In rhythmic song, staying its dazzling flight
With airy wing scarce bent the flowering crown.

A sombre throng around the tree was massed;
Each one had come, with close-drawn cloak,
Hiding the secret dormant of his soul,
With knife-thrust in his heart, and knife held ready.
Each one with claws, and yet with greetings
In his hands, the mask upon his face.

All sadness; and the Bird of Paradise
Did but accentuate with sweetest song
The secret grief, the damp, pale lips
Of each and all. Loudly it wept
And in the streaming tears that silently
Furrowed our cheeks, the Heavenly Bird was weeping.

It sang; our slower speech, our every word
It did transform, as though intoxicate,
Into its own delirium of joy.
From out the vast of Heaven, with arduous toil

It did dissolve and free the voiceless soul;
The crude, hard soul which, since our birth,
Coiled dumbly in the throat, has lain asleep.

And, as though drawn in darkness to the earth,
Downward it rushed; the Voice divine,
Reft of its glorious pinions. . .further still
To lower depths descended than ourselves
Do know; then, rose its flight, gaining new impetus,
And with the flight, upward the abyss was drawn.

And so down it rushed, like eagle to the assault,
The Bird Divine, its lovely plumage dimm'd
To dullest black, all brilliance gone; like swords
The stiffened feathers—hardly had it reached
With ready, open claws, the victim, suddenly
Upward it bounded, bearing its prey.

And as it rose, its golden hue returned:
Our rancorous thoughts, likewise transformed, rose also,
And our funeral garments, rising, changed
From dark to light, to silver, then to gold;
Our hair, now turned to grey with passing years,
Displayed the ardent colors of our youth.

And thus from out the narrow cloistered walls
Of custom we broke free; then at the foot
Of the great flowering Tree we found ourselves
And saw, but with a new and different vision,
As if beyond the present; hence,
Our life, and ourselves with it, were transported.

Under that spreading Tree the crowd now was
Gentle and harmless, like a field of corn
Bending in slow and ample undulations.
The glorious Song outpoured alike on all;
A breeze most lightly stirred the wings of gold.

Then spake the ethereal Voice: "O Man, it is
Thy weeping, like an airy veil, that lays
A soft transparent shadow on the eyes
Sated with seeing; let it overflow
And take its course; the furrows in thy cheeks
Shall now be filled with rivulets of light.

The joy that thou has lost, O Man,
Seek in thy pain, seek it, until thou find
This or another, maybe more sweet and pure—
For joy is like a tree of sombre bark,
And wood within like to the plum and blackthorn,
Yet often upon the crown will flower a rose. . .
O Man, this is the Tree where Woman first

Did seem to hear from out the Leafy Bower
Perfidious hiss within the foliage hid. . .
Here, where the twisting Serpent met Eve's gaze,
My wings I spread; and this shall always be,
Where'er was bitterness, thou shalt have sweetness.

A power, stern, breaks and wears away
The rocky mountain pass, but thou shalt find
The steps and pathways where that strife has passed;
A thousand furies waste and rend the earth,
And pass away; the empty tracks of evil
The caves and valleys—here behold them filled
With azure waters; here behold the rivers,
Here the lakes, the good alone reflecting. . ."

Francesco Chiesa

CHAPTER VIII

Transmutation and Sublimation of Sexual Energies

The problem of sex, the problem of how to deal in a sane and constructive way with the sexual drive, has confronted humanity ever since the beginning of civilization. But, for various reasons, this problem has now become more compelling, and public awareness of it is more acute; to use a current phrase, humanity has become definitely sex-conscious.

The crisis in the relations between the sexes is not isolated, but forms part and perhaps can be said to be the outstanding aspect of the general crisis which is deeply affecting the very foundations of existing civilization.

The authority of the religious and moral principles on which our civilization was based, the rules and customs which were formerly taken for granted and accepted (even if not always consistently applied) have lost or are rapidly losing their prestige, their binding and regulating power; even more, the younger generation is actively, and at times violently, revolting against them. The main cause of this crisis has been the fact that, while the religious fervor and the unquestioned acceptance of the theological and moral conceptions of the past have been rapidly losing their grip, the older and rigidly orthodox groups have attempted by sheer authority to enforce the strict rules, condemnations and prohibitions based on those theological and moralistic foundations.

Thus, in the past, in the sexual domain an attitude prevailed which led public opinion to regard the biological instincts and the human passions as bad and impure. Therefore, the method enjoined for dealing with them was that of suppression, except when the sex urge could find a justified satisfaction in lawful marriage. The whole subject of sex was considered improper, and adults tried to keep young people ignorant about it as long as possible.

The weakening of the religious influence on which that attitude was based, and the realization of the injurious effects of that suppression on health and character evoked various movements of revolt. First we had the "return to nature," advocated by Rousseau and his followers; then the glorification of feeling by the romantic movement; later, revival of the hedonistic and aesthetic ideas of ancient Greece and the Renaissance, followed by the wave of philosophical and practical materialism, and the individualistic revolt against society and its norms as portrayed by Ibsen. Perhaps more important in modern society has been the influence of Freud and his followers of the psychoanalytic movement, which emphasized the psychopathological effects of sexual repression. All these concurred to foster and justify the uncontrolled gratification of all drives and impulses, the letting loose of every passion, the following of every whim.

But the result of this "liberation" did not produce the expected satisfaction and happiness. While it eliminated some of the drawbacks of the earlier rigid attitude and the consequent suffering, it produced other complications, conflicts and misery. The followers of uncontrolled sexual expression found, and are still finding, that excesses are necessarily followed by exhaustion or disgust; that the sexual drive and passion, even when not checked by moral considerations, cannot always find gratification owing to lack of suitable partners. Moreover, various drives often come into conflict with each other, so that indulgence in one requires the inhibition of another. For instance, a reckless yielding to sexual urge is apt to clash with self-preservation, creating a conflict between, for instance, lust and fear of disease. Further, an exaggerated sense of self-assertion may be in conflict with social mores and the consequent fear of the risks involved.

The lack of any stable guiding principle, of any clear scale of values, makes the individual insecure, robs him of self-reliance, and subjects him to the influence of other people and external circumstances. Moreover, ethical and spiritual principles or aspirations cannot be eliminated as easily as many seem to believe; they persist in the unconscious owing to hereditary and environmental influences, and also exist latent in the true spiritual nature of man. When violated, they arouse conscious or unconscious protest and consequently intense inner conflicts.

For clarity's sake the picture of the situation has been over-simplified. In reality we are at present in a period of transition, of confusion and of cross-currents. In some places and groups the old conditions persist; old concepts and methods are still being enforced. In many cases a state of violent reaction and of conflict between the generations prevails. In the more advanced and enlightened circles the exaggerated nature of the reaction has been recognized and attempts are being made to find and adopt balanced views and sound methods.

It is apparent that neither of the two extreme attitudes can give satisfactory results. One might think that some compromise between the two could be the way out of the impasse, but while such a common-sense procedure might avert the worst results of those extremes, experience indicates that it cannot be considered a satisfactory solution.

However, there is another alternative, a more dynamic and constructive way of handling the problem. This is based on, and takes advantage of, a fundamental property of biological and psychological energies, namely, the possibility of their *transmutation*—a possibility existing in all energies.

The real nature of the process is not well known, but such is the case with all "ultimates." For instance, it cannot be claimed that we have grasped the essential nature of electricity, but we know enough about its manifestations and the laws regulating them to enable us to utilize electricity in many diverse and often complicated ways, as in electronics. It is the same in the psychological field; we need not ascertain the ultimate nature of the psychological energies and their transmutations in order to utilize them increasingly through a growing knowledge of the laws that govern them and by means of appropriate and efficient methods based on those laws. We can therefore proceed confidently in our examination of the methods to be followed in the utilization for constructive ends of surplus or excessive sexual drives. This is particularly valuable, for instance, in balancing the sexual appetites of man and wife in marriage, or adjusting to situations where normal sexual relations are not available.

The first rule is to adopt an objective attitude towards sex, free from the traditional reactions of fear, prudishness, and condemnation, as well as from the lure and glamor—often artificially fostered—by which it is generally surrounded at present. The sexual drive, like any other, is in *itself* neither "bad" nor "good." It is a biological function and, as such, it is not "immoral" but *pre*-moral. It has a great importance because it ensures the continuity of the animal species and of the human race. In animals it is subject to natural cyclic self-regulation. In civilized humanity it has become complicated through its close association with psychological functions, such as emotion and imagination, and with social and ethical factors which have partly over-stimulated, partly inhibited it. Therefore, the objective scientific attitude towards the sexual drive should be twofold: we should, on the one hand, eliminate the fears and condemnations, which have the effect of repressing it into the unconscious, as psychoanalysis has demonstrated; and, on the other hand, we should exercise a calm but firm control, followed by an active process of transmutation whenever its natural expression is unwarranted.

The processes of psychological transmutation and sublimation are symbolically indicated—although in obscure and abstruse ways—in the writings of alchemists (Jung, 9b). Other hints can be found in the works of writers on asceticism and mysticism, such as Evelyn Underhill. In the modern approach to the subject we find the following significant statement by Freud: "The elements of the sexual instinct are characterized by a capacity for sublimation, for changing their sexual aim into another of a different kind and socially more worthy. To the sum of energies thus gained for our psychological productions we probably owe the highest results of our culture." (Freud: *Ueber Psychoanalyse*, Leipzig und Wien, Deutike, 1910, pp. 61-62)[1]. This statement is important, for in it

---

[1]Many other psychologists have recognized the process of sublimation and dealt with it more or less extensively. Among them are Havelock Ellis (5), McDougall (11), and Hadfield (7). An accurate survey of the subject with many quotations and bibliographical references has been made by J. Trevor Davies in his book *Sublimation* (1947) (3). The theoretical problems and the differences of opinion aroused by the subject do not prevent—in this as in other cases—effective use of the *process* of psychological transmutation.

Freud himself shows the fallacy of considering the physical and instinctive aspects of sexuality separately and independently from its emotional and other psychological aspects. Yet this fallacy is committed by some investigators having a materialistic bias. Such a purely zoological consideration is altogether one-sided, and while those investigators have piled up a huge mass of facts, the neglect of their vital connection with the psychological aspect of sex, which is the truly *human* one, vitiates the conclusions drawn from them. James Hinton wittily remarked over half a century ago that to deal with the great fact of sexual love merely from the physical side would be like thinking, during a concert by Sarasate, of the cat's bowels and the horse's tail used in making the violin strings and bow (Ellis, 6).

In seeking to define the nature of sexuality we find in it three principal aspects:

1. A sensual aspect: physical pleasure;

2. An emotional aspect: union with another person;

3. A creative aspect: the birth of a new creature.

This classification does not claim to be scientifically accurate, but constitutes a practical aid in the process of transmutation. Each of the aspects mentioned can be transmuted or sublimated in accordance with its own specific nature.

Moreover, transmutations can take place in two directions. The first is the "vertical" or inward direction. Many instances of this kind of sublimation are offered by the lives and writings of the mystics of all times, places and religions. Their autobiographies furnish most interesting evidence of the nature of this process, its crises and vicissitudes, the suffering it entails as well as the joys which reward its stress and strain. All of them speak of the "bliss" they experience—which, however, they regard as a possible hindrance if one becomes attached to it. One can also observe the different steps leading from human love to love for a higher Being, such as the Christ, or for God Himself; this is the sublimation of the emotional aspect. They aspire to union with the Christ within, and some of them speak of it as the "mystical marriage." In psychological terms one would say that the goal of spiritual synthesis is the union of the personality with the spiritual Self, the first representing the negative feminine pole, the other the positive masculine pole. This polarity is a reality and not just a simple symbolical transposition of a biological fact. It is one of the fundamental aspects of the spirit-matter polarity and is, so to speak, its reflection on the psycho-spiritual level, as sexual polarity is its expression on the physical level.

Let us pause here for a moment in order to dissipate certain confusions and misunderstandings that might arise. While the process of transmutation and sublimation can frequently be observed, one must not infer therefrom that *all* spiritual love is "merely" the outcome of sublimated sex, that it is possible to "explain away" a higher psychological or spiritual manifestation by attributing its origin to biological sources or drives. The true nature of mysticism cannot be considered, as some investigators have maintained, to be merely a product or by-product of sex. On the one hand, one finds many people whose normal sexual life is inhibited yet who show no trace of mysticism; on the other hand, there are instances of people leading a normal sexual life, raising a family, etc., and having at the same time genuine mystical experiences.

The spiritual life and consciousness belongs to a definite psychological level and has a quality which is specific and not derived. The transmuted energies reach up to it from below, as it were, and give it added vitality and "heat," but they neither create nor explain that higher life. The creative aspect can be sublimated in this "vertical" direction in the formation of a new regenerated personality. The growth of the "inner man" calls for these creative energies, and in accordance with the degree to which the individual employs them new spheres of action of increasing vastness will open up before him.

The second direction of the transmutation process is "horizontal" or external. Here also we find three kinds of transmutation, corresponding to the three aspects. The first, rather than being actual transmutation, consists of the substitution of other pleasures of the senses for sexual pleasure, from simple enjoyment of food to the enjoyment of contact with nature and to aesthetic pleasures by the cultivation of the appreciation of beauty through sight and hearing. The second consists of an enlargement or extension of love so as to include a growing number of individuals; the third produces or fosters artistic and intellectual activities.

When the physical sexual expression of human love is blocked for some reason, its emotional or feeling manifestations can be enhanced and reach a high level of ideal, "platonic" love. Further, independently of any obstacle to the free and complete expression of love, a gradual process of transmutation takes place normally and spontaneously in harmoniously married couples. At the beginning, the sexual and intensely emotional manifestations of love generally predominate, but in the course of years and decades this passionate aspect cools off and is transmuted into tender feeling, increasing mutual understanding, appreciation, and inner communion.

The love-energy derived from sexual sublimation can and does expand beyond love of one individual. It extends in concentric circles or spheres, encompassing ever larger groups of human beings. In the form of compassion it is poured upon those who suffer; then it undergoes a further transmutation and becomes a motive power for social and philanthropic action. Sublimated love-energy can also be expressed as comradeship and friendship for those with whom we have a common basis of understanding, aims and activity. Finally, it can reach out further until it radiates as brotherly love upon all human beings and upon all living creatures.

The third kind of transmutation of the sexual energies is into creative activities of an artistic or intellectual nature. The following statement by a great philosopher, Arthur Schopenhauer, strongly bears out this point:

"In the days and in the hours in which the tendency to voluptuousness is stronger . . . just then also the higher spiritual energies . . . are apt to be aroused most strongly. They are inactive when man's consciousness has yielded to lust, but through effective effort their direction can be changed and then man's consciousness is occupied, instead of with those lower and tormenting desires, by the highest activities of the mind."

There appears to be a deep similarity between sexual energy and the creative energies operating at other levels of the human being. Artistic creation offers a particularly suitable channel for sublimation, and many instances can be found in the lives of great artists, writers and composers. One of them, which has a special significance, is that of Richard Wagner. As is well known, he was at one time passionately in love with a married woman, Mathilde Wesendonck, to whom he gave music lessons and in whom he found an understanding of and a devotion to his genius which he missed in his first wife, Minna. After a short time they resolved to renounce the consummation of their love, and Wagner left Zurich and went, or rather fled, to Venice. At first his desperate mood induced ideas of suicide, but soon he set himself to write both the libretto and music of *Tristan and Isolde*, and in a kind of creative frenzy, completed the opera within a few months. During this period he wrote many letters to Mathilde and kept a diary intended for her. These were published after his death and in them one can clearly trace the gradual cooling off of his passion as he gave expression to it in the poetry and music of his opera. The completion of the work found him so detached that he wrote to Mathilde in a rather tepid and much lighter vein, and even paid her a short visit on purely friendly terms. That Wagner was aware of this process of sublimation and consciously fostered it is evident from a letter to Liszt: "As in my life I have never enjoyed the true happiness of love, I want to raise a monument to this most beautiful of all dreams, in which this love shall be fully satisfied, from beginning to end. I am planning a 'Tristan and Isolde'."

Transmutation and sublimation is a process that can be either spontaneous or consciously and deliberately fostered and brought about. In the latter case, there is ample scope for the effective application of the facts and laws ascertained or rediscovered by modern dynamic psychology, and for the use of active techniques based on them. Here are some practical methods for such applications:

1. A firm conscious *control* of the drive to be transmuted, in which, however, care should be taken to avoid any condemnation or fear of it, as this could result in its repression in the unconscious. Non-condemnation of the drive, as such, does not imply a lack of realization of one's serious responsibility for the consequences, both individual and social, of its unregulated expression. Control can be helped by simple physical means, such as brisk muscular activity and rhythmic breathing; but the most effective, and at the same time the higher, way of con-

trolling both the sexual and the power drives is the acceptance and recognition of every human being as a "Thou" to be respected, and not as an "object" for the gratification of our pleasure, an "it" to be dominated and exploited. The reality of such a basic "right relation" to our fellowmen and our duty to recognize it have been convincingly expounded and emphasized by Martin Buber (2).

2. The active release, development and expression of the various aspects of personal and spiritual love—love for one's mate; love for others, beginning with those close to one and expanding to include increasing numbers of human beings in ever-widening circles and "upwards" towards God or the Supreme. The emphasis should be put on the *expression* of love—in understanding and cooperation in altruistic and humanitarian activities.

3. The deliberate projection of one's interest, aspiration and enthusiasm towards some *creative work* into which all one's energies can be poured. Various techniques for creative expression can be used for this purpose, such as drawing, writing, movement (Assagioli, 1).

4. The use of *symbols*. These exercise a strong attractive power on all our energies, conscious and unconscious, and specifically foster the process of transmutation. Jung in his *Contributions to Analytical Psychology* (9) went so far as to state: "The psychological machinery which transmutes energy is the symbol." There is a great variety of symbols having an anagogic (uplifting) influence that can be made to serve this process, of which ideal human figures or "models" constitute an important class. Two types of these ideal figures, different and in a sense opposite, are respectively suited to men and women. A man may visualize some hero or a human-divine Being, such as the Christ, or he can use the image of an ideal woman like Dante's Beatrice or the Madonna. Inversely a woman can take as a model the highest type of womanhood her imagination can conceive or an image of the ideal Man. The influence of such "images" is beautifully expressed in the Indian saying: "Ganga (the sacred river) purifies when seen and touched, but the Holy Ones purify when merely remembered."

A simple and effective symbol is the lotus plant which transmutes the mud and water of the pond into the delicate substance and beautiful form and hue of its flower. This it does through its own inherent vitality and through the life-giving energy of the sun's rays. Desoille in his therapeutic method of the guided day-dream (4a) has made use of symbolic movement upward for the purpose of sublimation and transformation. Kretschmer (10) has summarized various techniques of imagery which can be used to foster this process of sublimation.

Other anagogic symbols may be produced spontaneously in dreams and in free drawing; Jung and his followers (E. Harding (8), F. Wickes (13) and others) have made an extensive study and application of them.

5. Close psychological *communion* with individuals or groups who have realized, or are striving to realize, the same aim. As there are chemical catalysts, so there are "human catalysts," whose influence, radiation, and the "atmosphere" they create, greatly facilitate psychological transformations.

The importance and value of transmutation and sublimation—not only of the sexual energies but of all other drives—should be more widely known and appreciated, and the methods for putting them in operation should be more extensively applied in psychotherapy, education, and self-actualization.

The process of transmutation and sublimation may be compared to the regulation of the waters of a great river, which prevents recurring disastrous inundations or the formation of unhealthy marshes along its banks. While a portion of the water is permitted to flow freely to its natural destination, the remainder is diverted through proper channelling to appropriate mechanisms that transform its energy into electricity to be employed as motive power for industrial and other purposes. In a parallel way, the conscious or unconscious drives, which produce so much individual suffering and social disturbance, can become, if rightly controlled and channelled, the springs of activities having great human and spiritual value.

REFERENCES

1. Assagioli, R.: "Creative Expression in Education," *American Journal of Education*, 1963, No. 1.
2. Buber, M.: *I and Thou*, New York, Scribners, 1958.
3. Davies, J. Trevor: *Sublimation*, London, Allen & Unwin, 1947. New York, Macmillan, 1948.
4. Desoille, R.: *Exploration de l'affectivité subconsciente par la méthode du rêve éveillé. Sublimation et acquisitions psychologiques*, Paris, D'Artrey, 1938.
4a. Desoille, R.: *Le Rêve éveillé en psychothérapie*, Paris, Presses Universitaires de France, 1945.
5. Ellis, H.: *Little Essays of Love and Virtue*, New York, Doubleday, 1962.
6. Ellis, Mrs. H.: *Three Modern Seers: Hinton, Nietzsche and Carpenter*, London, Stanley. 1910.
7. Hadfield, J. A.: *Psychology and Morals*, London, Methuen, 1923. New York, McBride, 1925.
8. Harding, M. E.: *Psychic Energy. Its Source and its Goal*, New York, Pantheon Books 1947.
9. Jung, C. G.: *Contributions to Analytical Psychology*, New York, Harcourt Brace 1928.
9a. Jung, C. G.: *The Integration of the Personality*, London, Kegan Paul, Trench Trubner, 1940. New York, Farrar & Rinehart, 1939.
9b. Jung, C. G.: *Psychology and Alchemy*. Collected Works, Vol. 12, London, Kegan Paul, 1953. New York, Pantheon. 1953.
10. Kretschmer, Jr., W.: *Meditative Techniques in Psychotherapy* (translated by Wm. Swartley), New York, Psychosynthesis Res. Found., 1959.
11. McDougall, W.: *The Energies of Men*, London, Methuen, 1932. New York, Scribner, 1933.
12. Sorokin, P. A.: *The Ways and Power of Love (Types, Factors and Techniques of Moral Transformation)*, Boston, Beacon Press, 1954.
13. Wickes, F. G.: *The Inner World of Man*, London, Methuen, 1950. New York, H. Holt, 1948.

Part Four

APPENDIX

HISTORICAL OUTLINE OF PSYCHOSYNTHESIS |
ROBERTO ASSAGIOLI — BIBLIOGRAPHY | PICTURES
AND COLORS — THEIR PSYCHOLOGICAL EFFECTS
| INITIATED SYMBOL PROJECTION | MEDITATIVE
TECHNIQUES IN PSYCHOTHERAPY

A HISTORICAL OUTLINE OF PSYCHOSYNTHESIS

A beginning of my conception of psychosynthesis was contained in my doctoral thesis on Psychoanalysis (1910), in which I pointed out what I considered to be some of the limitations of Freud's views. In 1911 I presented my view on the unconscious in a paper at the "International Congress of Philosophy" in Bologna.

Then I gradually developed my ideas and combined in my psychotherapeutic practice the use of various techniques of psychotherapy, presenting my views in many lectures and published articles and pamphlets, among which was one in English in the year 1927 with the title "A New Method of Healing—Psychosynthesis."

In 1926 the "Istituto di Psicosintesi" was founded in Rome with the purpose of developing, applying and teaching the various techniques of psychotherapy and of psychological training, aiming to achieve the psychosynthesis of patients and, in the educational field, of pupils. World War II halted these activities, but from 1946 onwards courses of lectures on psychosynthesis, on psychological types, etc., were given in Italy, Switzerland and England; and further articles and pamphlets were published in various languages. (See Bibliography.)

In 1957 the "Psychosynthesis Research Foundation" was incorporated in the United States and the "Istituto di Psicosintesi" resumed its activities in Florence, Italy (Via San Domenico 16), with affiliated Centers in Rome and Bologna.

From 1960 to date Triant Triantafyllou, Ph.D., of Athens has translated and published in Greek various writings on psychosynthesis. In January 1969 he established the "Greek Association for Psychosynthesis" and opened the "Greek Center for Psychosynthesis," Kyvelis 5, Athens, Greece.

In 1964 "Psychosynthesis in Education, an Association for Personal and Spiritual Integration" was established in London under the leadership of Wm. Ford Robertson, M.D., O.B.E., dedicated chiefly to psychosynthesis in education.

In 1966 Juan Aleandri, M.D. and his colleagues incorporated the "Associacion Argentina de Psicosintesis," Juncal 2061, 1o B, Buenos Aires; followed in 1968 by the establishing of the "Instituto de Biopsicosintesis" at the John F. Kennedy University, Buenos Aires.

In 1965 the Indian Institute of Psychosynthesis was founded at Moradabad by Prof. J. P. Atreya, editor of the journal *Darshana*.

International Conventions on Psychosynthesis were held at Villeneuve near Montreux, Switzerland, in 1960 and 1961, and in Rome in 1967.

Roberto Assagioli

DR. ROBERT ASSAGIOLI — BIBLIOGRAPHY[a]

Gli Effetti del Riso e le loro Applicazioni Pedagogiche. (Rivista di Psicologia Applicata, Bologna, No. 2, 1906)

La Psicologia delle Idee-Forze e la Psicagogia. (Rivista di Psicologia Applicata, No 2-3, Bologna, 1910)

Trasformazione e Sublimazione delle Energie Sessuali. (Rivista di Psicologia Applicata, No. 3, Bologna, 1912) (Russian translation: "Psichoterapia," No. 3, 1912)

II Subcosciente. (Atti del IV Congresso Internationale di Filosofia, Bologna, 1911) ("Biblioteca Filosofica," 1911)

La Psicologia del Subcosciente: 1. La Psicoanalisi—2. Personalità alternantie e Concosciente. ("Psiche," No 2-3, Florence, 1912)

Psicologia e Psicoterapie. ("Psiche," No 3, Florence, 1913)

Gli Errori degli Scienziati. ("Psiche," No 4, Florence, 1913)

La Classificazione dei Sogni. ("Psiche," No 4, Florence, 1915)

L'Ecole Psychopathologique Americaine. ("Scientia," Milan, March, 1919)

La Psicologia e la Scienza della Sessualità. ("Bolletino dell' Associazione di Studi Psicologici," No 1, Florence, 1920)

A New Method of Healing: Psychosynthesis. (Istituto di Psicosintesi, Rome, 1927)

II Valore Practico ed Umano della Cultura Psichica. (Istituto di Psicosintesi, Rome, 1929) (French translation: "Bulletin de la Société Lorraine de Psychologie Appliquée," No 34-35, Lorraine, 1930)

Psicanalisi e Psicosintesi. (Istituto di Psicosintesi, Rome, 1931) (English translation: "Hibbert Journal," London, 1934)

Parole Franche agli Adulti. ("Rivista Montessori," Rome, 1931)

Sviluppo Spirituale e Malattie Nervose. (Istituto di Psicosintesi, Rome, 1933) (English translation: "Hibbert Journal," London, 1937)(German translation: "Wege zum Menschen," Monatschrift für Seelsorge, Psychotherapie und Erziehung, Göttingen, Mav. 1955).

La Musica Come Causa di Malattia e Come Mezzo di Cura. ("Rivista Internazionale del Cinema Educativo," Rome, 1934)

Contribution de la Psychologie à l'Education Interculturelle. ("Revue Pedagogique," No 3, Tournai, Nov. 1948)

Come si Imparano le Lingue col Subcosciente. ("L'Economia Umana," Rassegna Medica Internazionale, Milan, May-June, 1954)

Saggezza Sorridente. ("Fenarete," Milan, January, 1955)

Comprendere gli Altri. ("Fenarete," Milan, April, 1955)

La Psicologia e la Scienza della Sessualità'. ("L'Economia Umana," Milan, November-December, 1955)

II Mistero dell'Io. ("La Grande Ricerca," Rome, April-June, 1956) (Portuguese translation: "Monismo," Sao Vicente, Natal, 1959; Rio de Janeior, 1960)

Modi e Ritmi della Formazione Psicologica. ("L'Economia Umana," Milan, November-December, 1956)

Veleni e Farmaci Psicologici. ("La Grande Ricerca," Rome, July-September, 1956)

La Psicoterapia. ("Medicina Psicosomatica," Rome, 1957, No. 1)

---

[a]More important titles only

Music as a Cause of Disease and as a Healing Agent. (revised and expanded) (Psychosynthesis Research Foundation, U.S.A., 1956)
La Psicologia della Donna e la sua Psicosintesi. ("L'Economia Umana," Milan, March-April, 1958)
Dynamic Psychology and Psychosynthesis. (Psychosynthesis Research Foundation, (U.S.A., 1959)
Psychologie Dynamique & Psychosynthèse. ("Centre de Psychosynthèse," 11 rue Franquet, Paris 15e.)
Self-Realization and Psychological Disturbances. (Psychosynthesis Research Foundation, U.S.A., 1961)
La Psicologia e l'Arte di Vivere.(Isituto di Psicosintesi, Florence, 1962)
Psicologia dinamica e psicosintesi.(Istituto di Psicosintesi, Florence 1962)
L'educazione dei giovani particolarmente dotati.(Istituto di Psicosintesi, Florence, 1962)
Pictures and Colors (Their Psychological Effects) (Psychosynthesis Research Foundation, U.S.A.)
The Balancing and Synthesis of the Opposites. (Psychosynthesis Research Foundation, U.S.A.)
Smiling Wisdom. (Psychosynthesis Research Foundation, U.S.A.)
The Training of the Will (Psychosynthesis Research Foundation, U.S.A., 1966)
Jung and Psychosynthesis (Psychosynthesis Research Foundation, U.S.A., 1967)
Psychosomatic Medicine and Bio-Psychosynthesis (Psychosynthesis Research Foundation, U.S.A., 1967)
The Psychology of Woman and Her Psychosynthesis (Psychosynthesis Research Foundation, U.S.A., 1968)
Symbols of Transpersonal Experiences,("Journal of Transpersonal Psychology," Spring 1969.)

PICTURES AND COLORS: THEIR PSYCHOLOGICAL EFFECTS

By Roberto Assagioli, M.D.

Pictures and objects of various kinds (paintings, drawings, and all objects of art) often have a great suggestive power, especially upon those who belong to the visual type. Their influence is twofold: on the one hand, this is due to the intensity of their expressive power or the charm of their beauty, and on the other, to their inherent meaning.

This double combination explains the enormous influence of works of art, an influence which has inspired millions of people through all the ages and has often moulded a whole period or an entire nation.

Thus, it would appear that in works of art there is much more than mere aesthetic value; they constitute living forces, almost living entities, embodying a power which has suggestive and creative effects. Therefore we should not allow this force to remain unused, or subject ourselves to it unconsciously and without definite purpose; instead, we should learn to use it deliberately for the further development of our personality.

To obtain the full benefit of this influence, it is necessary to observe the picture or object in the following way. We must contemplate it intently, in a state of sympathetic and quiet receptivity, and for a certain length of time, until we become wholly absorbed by it; until we feel ourselves to *be* the thing or picture we are contemplating.

For instance, if we look at the statue of Michelangelo's "Moses" (or even a reproduction of it), we should be able to *feel within ourselves* that wonderful, sustained power which permeates it. Or, if we contemplate the resurrected "Christ" of Fra Angelico, we should feel that it is *our own spirit* that has risen from the tomb; which has broken all bonds and is now free from all limitations, and manifesting as triumphant power radiating light around us.

To achieve these things, a certain degree of method is necessary, as in the case of making a collection of maxims and quotations from readings. We should collect and arrange a series of pictures, etc., expressing the quality or virtue we wish to acquire, using them *regularly* for that purpose and alternating them, when necessary.

Sometimes it is better to separate the different elements instead of using the combined influences of the chosen object; i.e., to take one portion at a time. For, though a single element is perhaps more restricted, it is also more concentrated and will help to bring about the desired result more quickly and effectively.

We can divide the elements into the following categories: (1) Lines and forms; (2) Colors.

Lines and Forms

It might surprise some readers to know that a mere line may have a definite psychological effect. But it is a fact, and some individuals feel these effects intensely and spontaneously. Many are more or less affected by them without being aware of it.

Straight lines, sharp angles, and broken lines produce very different impressions from curves, broad arches, and sinuous (wavy) lines. The former are, in a general way, suggestive of the masculine qualities, while curves and all their derivations are more expressive of the feminine characteristics.

Thus, the prevalence of straight lines gives the impression of firmness, hardness, decision, active and one-pointed energy; sharp angles turned upwards suggest aspiration and mysticism of an austere, transcendental type. It is typical of the pure Gothic style and of sharp, rocky mountains. Curves, generally speaking, suggest softness, breadth, expansion, rhythmical motion, change, plasticity, restfulness, kindness, love and passivity, and, in some cases, even sensuousness.

In architecture, we find curves predominating in the Baroque and Rococo styles, while Romanesque art represents the more harmonious blend of straight lines and curves.

In Nature, curves prevail in the watery elements; in the sea, with its rhythmic motion and endless waves, and in the clouds.

These general characteristics are sufficient to give us the key for the use of lines for different psychological purposes. If these principles were more widely appreciated and applied, then both the outer aspects of our buildings and their interior design would create a much more harmonious and helpful environment, intelligently adapted to our various needs and occupations. For instance, curves should provide the dominant note to places intended for rest and the pleasurable activities of social life, while the sterner, straight lines are more appropriate for places of work, such as factories, offices, and studios.

But we can use lines for psychological purposes also in their simplest and most elementary form, by just drawing a few lines on a piece of paper, or a single object of a certain shape, and then concentrating upon them. If we contemplate them in a receptive attitude, their influence will penetrate us and often awaken a response surprising in its directness and intensity. This offers us a very simple and pleasant method of achieving our aims.

The real connection between lines and their psychological qualities is clearly revealed in our handwriting, and creates the basis of graphology or personality description through the study and analysis of handwriting. This offers another method of applying the above principles, for by deliberately changing our style of handwriting and adopting a style which expresses the qualities we lack, it will help us to cultivate those particular qualities. I know that definite results have been achieved in this way.

Colors

Colors have a more obvious effect upon many individuals and often a more powerful influence than lines.

It is generally admitted that each color has a distinct psychological quality of its own, and consequently a definite effect. There is still some diversity of opinion regarding the specific quality and effect of each color, and further investigation and experiments are still needed to give more light on this fascinating subject; but there are some points which can be considered as practically ascertained.

For instance, it is now generally accepted that so-called "cold" and subdued colors have a quieting effect, and that "warm," vivid, and bright colors have a stimulating or exciting influence. Certain shades of blue are usually considered as having a soothing, harmonizing effect; light green is refreshing; red and bright yellow are usually stimulating, while pink suggests serenity and happiness.

Miss Beatrice Irwin, author of *The New Science of Colour*, says: "Colour always has one of three effects upon us—sedative, recuperative or stimulating.

"A colour is sedative when it has the power to induce contemplation, reflection, indifference, resignation, inception, coagulation, melancholy. It is recuperative when it can create conditions of change, balance, expansion, generosity, contentment, conception, cohesion. And stimulating colours are those which can excite hope, ecstasy, desire, aspiration, ambition, action, or which can cause liberation of thought and emotion through achievement, dispersion, joy, peace, spiritual renewal and fresh growth."

The colors selected by women in their dress have a profound effect upon them, and usually satisfy (consciously or unconsciously) their psychological needs, besides exerting influence upon men who do not so express themselves. But perhaps the greatest scope for the influence of color is in the home.

The general principle for lines can be applied also to colors. Soothing colors are the best for places of rest and relaxation; bright, cheerful colors for private and public dining-rooms, clear or whole tones for places of work, etc. These are only general indications but the principle can be adapted and varied according to the particular conditions and individual needs. Sunny rooms require different shades from those facing north and, on a wider scale, the color tones necessary in southern climates differ from those better suited to the cold climates of northern countries.

The influence of color as a therapeutic agent is also becoming increasingly recognized. I think in this respect it opens up great possibilities, but as a science it is still in its infancy and needs, as yet, to be used with much care. Even slight differences of shade and tone can produce widely different effects; much depends on the quality of the pigment used, and whether the color is reflected from a solid basis or background or is transmitted through a transparent medium.

The individual constitution and temperament of the patient is also an important factor. A color which mildly stimulates one person in a beneficial way can excessively excite another. Or a color which is agreeable and soothing in one case may not produce the slightest effect in others. Thus, much scientific experiment and accurate differentiation is needed, but the beneficial results well justify further research.* But, apart from these more thorough and systematic investigations, each individual can experiment for himself with all these visual methods—pictures, lines, and colors. And each experiment can represent for us a pleasant and entertaining psychological game, with a resulting very definite gain for each one of us.

INITIATED SYMBOL PROJECTION

(Based on unpublished manuscripts by Hanscarl Leuner, M.D., Psychiatric Hospital, University of Göttingen, and H. J. Kornadt, Ph.D., Psychological Institute, University of Würtzburg, West Germany. Translated, edited, and amplified by Wm. Swartley[a], Ph.D.)

Initiated Symbol Projection (ISP) is both a psycho-diagnostic and psycho-therapeutic technique. The following is a discussion only of the diagnostic implications of the new technique. Developed in West Germany since 1948 largely as a therapy, only more recently have standard diagnostic procedures been established based on clinical success. The first carefully controlled experimental studies reported upon in the following compare the technique with other diagnostic methods, in order to clarify the special advantages of the new process. The results present evidence for both psycho-diagnostic and therapeutic theory, and offer an improved means of gathering controlled data regarding some of the least known areas of psychological functioning.

Historical Introduction

Initiated Symbol Projection has three major roots by which it becomes part of the development of: 1) psycho-therapeutic techniques, 2) projective diagnosis and 3) phenomenological description of psychological processes.

*We draw particular attention to the fine research work already carried out by R. Gerard, Ph.D. of Los Angeles. See "Differential effects of colored lights on psychophysiological functions"; doctoral Diss. (Univ. California, Los Angeles 1958). "Color and emotional arousal"; 66th annu. Conv. Amer. Psychol. Assn., Washington, D.C. 1958; *Amer. Psychol. 13*: 340.

[a]Self Analysis Training Institute, Philadelphia, Pa.

1) *Therapeutic Techniques.* It was Josef Breuer who named the Catharsis technique which, according to Ernest Jones (10), was actually discovered by his famous patient, Anna O. Breuer observed, when he *allowed* his hysterical patient under auto- or therapist-induced hypnosis to repeat the disagreeable events of her day, *including terrifying hallucinations,* she felt relief. Symbol Projection therapeutically can be classified as a cathartic technique. However, ISP requires no or only the lightest hypnosis. Also, Symbol Projection initiates what can be termed a "symbolic catharsis," effected by psychological experiences during initiated visualization related to phantasy and hallucination, rather than recovery of suppressed memory. The older cathartic techniques most similar to ISP are those of Silberer (23), L. Frank (5), and K. Tuczek (24).

Freud discarded Hypno-Catharsis because he was unable to hypnotize all patients, at least as deeply as he believed was required. Later he decided hypnosis conceals transference and resistance, the analysis of which became essential in his treatment. While evolving his Free Association technique, Freud used what he called a "concentration" technique. He asked his patient to concentrate on a symptom and when no progress was being made, he would press his patients' foreheads and *assure* them some thought would come into their mind. Initiated visualization differs from Suggestion techniques in that less threatening "symbolic experiences" are sought, rather than recovery of a memory, or direct manipulation of a symptom.

Freud's Free Association technique is similar to ISP in that, like Dream Analysis, it is a combined diagnostic and therapeutic technique. Freud turned to Dream Analysis because it avoided some of the diagnostically and therapeutically superficial circular thinking characteristic during Free Association. Two major limitations of Dream Analysis largely overcome by the Symbol Projection technique are:
1) passive dependence on the uncontrolled appearance of dreams and
2) the difficulty, perhaps impossibility, of full analysis of what Eric Fromm has called "The Forgotten Language" of dreams into words of conscious thought. Symbol Projection permits the initiation of psychological experiences similar to dreams almost at will.

ISP is also a radical departure from strictly analytical techniques, in that, although some use is made of the analytic method, much diagnosis and therapy remains *non-analytic*. Clinical experience has demonstrated in many cases "symbolic-experience" during ISP requires no analysis for either meaningful diagnosis or therapeutic effect.

Freud realized that dreams have certain common themes, such as the incest motive, a knowledge of which aids the obscure process of dream interpretation. However, Dream Analysis resists scientific, especially experimental, control. Symbol Projection offers a new, simple method of testing the validity of Freud's conception of universal themes of dream symbolism.

Jung, after losing interest in his Association Test which is part of the history of projective psycho-diagnosis, has also concentrated on the problems of dream analysis by attempting to describe more accurately common symbolic themes, or Archetypes as he has termed them. Unfortunately, Jung's work toward increasing scientific control over the interpretation of dreams by reference to mythological and alchemical literature leaves much to be desired, especially in terms of experimental demonstration of the validity of his Archetypes.

Jung has emphasized the importance of the analysis of a *series* of dreams. He sponsors a distinctive world-view from Freud's. Freudian type analysis is characteristically more reductive in terms of the patient's past life and instinctual drives, more or less sexual in character during various periods of Freud's thinking. Jung's analysis is generally more psycho-*synthetic*, seeking to comprehend man in terms of basic motivations toward integration of psychological components in human beings. Several of Jung's ideas are fundamental in the use of ISP as a therapy, for instance, the "confrontation" and "initiated-unions of symbolic opposites." Also, analysis is not the ultimate for Jung as it was for Freud. Jung is largely satisfied to lead his patients to a "big dream," which proves unanalyzable, if its therapeutic effect is obvious.

Jung has only vaguely described his Active Imagination technique. It is similar to ISP except Jung encourages his patients to visualize alone rather than in the presence of the psychologist. Jung seems to fear the psychologist's presence during Active

Imagination would reduce the essential spontaneity and value of the visualization. Experiments with ISP have demonstrated the opposite to be true, if the psychologist is sufficiently skilled to encourage and aid visualization by offering helpful symbols when visualization bogs down, or becomes too frightening.

Among the few systematic predecessors of ISP is the *Autogene* Training Technique of J. H. Schultz (21,22), the first stages of which are often incorporated directly into the new technique. ISP is especially related to the "Higher Stages" of Schultz's technique, which, unfortunately, he and his followers have described only in the vaguest form. The first two symbols of Carl Happich's historically important technique of meditative-psychotherapy (6,7,8) have also been incorporated into the new technique. The emphasis on initiating visualization *down*ward, as well as the upward direction emphasized by Happich, was taken from the Waking Dream (*Rêve Eveillé*) technique of Robert Desoille (2,3,4).

2) *Projective Techniques.* Jung's Association Test of 1906 introduced experimental controls into the realm of "Depth Psychology." His standard list of key words was an early attempt to introduce experimental controls into Freud's Free Association technique and can be viewed as an early form of a projective test. Unfortunately, the value of Jung's test is limited by the nature of Free Association, which time has demonstrated has only a limited diagnostic value.

Jung's test stimulated Rorschach, whose projective test appears to evoke responses of greater diagnostic significance. Although Rorschach and his followers have attempted to introduce scientific controls over the interpretation of responses to the ten standard ink blots, interpretation of Rorschach protocols remains subjectively determined in important respects.

Other projective tests have been developed as the Thematic Apperception Test, and Rosenzweig's Picture Frustration Test; each test designed to compensate for limitations of earlier tests. The difficulty has been to devise a test which evokes significant projection from "deeper levels" of a personality, yet retain scientific controls and experimentally justify the interpretation of test responses.

The Initiated Symbol Projection technique minimizes two

major limitations of existing projective tests. First, the essential spontaneity of psychological manifestations revealing underlying psycho-dynamic organization is less "dampened" by the introduction of scientific controls over the interpretation of test responses. Secondly and more important, the new technique permits the psychologist to more actively participate and influence the rapid flow of diagnostic manifestations, yet without harming the essential validity of the test responses.

Viewed in one way, the task presented the subject during ISP stands between the task presented by the TAT and Rorschach tests. That is, the stimuli presented during ISP diagnosis are less structured than the TAT plates and, in one sense, more structured than Rorschach plates. However, viewed from a different perspective, the symbol-stimuli presented during ISP are less structured of content and thus permit a greater variety of projection than even the Rorschach plates. If measured by the variety, "depth" and obvious diagnostic significance of the responses it evokes, the ISP method ranks high among projective instruments.

Initiated Symbol Projection offers refinements of two methods of validating its diagnostic relevance. The first, which could be called the *method of consistent projection*, is the one usually applied to validate the interpretation of projected responses. A projective test is administered to a group of persons who share the same maladjustment, seeking some consistency among their responses. Or, the same person is re-administered a test after a specific improvement or deterioration is established, seeking a consistency between the changes of personality and changes among the responses to the same projective test administered before the changes.

Even using the method of consistent projection to assess validity of diagnosis, ISP has several advantages over most projective instruments. First, the less structured character of the symbol-stimuli allows frequent re-administration revealing subtle changes during therapy. Secondly, because the stimuli which evoke projection are symbols rather than vague pictures or ink blots, the projected responses are reactions to symbols, thus lowering the "depth" of diagnosis to the psychological "level" where depth psychologists have found treatment most effective. If Freud's and Jung's observations of basic symbolic motives among unconscious manifestations are correct, symbols should provide the basis of both more meaningful and obvious diagnostic categories than have been evolved for the TAT or Rorschach tests. It is remarkable that so much use has been made of symbols in therapy, yet so few methods have been found to use symbols during diagnosis.

A second means of determining the validity of a diagnostic technique could be called the *effect of indicated therapy method,* a method which is not so directly· applicable to validation of most diagnostic techniques as it is to Symbol Projection. The great limitation of most psycho-diagnosis is that the raw test responses must be interpreted into scientific terminology, which must then be re-translated into a therapeutic goal. The value and necessity of such a process which imposes several intermediary steps between diagnosis and therapy is open to question. Ideally, a diagnosis would indicate treatment without intermediary steps. Symbol Projection, because it is equally a diagnostic and therapeutic technique, offers a rare opportunity to obtain a diagnosis *in symbolic terms* which is immediately applicable to therapy conducted on the symbolic (non-analytic) level. Clinical experience has demonstrated that the source of most psychological maladjustment lies (in "psychological space") on an infantile or primitive, and largely pre-conscious level. On that level thinking appears to take place largely in a "symbolic language" and thus the unresolved conflicts of childhood are best and most easily expressed *and treated* in largely symbolic terms. The best demonstration of the validity of a diagnostic technique is the beneficial effects of unquestionably indicated treatment, whether in symbolic or other terms.

3) *Phenomenological Description of Psychological Processes.* The visualized experiences initiated by the new technique possess the same phenomenological characteristics as the subjective *Anschauungsbilder* (images) described by V. v. Urbantschitch (25) and the *Eidetik* phenomena studied by E. R. Jaensch and his associates (9; see 13). The relation between *eidetischen* experiences and the dream mechanisms described by Freud were already recognized by Paul Schilder in 1926 (20), Bibring-Lehner (1), and even by

Jaensch himself. O. Kroh said the possibility of observing effective experiences by an *eidetischen* method was a significant new approach to depth psychology (12). The *Bildstreifdenken* (picturestrip-thinking) described by Ernest Kretschmer is also a closely related phenomena (11).

Test Procedure

The subject is seated in a comfortable chair or on a couch, asked to close his eyes, and induced to relax by one or more methods. In most cases, the use of the first two stages (1 — Suggestion of Bodily Weight inducing muscular relaxation; 2 — Suggestion of Bodily Warmth inducing vascular relaxation) of J. H. Schultz's *Autogene Training*, or a light hypnoid state have proved valuable. Deep and regular breathing are encouraged, similar to Schultz's Fourth Stage.

Then, in a psychological state characterized by diminished consciousness of the outer world, reduced conscious criticism and self-control, the subject is asked to visualize a standard series of twelve symbol-motives, presented verbally by the psychologist. For instance, the subject is first asked, "Try to visualize yourself in a meadow."

Such vague, unspecific symbol-stimuli act like a "center for crystallization" of a specific type of visualization which differs from mere images, daydreams, or most phantasy. In the phenomenology of medical psychology, they are similar to "hypnagogic visions." Such "visions" differ from similar phenomena; first, in the clarity of their form and content, which permits exact description. Secondly, such visualizations have a distinct "life of their own" which, although never completely beyond conscious control, is determined largely subjectively and unconsciously. This type of visualization has been termed *autochthonous,* that is, largely independent of conscious control. Leuner has designated them *katathyme* visualizations, the concept stemming from H. W. Maier and used by E. Breuler and E. Kretschmer to describe the inter-dependence of an affective and bodily reaction. The ISP technique is known in Germany as *Experimental katathymes Bilderleben,* which is abbreviated as EkB. (14,15,16,17,18,19).

Such induced visions contain meaningful symbols, analogous to the symbols of dreams. The symbols which appear during ISP differ from those in dreams in their comparative simplicity and clarity of content. Confusing, secondary influences of such factors as the degree of body tension, the amount of sleep, etc., are also considerably reduced compared with their effect on dreams. Most important, relevant psycho-dynamic organization of affect is usually projected into such visualizations far more clearly than is found in dreams.

Despite the unprecedented degree of freedom to project into initiated visions, the method permits an experimental control of diagnostic standards. An outline of the twelve symbolic motives verbally presented to the subject is given below, together with the briefest indication of their significance. The twelve motives were selected pragmatically after clinical experience, exactly as Rorschach chose his plates. An introduction to the experimental justification of their indicated importance is found in the latter part of the present paper as well as six papers by Leuner.

1. A Meadow:

The meadow, also the first symbol in Happich's technique, has proven a good initiator of visualization. The symbol of a meadow serves as a kind of "psychological Garden of Eden," that is, a good beginning of a (psychological) development during which something went wrong. A meadow, readily accepted by most adults and children as an easy start for induced visions, is a neutral or positive center for the play of their imagination, even if they have grown up in a city. The meadow suggests a return to nature and a fresh beginning. Many subjects first visualize a meadow which they have visited in outer life. They are encouraged to walk through the meadow describing verbally what they see and the emotions they experience. They are stimulated to continue walking and describing their experiences until they find a part of the meadow or another meadow which they have never seen in the outer world, and into which they can thus project more freely. If unable to do so, introduction of the following symbol motives usually induced them to visualize unfamiliar territory which is able to receive more spontaneous and diagnostically more significant projections.

Diagnostically, the length and greenness of the grass in the visualized meadow appear meaningful from clinical experience.

Like the brilliance and warmth of the sunlight in the meadow, the condition of the grass seems to give a rather accurate indication of the subject's "general psychological health." Short, closely clipped grass is often a sign of unhealthy psychic mechanisms; for instance, over-intellectualization at the expense of the full expression of the subject's emotional life. Some subjects appear so alienated from their own inner life that they are only able to visualize a desert, and must be encouraged to continue searching under each stone for a single blade of grass. (An example of clearly indicated "symbol-therapy" in the last case would be to encourage the patient to search for some water to pour on the blade of grass to make it grow.)

II. Climbing up a Mountain:

Also Happich's second motive, a mountain, initiates "psychological movement" upward in symbolic space. The fundamental difference and effect of initiating visualization upward or downward has been emphasized by Desoille. The height of the mountain which subjects visualize themselves climbing indicates, according to both clinical and experimental evidence partially reviewed in the latter part of the present paper, the subject's level of aspiration regarding whatever the visualized mountain symbolizes to them. The nature of the obstacles most subjects spontaneously visualize as blocking and impeding their climb is the subject's "self-diagnosis" in symbolic terms of the psychological hindrances which they are aware, at least unconsciously, impede their psychological growth.

Often subjects will visualize a small hill, perhaps one they have climbed in the outer world. In such cases, they are instructed to look around from the top of the hill seeking any higher mountains in the distance. If they can see any mountains, they are asked to climb the highest they can see.

III. Following the Course of a Stream:

The amount of water flowing through the visualized stream is an indication of the total psychic energy (libido) which flows through a subject's psychic structure. The depth and breadth of the stream appear closely related to ordinary descriptions of a person as "deep," "shallow," "broad-minded," or "narrow." The obstacles which impede the flow of the stream are symbolic expressions of conflicts and complexes which subjects are aware, at least unconsciously, are disturbing the free expression of their psychic energy. The turbulence of the stream is a sign of the degree to which the subjects are disturbed by their own complexes. The clearness or relative cloudiness of the stream indicate subjects' awareness of the nature and components of their libidinal energy.

IV. Visiting a House:

The visualized house serves as a symbol of the subject's self. The more imaginary the house, the clearer the symbolism. Often subjects will explore a house with which they are familiar in outer life before they can be initiated into the exploration of an imaginary house. The contents and size and relationship one to another of the rooms in the house symbolize the components or functions of the subject's psychological make-up, as well as the relationships between the various components, whatever they might be.

V. The Ideal Personality:

Subjects are induced to "hear" in their imagination the first name of a person of the same sex. Then they are asked to visualize an imaginary person called by the name. As a rule, the visualized person possesses the personality which the subjects believe they should or could develop. Often the visualized personality is the opposite of a subject's own personality and represents a synthesis of the qualities visualized in the ideal personality with the personality of the subject, an obvious goal of therapy.

VI. Unconscious Affective Relationships Symbolized by Animals:

In the meadow, or in some symbolic location which proves more favorable, the parents, siblings, marriage partner, etc., are summoned. However, in order to allow clearer expression of the subject's affective relationship with such persons, instead of asking subjects to visualize the body of their mother, they are asked to visualize a cow, which clinical and experimental evidence has demonstrated is in most cases a very adequate symbol for the mother figure. Most subjects are able to project their true affective relationship with their father into the form and behavior of an elephant or bull. The diagnostic implications of a threatening elephant or bull are in most cases obvious, as is conflict between two animals.

VII. Unconscious Attitude Toward Sexuality:

A. *For Males:* The subject is asked to visualize a rose bush. The luxuriance of its growth, the richness of its color, the degree to which the blossoms have opened or are still growing, all have proven to symbolize by projection the psycho-sexual development of male subjects, as does the subject's ability to pick the visualized flower without being pricked.

B. *For Females:* Female subjects are asked to visualize themselves walking home along a road at dusk after an exhausting walk through the countryside. Then they are instructed to visualize an automobile coming along the road behind them which, when it reaches them, stops and the driver asks if they want a lift home. The sex and appearance of the driver, as well as the color and size of the automobile have demonstrated diagnostic significance regarding the sexual development of most feminine subjects. Especially significant are signs of resistance, such as when a subject can visualize the road, but no car appears, or the car disappears into the air as she enters it.

VIII. Pool of Water in a Swamp:

The subjects are asked to visualize a swampy pool in the meadow (a place for symbolic retreat if subsequent visions become too fearful). They are instructed to look down at the mirroring surface of the pool. Very often, a horrible animal will rise up out of the swampy pool. Or else a strange figure of the opposite sex of the patient will come from the pool, usually a variation of a naked man who appears sexually threatening, or else an ethereal feminine form. These figures generally represent disturbances in the sexual sphere of the subjects, especially repressive and regressive tendencies.

IX. Waiting for a Figure to Emerge from a Cave:

The subjects are instructed to visualize themselves waiting in the dark behind a protective tree for the emergence of someone or something from a cave. In most cases, a real or mythological-like figure or figures appear, either a parent, friend, a dragon-killer, a goddess, a giant; also all kinds of animals, more or less aggressive in nature. Such forms are usually symbolized projections of suppressed or undeveloped areas of the subject's personality.

X. Eruption of a Volcano:

The violence of the eruption, which is closely related to the ease with which a subject can visualize the beginning of the eruption, as well as the character and amount of material erupted by the volcano have proven to be a good index of the nature and amount of affective tension a subject has stored within himself. The ease by which a subject can release such tension and the way he does it is also frequently projected into the eruption of the volcano.

XI. The Lion:

The behavior of a lion during visualization serves as an indicator of the subject's ability to express himself. The lion is confronted during visualization with any persons who are known to oppose the subject in outer life. The lion can either fall upon them and eat them, or lie at their feet, either case usually reflecting the subject's ability to overcome his opponents in life.

XII. An Old Picture Book:

In the cellar of the visualized house, the subject is led to visualize himself digging a hole in an earthen floor. The subject is told to seek an old book buried there; a book which contains many pictures. When the book is found, the subject is asked to describe some of the pictures it contains. This symbol gives the subject an opportunity to project freely into the contents of the book. Usually the pictures relate to things visualized during the presentation of the first eleven symbol motives and often compensate somehow for what was left unsaid and unresolved during the earlier visualizations.

Experimental Comparison with Other Diagnostic Techniques

Systematic studies of Initiated Symbol Projection have been made using thirty subjects, largely students in a German University. Among other things, the studies compared ISP with other diagnostic techniques. The personality of each subject was assessed using three projective techniques: the TAT (all twenty pictures), Rosenzweig's Picture Frustration Test, and Jung's Association Test. In addition, a detailed case study of the life history, emotional relationships, interests, conflicts, etc., was made of each subject. About eight hours was given for evaluation of each subject.

The thirty subjects were administered under standard conditions and in constant sequence the twelve symbol motives which compose ISP as a diagnostic procedure. Each subject was asked one hundred standard questions during diagnosis and an evaluation was made on nineteen points, such as each subject's attitude toward his parents, his psychosexual development, the amount of aggression present, his level of aspiration, etc.

No attempt will be made here to present the statistical and detailed information gathered during the study. Instead, only several examples which demonstrate the implications of the investigation can be presented.

For instance, there appears to be a demonstrable relationship between the subjects':

Level of Aspiration based on 1) A rating made from an independent study of the case histories, and 2) the subjects' TAT responses, and

The 1) height and 2) accessibility of the top of the visualized mountain (Standard Symbol Motive II).

An example is the responses of two subjects determined to have a low and high Level of Aspiration respectively:

Subject I—Level of Aspiration—Low

Case History: The subject, a 19 year old girl, hardly knew her father. She had always felt herself rejected by her mother, who she believed favored her brother. Her reasonable requests were rejected by her mother with the remark, "First bring home good grades." In spite of an I.Q. of 115, she failed high school. She had largely resigned herself to a life of frustration. She was working as a house maid. Her most prominent desires were primitive desires for food and a wish to be left "in peace."

TAT Responses: Her TAT responses included for Plate 1, "This young boy is very talented. His musical talent is not valued at home. His parents do not want to pay for his violin lessons. He enjoys making music for himself, but when someone comes or he must perform for others, then he has inhibitions and cannot do it. And so he sits alone and considers how different everything would be if people, above all his parents, had more understanding for his music. It looks as though he has no joy in his work without this."

Other TAT responses included another story with the "unsuccessful efforts" theme and four stories in which accomplishment was experienced as an obligation or otherwise viewed negatively. Three other stories dealt with the "renunciation of all wishes" and the senselessness of life.

Conclusion: According to all information gathered, the girl's effective level of aspiration was judged "very low."

Initiated Symbol Projection Responses: Her response to the Mountain Motive was "The mountain stands on a meadow. A zig-zag path leads up to it. It is approximately fifty meters high. Only a hill actually. A round, pointed sort of a flat summit. First one sees bushes along the way. Then the path goes on further, like a winding road. There is a bench. Then one goes somewhat higher again. Still more bushes. Then come trees. Then one is on the summit. (Question—Was it difficult?) Yes, rather steep. There are rocks on the way and tree roots. And on the top is another bench."

Compared with symbolic experiences of other subjects, her mountain was "extremely low" and the ascent "easy."

Subject II—Level of Aspiration—High

Case History: The subject, a thirty-one year old female, has highly ambitious goals, yet suffers deep doubts about her abilities. She comes from a family with social position and places much value in "social climbing." She felt that too many demands were put upon her as a child. She became a teacher, but was not satisfied with her social position and successes. She could not reach her ultimate goal, the accomplishment of something unusual in the literary world, because of her excessive self-criticism. At thirty she finally began to study in the face of great personal sacrifice. She hopes to fulfill especially high cultural and scientific standards.

TAT Responses: Her response to the first plate was: "Like Menuhin when he was a young boy. He is a young boy who has the desire to become a great violinist. He received the violin as a present and now practices industriously. But he realizes that art is lofty and that he is still far away from it. He wonders if it is worth following this pathway. He has phantasies about how it would be *If* . . . But failures oppose them."

Three more of her TAT stories dealt with the "way to success in life," two others concerned what had been accomplished in life.

Conclusion: From all evidence, the second subject's level of aspiration was judged to be "high."

ISP Responses: She said, "The mountain is 2000 meters high. It has a very sharp and steep slope and a very pointed summit. In order to climb it, I must go along the slope. I try it putting one foot in front of the other as on the edge of a roof. I have to use my hands to help myself. Now I slip—get my balance again. I sit down and pull myself along gradually. The ridge is sharp as a razor blade. Now I am hanging there tightly. It will not go. Now I can go on a bit further. I slip again. Above I can support myself. Now I am almost to the top. I have to pull myself high onto the summit. It is very pointed on top."

Compared with other subjects, the girl climbed "higher" and "steeper" and with greater difficulty than most subjects.

* * * *

Conclusion

This is not the place to present more than an indication of the nature of a new projective technique, the experimental procedures which have been applied to its study, or the promising data which has been collected. Here it seems worthwhile only to indicate some of the conclusions regarding the nature of projective diagnosis which the new technique has clarified:

1. It appears clear that the presentation of certain symbol motives initiates diagnostically meaningful projection in many subjects.

2. That the choice of diagnostically fruitful symbol motives for presentation can be made pragmatically from clinical experience.

3. That diagnosis based on subjects' responses to a series of standard symbol motives can be experimentally justified.

4. That Initiated Symbol Projection has certain advantages over existing diagnostic techniques, such as:

   a. The large degree of freedom which it allows, once projection has been initiated by a symbol motive, as subjects are less "confined" during projection than while using a picture, ink blots, etc., to introduce controls over interpretation.

   b. That symbol motives initiate projection from "deeper levels" of a personality than most projective tests, yet because the areas of personality from which projection is tapped are so basic, the diagnostic implications gained from such projection are 1) more obvious, 2) diagnostically meaningful, 3) can be experimentally validated with more surety, and 4) are directly applicable to therapy without intermediary analysis or interpretation.

BIBLIOGRAPHY

1. Bibring-Lehner, G.: Ueber die Beeinflussung eidetischer Phaenomene durch labyrinthaere Reize, Z. Neurol. & Psychiat., 1928, 112, 496-505.
2. Desoille, Robert: Exploration de l'Affectivité Subconsciente par la Méthode du Rêve Eveillé (with preface by C. Baudouin), Paris, D'Artrey, 1938.
3. —— Le Rêve Eveillé en Psychothérapie, Essai sur la Fonction de Régulation de l'Inconscient Collectif, Paris, Presses Universitaires de France, 1945.
4. —— Psychanalyse et Rêve Eveillé Dirigé (with case histories by Doctors Y. Fayol, S. Leuret and M. Violet-Conil), Paris, Chez Le François, 1950.
5. Frank, L.: Affektstoerungen, Berlin, Springer, 1913.
6. Happich, Carl: Das Bildbewusstsein als Ansatzstelle psychischer Behandlung, Zbl. Psychother, 1932, 5, 663-677.
7. —— Bildbewusstsein und schoepferische Situation, Deutschen med. Wochenschrift, 1939, 2, 68.
8. —— Anleitung zur Meditation, (1st Edition 1938) 3rd Edition, Darmstadt, Roether, 1948.

9. Jaensch, E. R.: *Ueber den Aufbau des optischen Wahrnehmungs und Erkenntnisvorganges*, Leipzig, Barth, 1927.
10. Jones, Ernest: *Life and Work of Sigmund Freud*, Vol. I, New York, Basic Books, 1953, p. 223.
11. Kretschmer, Ernest: *Medizinische Psychologie*, Stuttgart, Thieme, 1956.
12. Kroh, O.: Neues zur Eidetik, *Psychol. Rundschau*, 1949-50, 1, 257-260.
13. Krudewig, M.: *Die Lehren von der visuellen Wahrnehmung und Vorstellung*, Meissenhein (Germany), Westkulturverlag A. Hain, 1953.
14. Leuner, Hanscarl: Kontrolle der Symbolinterpretation im experimentellen Verfahren, *Z. Psychotherapie und med. Psychol.*, 1954, 4, 201-204.
15. —— Experimentelles katathymes Bilderleben als ein klinisches Verfahren der Psychotherapie Grundlegungen und Methode, *Z. Psychother. und med. Psychol.*, 1955, 5, 185-202.
16. —— Experimentelles katathymes Bilderleben als ein klinisches Verfahren der Psychotherapie: Auswertung und Belege, *Z. Psychother. und med. Psychol.*, 1955, 5, 233-260.
17. —— Symbolkonfrontation, ein nicht-interpretierendes Vorgehen in der Psychotherapie, *Schweiz. Arch. Neurol. & Psychiat.*, 1955, 76, 23-49.
18. —— Symboldrama, ein aktives, nicht-analysierendes Vorgehen in der Psychotherapie, *Z Psychother. und med. Psychol.*, 1957, 7, 221-238. See also 1960, 10, 45, and 1964, 14, 196-211.
19. —— Einfuehrung in das experimentelle katathymes Bilderleben. In *Aktuelle Psychotherapie*, Munich, Lehmanns Verlag, 1958.
20. Schilder, Paul: Psychoanalyse und Eidetik, *Z. Sexualwiss.*, 1926, 13.
21. Schultz, J. H.: *Das Autogene Training*, (1st Edition, 1932) 9th Edition, Stuttgart, Thieme, 1956.
22. —— *Uebungsheft fuer das Autogene Training*, Stuttgart, Thieme, 1953.
23. Silberer, H.: Bericht ueber die Methode, gewisse symbolische Halluzinationserscheinungen hervorzurufen und zu beobachten, *Jb. Psychoanal. u. psychopath.* Forschg., 1909, 1, 513-545.
24. Tuczek, K.: Ueber optische Phaenomene in der Katharsis, *Nervenarzt*, 1928, 1, 151-160.
25. Urbantschitsch, V. v.: *Ueber subjektive optische Erscheinungen*, Leipzig, Thieme, 1907.

MEDITATIVE TECHNIQUES IN PSYCHOTHERAPY

(Die meditativen Verfahren in der Psychotherapie)
by Dr. Wolfgang Kretschmer, Jr., M.D.
of the Tübingen University Psychiatric Clinic

Translated by William Swartley[a], Ph.D.
from
Zeitschrift für Psychotherapie und Medizinische Psychologie
(Vol. I, No. 3, May 1951)

The psychotherapist who wants to employ techniques of
meditation must first be able to meditate himself. The book by
the German psychiatrist, J. H. Schultz, called *"Autogenous Training"* (auto: self; genous: originated) and subtitled "Concentrated
Self-Relaxation" (*Das Autogene Training*, 9th edition, George
Thieme Verlag, Stuttgart, 1956 and *Ubungsheft für das Autogene
Training*, 8th edition, Thieme, Stuttgart, 1953), offers a step-by-
step introduction to one technique of meditation. However, with
meditation, as with psychotherapy, a study of the literature is
seldom enough. A personal dedication is necessary. Without it,
individual practice of meditation can be dangerous; especially the
advanced stages of genuine meditation described by Schultz. In
these advanced stages, after a general bodily relaxation has been
achieved, symbolic fantasies are skillfully induced. Then colors
and objects are visualized. One endeavors to experience a symbolic representation of ideas which are understood only abstract-
ly, of one's feelings, of friends, and finally of higher moral questions, in a way which allows the psyche to make unconscious
tendencies symbolically visible. Dreams are similar to meditation,
except meditation gains the reaction of the unconscious by a
systematic technique which is faster than depending on dreams.
But the Schultz technique only serves to raise, with a special
emphasis, the question, "What is the goal of meditation?" Schultz
sees this question clearly, but that this question is basically a religious one, or at least connected with religion, Schultz does not
conclude. Therefore, he limits himself to the formulation of "basic

[a]Self Analysis Training Institute, Philadelphia, Pa.

existential values." This means the meditator is encouraged to strive toward a reasonable view of life orientated toward self-realization, psychic freedom and harmony, and a lively creativity. At best, one achieves a Nirvana-like phenomena of joy and release. Maybe Schultz conceals decisive experiences which go further; because of the basically unlimited possibilities of meditation, we can always await such an extension of his ideas.

The technique developed by Carl Happich, the former Darmstadt internist, is meditation of the most systematic kind, and also of the widest human scope. It begins with physiology and ends in religion. Happich developed it out of his literary and practical knowledge of Oriental techniques. He combined their wisdom with the experience of modern depth psychology. He set forth his fundamental principles in two small works entitled, *"Symbolic Consciousness as the Starting Point of Psychic Treatment"* (*Das Bildbewusstsein als Ansatzstelle psychischer Behandlung*, Zbl. f. Psychotherapie, Bd. 5, 1932) and *Symbolic Consciousness and the Creative Situation"* (*Bildbewusstsein und schopferische Situation*, Dtsch. med. Wschr. 1939, Nr. 2), and beyond these left only a small *"Introduction to Meditation"* (*Anleitung zur Meditation*, E. Rother, 3rd edition, Darmstadt, 1948), which is concerned with religious symbolism. Unfortunately, he did not live to set forth his life experiences in a grand scientific frame. His importance lies, above all, in the practical techniques which he began to spread among theologians when physicians demonstrated no interest in them.

Happich took the level of consciousness he called "symbolic consciousness," which seems to lie between consciousness and unconsciousness, as the point of departure for all creative production and, therefore, also for the healing process. On this level the "collective unconscious" can express itself through symbolism. It is in the activation of the possibilities of symbolic expression that Happich, as Schultz, sees the point of departure for meditation and its therapeutic possibilities.

How can we proceed practically? Assumed, as always, is the bodily solution which is attained systematically with the Schultz method or by more direct means. Happich placed great value in breathing as a graduated measure of the affective state which alters itself in the permissiveness of meditation. He encouraged, both before and during the therapeutic session, an increasing passivity of respiration. Most men can only achieve this through progressive breathing exercises.

After some experience with physiological reactions to breathing exercises has been gained, the first psychological exercise, the so-called "Meadow Meditation," can be attempted. The meditator must repeat to himself the words of his meditation-master and imagine that he (the meditator) leaves the room, goes through the city, over the fields, to a meadow covered with fresh grass and flowers, and looks upon the meadow with pleasure. Then, he psychically returns the same way to the room, opens his eyes, and relates what he has experienced. When this exercise can be done freely (which usually requires a number of sittings) it is followed by the "Mountain Meditation."

The meditator, as in the first meditation, goes into the country and then slowly climbs a mountain. He passes through a forest, and finally reaches a peak from which he can view a wide expanse. In the third step, the "Chapel Meditation" is explored. In it, the meditator passes through a grove and reaches a chapel which he enters and where he remains for a long time. Lastly, Happich has the meditator imagine himself sitting on a bench by an old fountain listening to the murmur of the water.

What does all this mean? One who is familiar with dream symbolism knows immediately that the three central symbols (meadow, mountain, and chapel) to which the meditator is led have an "archetypal" significance even though, in everyday life, they are quite ordinary and in no way help to bring about an especially deep knowledge.

However, when a certain depth of meditation is attained, such symbols lose their ordinary meaning and their symbolical value is slowly revealed. As the meditator returns to the meadow, he does not experience things as he would in the ordinary world. Rather, the meadow provides a symbol of the hypnotic level of consciousness and stimulates the emotions on this level. The individual takes an ordinary situation as the means of experiencing the primordial content of the symbol of the meadow. The meadow presents youthful Mother Nature in her serene and beneficent aspect. In contrast, a forest is also inhabited by demons. The meadow represents the blossoming of life which the meditator seeks. It also represents the world of the child. When one meditates on the symbol of the meadow, he regresses to his psychic origin in childhood. Once there, he does not uncover sexual dreams of his childhood as might be expected. Nor does he find a "stump," which can also be a meaningful symbol. Rather, he returns to the positive, creative basis of his life.

Every healthy man has in his psychic depths something corresponding to this meadow. He retains within him an active and creative "child." When a man is psychically sick, this "child" loses its positive and creative power. As the realm of this "child" is revealed through meditation on the symbol of the meadow, the meadow becomes a point of departure and crystallization for other symbols related to this psychic realm. These self-crystallized symbols are unmediated expressions of the individual's adaptation to the realm of the "child" within his psyche. A healthy man will have a satisfying experience of a meadow in the flush of Spring. He will populate the meadow with children or with the form of an agreeable woman. He will, perhaps, pick flowers and so on. In this way, the meditator discovers a symbolic representation of his psychic condition.

The psychically ill find it impossible to visualize a fresh meadow and during meditation cannot find one. Or the meadow may be seen as wilted or composed of a single stump. Or all sorts of disturbing, negative symbols may be scattered around. From such manifestations of illness, one gains a diagnosis which must then be translated into a therapy. Often, the meditation must be repeated many times until the crippling effects of the fundamental psychic problem are undone and the meditation can proceed normally. Analytic conversation with the psychotherapist normally aids the whole process.

In climbing the mountain, the meditator will generally symbolize some obstacle in his way so that he must prove himself. Climbing in this psychic sphere always implies "sublimation," in the Jungian rather than the Freudian use of the term. The words transformation, spiritualization, or humanization might convey the idea better than the word "sublimation." In any case, the climbing is a symbol of a movement during which man demonstrates his capacity to develop toward the goal of psychic freedom, the peak of human being. The passage through the forest on the way up the mountain gives the meditator the opportunity to reconcile himself with the dark, fearful side of nature. With the symbol of the chapel, the meditator is led into the innermost rooms of his psyche where he faces the simple question of how he relates to the possibilities of psychic transformation within man. When the meditator is able to comprehend the symbolic significance of the chapel, he can learn to use it to uncover and face in himself the central problems of human life. The chapel also provides a stage on which the resolution of these central human problems can be symbolically revealed. It is Happich's idea that the "religious function" is the most intimate and not an invisible factor in human life. Further, he believed that man, if he will be really healthy and psychically free, sometime and somehow must face these questions. One cannot avoid the fact that the special efficacy of Happich's therapy was the result of his religious attitude. He developed a Christian meditation.

That his system of meditation is based on sound psychological principles is confirmed by the work of the Jungian school. Dreams have been recorded where a mountain is seen in a landscape and on the mountain stands a church. Such symbolic pictures have been valued psychically as an indication of the end of the process of "Individuation," as a symbol of the attainment of "spirituality." But in meditation one does not wait until the needed symbols are produced spontaneously, as during dream analysis. Rather, the meditator is forced to occupy himself with certain symbols selected by the therapist until he has explored the fullness of their meaning.

Happich directed his meditators to a higher step which he called "Design (or *Mandala*, a Sanskrit word literally meaning circle, but more specifically an abstract design used especially in Tibetan Buddhism as a stimulus during meditation) Meditation." The design which is meditated upon is a kind of condensation, an abstraction of many symbols which are united into a generalized form. In the course of meditation on these designs, the meaning of the inherent symbolism can become obvious. With mandala meditation, the goal is not the production of extensive fantasy, but rather a lively meditation revolving around the central meaning of the design. Eventually, the meditator is directed to psychically identify himself with the symbol and to integrate the meaning of the symbol with his psychic life. Properly speaking, these designs are not used as a technique of therapy, but rather in furthering the highest development of personality. An example of what can be experienced through meditation on a design can be read in the opening of Goethe's *Faust*, where Faust beholds the design of the macrocosmos.

A still more abstract form of meditation is "Word Meditation," directed toward unfolding the central human importance of a word or a saying. Meditation on designs and words are of the greatest importance in furthering religious development.

Happich holds the healthy principle of the equality of rational and irrational activity during the course of meditation.

On the other hand, one should not meditate on symbols or designs which stimulate dangerous negative emotions, as for example, a snake or a scorpion. The subject of meditation should be purified through thousands of years' experience of the wisest men, and be of proven value as is the case with many Egyptian, Hindu, and German symbols and also the holy symbols of the Greek church. The first requirement of such symbols is the impression of their positive transforming power, which can be regulated by man's psyche.

R. Desoille, a Frenchman, described one of the newest and most original techniques in his book entitled, *"The Waking Dream in Psychotherapy, an Essay on the Regulatory Function of the Collective Unconscious."* (*Le Rêve Eveillé en Psychothérapie*, Presses Universitaires, Paris, 1945. See also *Psyche* 1947, Number 2 and *Psychanalyse et Rêve Eveillé*, Paris 1950.) His procedure is not meditation in the classical sense. The emphasis is shifted toward more conventional depth psychology. But it deserves discussion as a technique of actively relating to the unconscious.

Desoille treats his patients in a state of limited consciousness, in which he suggests that symbols be plastically visualized and actively experienced. He directs his patients to psychically wander wherever they choose, availing themselves of any means, a kind of wandering into which most patients soon fall. They experience, for example, the climbing of a mountain or a tower, ascent into the clouds, etc. Especially important is the climbing, for reasons already discussed. In this wandering, all possible hindrances are eliminated. As in dreams, various symbolic forms are manifested from the "Personal and Collective Unconscious"—in both auspicious and horrible aspects. Meeting "Archetypal" symbols is considered especially effective. The patient relates his psychic experiences as he has them, and the turning point of the method is the therapist's reaction to them. As he is informed in each moment of the psychological scene, the therapist suggests to the patient a symbolic means of changing his (the patient's) situation by climbing or descending. The therapist does not suggest the whole fantasy; rather, he gives only a direction and maintains control of the fantasy by offering helpful symbols which can serve as points of crystallization for the fantasy. The technique is a good one. In the climb, Desoille realizes and makes use of the human ability for creative sublimation. In the descent, the patient comes to know psychic productions from the sphere of man's instinctual nature. The patient is led to the psychological execution of what Goethe poetically described as the way "from heaven through the world to hell." In other words the therapist penetrates the patient's conscious self-image and provides symbolic expressions of inherent libidinal tendencies which motivate men on various psychic levels. Decisive for Desoille is the experience of meeting the "Archetypes" which lead man to the absolutes of existence and the last decision, a decision of absolute and vast importance.

Desoille's valuation of the "Collective Unconscious" is more radical and consequential than Jung's, in that he (Desoille) holds that the meeting with the "Collective Unconscious" is a decisive and unavoidable presupposition of the therapeutic process.

Desoille holds that when the patient can relate himself to the "Archetypes of the Collective Unconscious," he can find in them the appropriate adjustment to the problems of life. The patient must learn to control the "Archetypes" within himself, to be free from them, and thereby lose his fear of them. He can then comprehend and resolve his personal conflicts within the larger context of man's inherent problems. Thus, the patient experiences his personal conflicts as having an impersonal and collective background. The motivational (libidinal) conflict is not resolved by being transferred upon the therapist, as in psychoanalysis; rather, the patient uncovers, in himself, the basic roots of the conflict. The goal of the technique is to direct the patient toward the fulfillment of his human potentialities through the creative development of man's basic biological impulses into a higher and harmonic order. With this idea, Desoille enters the realm of ethics and religion. Religious sensitivity is, for Desoille, the highest psychic state and the source of great activity.

Desoille's techniques require the therapist to possess a rare knowledge and understanding of symbolism and great psychological intuition in order to evaluate the waking dreams of his patients and to retain control of the process of psychological development which the waking dreams initiate.

The technique is, in a unique way, both diagnostic and therapeutic and the seemingly irrational procedure is worthy of note. Penetration of the psychic situation using intellectual analysis is given up. The therapeutic principle lies in the acceleration and furthering of effective development. It is a healing process which seeks the maximum transcendence of psychic limitations through symbolic ascensions and descensions. In this simple but most important principle, an earnest reminder can also be seen. Any therapist who would lead others to psychic heights and depths must, himself, be able to attain these heights and depths of the psyche. Contemporary psychotherapists will have to begin by training themselves to ascend and descend through their own psyche and thereby experience the manifold components within man and the driving forces behind human life. Who will accept Desoille's hypothesis and begin to look up and climb?

Walter Frederking calls his psychotherapeutic technique "Deep Relaxation and Symbolism," which he sketched in "Psyche," 1948, Number 2. Frederking's technique is unsystematic, which implies nothing about its value.

Frederking also seeks freedom from dependence upon dreams by stimulating the unconscious to spontaneous productions of other kinds. To do this, he directs his patients in a progressive bodily relaxation during which they continue to describe their discoveries. One could also say he simply allows fantasy. The patient soon progresses from unclear visions to increasingly clearer productions of a kind of "symbolic strip thought." This symbolic thought, which has a significance similar to dream life, is allowed to flow by, scene by scene. The patient is both the playwright and the actors. He meets the contents of his "Personal Unconscious" and, to a degree, the "Collective Unconscious" and is able to relate their contents directly and dramatically to his psychic problems. One could also say that the patient is directed to enter "hell" to conquer the fiendish demons. This meeting with generally unrecognized aspects of himself brings about a spontaneous healing through various transforming symbols. Frederking holds that "in dreams and symbols man is led through every sphere of the psyche, during which the forms of psychic force are able to resolve themselves without the use of other means and deep-going transformations are effected."

Frederking also allows the therapy to be regulated by the autonomous healing force of the psyche. The technique is also irrational. Frederking knows, as all who work in these spheres know, that the therapist is in no way indifferent during the course of the therapy. It is true that he only occasionally injects himself to clarify and point out the course of the healing. But the therapist knows that the patient can only experience the most significant symbols when his inner development allows him to do so. Although the therapist remains essentially passive and does not interfere, the patient is still in the therapist's psychic field and may receive direction or formulation of impulses.

Friedrich Mauz has described another technique in an article called "The Psychotic Man in Psychotherapy." (Archiv für Psychiatrie, 1948) This technique is not meditation in the strictest sense, but it is related to it in many ways. With psychotics, the previously described methods are very dangerous and, therefore, rejected. Accordingly, the Mauz method is a severly restricted form of meditation in which the unconscious is most carefully tackled and channelled into productive performance.

Mauz does not mention preference for any technical preparation. The technique develops directly out of conversation which reveals the extent to which the patient's life is ruled by conditioned reflexes. This conversation is almost a monologue in which the therapist depicts the patient in plastic and sympathy-evoking representative pictures from childhood: the experience of a procession, Christmas celebration in the family, a children's song, etc. The depiction must have, for the patient, an appropriate and intuitive power as a "solvent picture." It should unlock and enliven the suppressed emotions of the psychotic so that later a real conversation can develop.

Mauz aims, as does meditation in other respects, at the

emotional level of the patient. Basically, he also leads the patient to the Happich childhood meadow, the creative ground of the psyche. But rather than wait for the patient to produce, Mauz impregnates the meadow with symbols he knows will awaken positive feelings and meanings within the patient, such as the "security" of childhood with its guiltless pleasures. Through such feelings and symbols, the psychotic can again connect with the world around him. The creative power which flows from these feelings and symbols aids in closing the breach in the patient's personality.

It is noteworthy how Mauz describes important fundamental principles of meditation which he apparently discovered completely intuitively in actual human behavior. The symbolic scene is the effector of the therapy, but only if it is experienced as real and actual; that is, as in meditation. "The picture must be personal and impersonal at the same time." It leads into the "sphere of impersonal knowledge and reality." "All that is loud, obtrusive, and harsh must be avoided." The decisive experiences of the past present themselves in the stillness. We must "identify ourselves with the psychotic opposites." "The therapist mixes himself into a common solution with the patient and allows his own comfort to wait." One could say that the therapist must meditate on the patient. He must allow himself to be caught by the patient as the patient is caught by formulations of his psychic power. This is the mystical unity between the therapist and the sick. One must "not only analyze the illness," but also "know the possible health." The therapist must have before him a conception of the completely harmonic man and seek where he can find it again to develop it.

What happens here is biologically and psychologically one. "The emotion of security," says Mauz, "is both vegetative and psychic." With this idea Mauz grasps the whole anthropological aspect of therapy.

Decisive for Mauz before all else, is "the simple human relationship." It appears most significant to the writer that a professional scientist like Mauz comes through his experience with meditation with the conclusion that "humanness" is the highest principle of therapy, an idea which is still far from scientific medicine today.

Now to gather together the viewpoints which characterize

and are combined in the various techniques. All involve the active provocation of the unconscious, as the writer wishes to call it, in which the therapist chiefly has the function of a "birth helper." The patient is directed to place himself in relation to his unconscious, and thus make its creative possibilities available in the healing process. In contrast with the conscious, passive attitude employed in analytical methods of treatment, one takes an active, conscious, and oriented part in the healing process when using meditative techniques. Also in contrast with analytical methods, the meditative technique strives for a goal-directed, but individually adapted, formulation of man's nature in which a picture of the transformed man stands in the background. In this respect, Frederking is a relative exception. In contrast with analytical techniques, the basic exercises of meditation may also be used by normal adults who, because of their greater ego strength, can use them to facilitate their psychological growth much more rapidly than patients.

There is value in the analysis of abnormality, but emphasis on the analytical is usually emphasis on our psychic past. During meditation, there is more dependence on the tendency toward health in the psyche. The orientation is synthetic rather than analytic.

Meditation helps the patient to an expanded consciousness and impersonal experience and knowledge. Meditation has an advantage in that it allows the transition to religious problems to consummate itself in a completely natural way. The course of therapy is shorter with meditation because one is not dependent upon the mood of dreams and comes more quickly, both diagnostically and therapeutically, to the psychic conflict. Finally, with meditation, the patient does not ordinarily transfer his problem onto the therapist and, therefore, the resolution of transference is usually unnecessary.

Opposed to the great range and efficiency of meditation is only one severe limitation. Meditation is limited by the subjectivity of both the therapist and the patient. Unfortunately, each successful therapist forms his own school. Desoille and Mauz certainly demonstrate most unusual intuitions and artistic ability. Not every patient is equally able to fruitfully experience the deeper levels of the psyche. Decisive is the problem of the psychic field of force described by Heyer, which is valid for all techniques which explore the deeper levels of the psyche. If the patient would resolve his intimate psychic problems, he must bring the symbols which expose them, either in dreams or in meditation, into higher levels of consciousness. Stimulation of the deeper levels of the unconscious is the art of psychotherapy, which really can be described only by the unscientific term "Exorcism." Exorcism is not only the result of a learnable technique, but is rather the result of the whole personal influence of the therapist on the patient. Therefore, with all these techniques, competent therapists are required. With one therapist, the patient may experience only the most banal contents of his unconscious; and with another, the patient may have a decisive experience of psychic depths. Thus, the psychotherapist must have a sense of vocation as well as a technique. A sense of vocation is the consequence of natural gifts and skill. Such skill is not learned as a craft nor as medical training, but rather through personal skill as it develops in the relationship between master and disciple. Great psychotherapy is unique and cannot be copied any more than a work of art. It is because the work of a master cannot be copied that one can learn from him.

Meditation has a good chance of eventually becoming one of the leading therapeutic techniques. All the newer systems with which the writer is familiar look for a development in this direction. But whether or not this development takes place depends completely on a deep-going reformulation of psychotherapeutic training and the practice of psychotherapy. It is of the greatest importance that psychotherapists continue to study meditation. We can only hope that meditation will continue to develop into a systematic technique which can aid men towards their goal of developing their highest psychic potentialities.

Persons interested in obtaining further information about psychosynthesis may write any of the following centers.

CANADIAN INSTITUTE OF PSYCHOSYNTHESIS, INC.
3496 Marlowe Avenue
Montreal, Quebec, Canada H4A 3L7

HIGH POINT FOUNDATION
Psychosynthesis Training Center
647 North Madison Avenue
Pasadena, Ca. 911201

KENTUCKY CENTER FOR BIO-PSYCHOSYNTHESIS, INC.
1226 Lakewood Drive
Lexington, Kentucky 40502

PSYCHOSYNTHESIS INSTITUTE
150 Doherty Way
Redwood City, Ca. 94062

PSYCHOSYNTHESIS RESEARCH FOUNDATION, INC.
40 E. 49th Street #1902
New York, N.Y. 10017

THE HILL CENTER FOR PSYCHOSYNTHESIS IN EDUCATION
Old Walpole Road
Walpole, N.H. 03462

INDEX

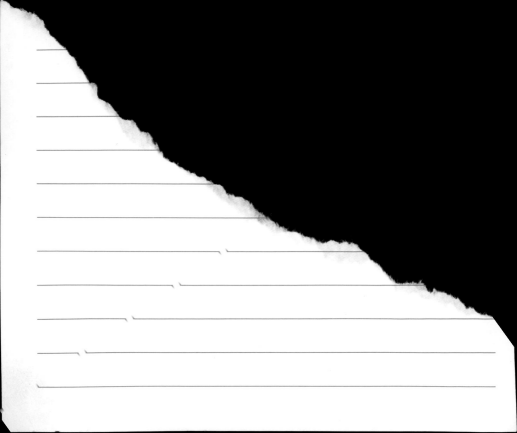

FOR THE BEST IN PAPERBACKS, LOOK FOR THE 🐧

In every corner of the world, on every subject under the sun, Penguin represents quality and variety—the very best in publishing today.

For complete information about books available from Penguin—including Pelicans, Puffins, Peregrines, and Penguin Classics—and how to order them, write to us at the appropriate address below. Please note that for copyright reasons the selection of books varies from country to country.

In the United Kingdom: For a complete list of books available from Penguin in the U.K., please write to *Dept E.P., Penguin Books Ltd, Harmondsworth, Middlesex, UB7 0DA*.

In the United States: For a complete list of books available from Penguin in the U.S., please write to *Consumer Sales, Penguin USA, P.O. Box 999—Dept. 17109, Bergenfield, New Jersey 07621-0120*. VISA and MasterCard holders call 1-800-253-6476 to order all Penguin titles.

In Canada: For a complete list of books available from Penguin in Canada, please write to *Penguin Books Canada Ltd, 10 Alcorn Avenue, Suite 300, Toronto, Ontario, Canada M4V 3B2*.

In Australia: For a complete list of books available from Penguin in Australia, please write to the *Marketing Department, Penguin Books Ltd, P.O. Box 257, Ringwood, Victoria 3134*.

In New Zealand: For a complete list of books available from Penguin in New Zealand, please write to the *Marketing Department, Penguin Books (NZ) Ltd, Private Bag, Takapuna, Auckland 9*.

In India: For a complete list of books available from Penguin, please write to *Penguin Overseas Ltd, 706 Eros Apartments, 56 Nehru Place, New Delhi, 110019*.

In Holland: For a complete list of books available from Penguin in Holland, please write to *Penguin Books Nederland B.V., Postbus 195, NL-1380AD Weesp, Netherlands*.

In Germany: For a complete list of books available from Penguin, please write to *Penguin Books Ltd, Friedrichstrasse 10-12, D-6000 Frankfurt Main 1, Federal Republic of Germany*.

In Spain: For a complete list of books available from Penguin in Spain, please write to *Longman, Penguin España, Calle San Nicolas 15, E-28013 Madrid, Spain*.

In Japan: For a complete list of books available from Penguin in Japan, please write to *Longman Penguin Japan Co Ltd, Yamaguchi Building, 2-12-9 Kanda Jimbocho, Chiyoda-Ku, Tokyo 101, Japan*.